6 W $2.95

5/30/79 cf 8/67 Sci Amer review
distinguish'g culture historian
vs culture process people
in archaeology (not prehistory)

HORIZONS
OF
ANTHROPOLOGY

HORIZONS

OF

ANTHROPOLOGY

EDITED BY *Sol Tax*

ALDINE PUBLISHING COMPANY / *Chicago*

Copyright © 1964 by Aldine Publishing Company
   All rights reserved
First published 1964 by
   Aldine Publishing Company
   64 East Van Buren Street
   Chicago 5, Illinois
Library of Congress Catalog Card Number 63-20409
Designed by David Miller
Printed in the United States of America

Second Printing, 1965

PREFACE

IN JANUARY, 1959, the Voice of America introduced a special English-language program of half hour broadcasts, presented in series under the title, "Forum: The Arts and Sciences in Mid-Century America." In the words of Walter Nichols, the originator,

The Forum lectures are designed to cover, eventually, the major fields of knowledge or cultural activity in which an understanding of the American experience or achievement is considered likely to be of interest or practical value to a sophisticated foreign audience. . . . The program's two most important objectives are: (1) to convey an understanding of current American thought and activity in the arts, the physical and natural sciences, and the social sciences; and (2) to gain added appreciation and respect for American intellectual achievement by displaying its best products.

When I was asked to develop a series on anthropology, it seemed an opportunity to display our changing science by discovering what anthropology in this country will be like tomorrow. A "senior" member of a learned profession, with too rare exceptions, implements ideas created when he was a junior scholar. At that time his voice was drowned out in the fame of his teachers whose ideas, in turn, dated from still earlier years. To break the chain, it was necessary to identify a wide variety of the best specialists still in their thirties, and ask them to discuss what *they* thought interesting and significant.

I trusted myself only to choose five young colleagues with diverse interests, whose competence was most commonly attested to. They chose the others of the nineteen who provide the substance of this book.

My instructions were limited:

> If you imagine that you are talking to a general audience at the University of Moscow, it will assure that the talk, though pitched high, will not assume any particular knowledge. Also, you will then keep away from our more parochial and professional issues. Otherwise, I suggest that each just say what is to be said about his topic in its broadest time–space, "whole–human" and cultural–social perspective, including the complex societies.

To unify the series, participants conferred in Chicago and in Berkeley and also exchanged plans and (eventually) completed papers by mail. Before they recorded their lectures, each had read most of the others. I avoided offering suggestions, but encouraged the others to criticism. My introductory and concluding lectures were written after reading the others. Several of the authors have modified and corrected their papers for publication in this book.

While the book was in press, a teaching assistant, helping me to select reading for an undergraduate course, compared a number of volumes of readings in general anthropology. Noting the overlap in the material of printed collections such as *Anthropology Today* and Morton Fried's *Readings in Anthropology*, he remarked that these Forum lectures surprisingly did not duplicate either of the other sets. Evidently the new generation either chooses different problems than the old or treats them differently. As one should expect in a growing science, anthropology has ever new horizons. Students who read this book are invited to work now on its successor.

                                                                    Sol Tax

CONTRIBUTORS

ROBERT M. ADAMS is Professor of Anthropology and Director of the Oriental Institute at the University of Chicago. One of his principal research interests has been the comparative study of early civilizations in the Near East and Middle America. More recently, he has been involved in intensive studies of urbanism and irrigation agriculture in Iraq and Iran.

PAUL J. BOHANNAN is Professor of Anthropology at Northwestern University. He has conducted extensive field work in Nigeria and Kenya and is the author of books and articles dealing with African cultures.

EDWARD H. BRUNER is Associate Professor of Anthropology at the University of Illinois. He has done field work among American Indians and in Indonesia, and has published many articles in professional journals.

IRVEN DeVORE is now with the Department of Anthropology of Harvard University. His research interests have been in the social relationships among primates, based on field observation in Africa.

SUSAN M. ERVIN is Assistant Professor in the Department of Speech and Research Associate of the Institute for Human Learning at the University of California at Berkeley. Her publications include research on children's reasoning and language and on bilingualism.

LLOYD A. FALLERS is Associate Professor of Anthropology at the University of Chicago. His special interests have been in traditional African cultures and in the distinctive characteristics of modern industrial societies.

MORTON H. FRIED is Professor of Anthropology at Columbia University. He has conducted field work in China, British Guiana and Formosa, and his publications include books and articles on modern Chinese culture.

CLIFFORD GEERTZ is Associate Professor of Anthropology and Executive Secretary of the Committee for the Comparative Study of New Nations at the University of Chicago. His major field work has been in Southeast Asia, and his special interests have been in comparative religion and in the economic development of underdeveloped areas.

JAMES L. GIBBS, JR., is Associate Professor of Anthropology at the University of Minnesota. He has published several papers on his field work among the Kpelle of central Liberia and has been honored for distinguished work as a teacher.

F. CLARK HOWELL is Professor of Anthropology at the University of Chicago. He has specialized in the study of early man and his evolution, and has conducted field work in Africa and Europe, most recently in Spain.

DELL H. HYMES is Associate Professor of Anthropology at the University of California at Berkeley. His field work with American Indians in the western United States has concentrated on linguistics and folkore; his present main interests are in the history of anthropology and the comparative study of the functions of speech.

ALAN P. MERRIAM is Professor of Anthropology at Indiana University. He has specialized in African studies and is a leading expert in the field of ethnomusicology.

FRANK B. LIVINGSTONE is Associate Professor of Anthropology at the University of Michigan. He has done research on the population genetics of the hemoglobins and blood groups in Liberia.

LAURA NADER is Assistant Professor of Anthropology at the University of California at Berkeley. She has done field work among the Zapotec Indians of Mexico and the Shia Moslems of Lebanon. Her publications include comparative studies of conflict resolution and social organization as well as ethnographic studies.

MANNING NASH is Associate Professor of Anthropology in the Graduate School of Business at the University of Chicago. His field work in Middle American and Southeast Asian ethnology underlies his principal concern with cultural change in relation to economic development.

EDWARD NORBECK is Professor of Anthropology and Chairman of the Department of Anthropology and Sociology at Rice University. His fields of special interest include ethnological theory and study of culturally elaborate societies, with particular emphasis on Japan and Pacific Ocean cultures.

STEVEN POLGAR is Director of Research Planned Parenthood —World Population. His field work includes research in Ghana and among Indians and Negroes in the United States. He is an action anthropologist specializing in public health and culture change.

MARSHALL D. SAHLINS is Associate Professor of Anthropology at the University of Michigan. His field work has been in Fiji, and his major theoretical concerns have dealt with problems of culture change and evolution.

SOL TAX is Professor of Anthropology at the University of Chicago and is Editor of *Current Anthropology*. His field work among Middle and North American Indians has resulted in such books as *Penny Capitalism* and *Heritage of Conquest*, and in the development of what is now called "Action Anthropology." He has edited many books, including the three–volume symposium, *Evolution After Darwin*. He was President of the American Anthropological Association in 1958-59 and in 1962 received the Viking Fund Medal in Anthropology.

ERIC R. WOLF is Professor of Anthropology at the University of Michigan. He has done field work in Puerto Rico, in Mexico, and in the Italian Alps, and is the author of *Sons of the Shaking Earth*, a study of cultural development in Middle America.

CONTENTS

HORIZONS
OF
ANTHROPOLOGY

1.

THE SETTING OF THE SCIENCE OF MAN

Sol Tax

MEN HAVE ALWAYS BEEN interested in studying themselves. The individual man spends his life understanding himself; a people provides itself with myths; nations write their histories. Therefore it is futile to speak of the beginning of the study of man. We usually refer back to classical Greece for the origins of the study of man, but the study is world wide—a philosopher can appear in any tribe—and it goes back anywhere that records carry us back. Yet, there are times when any science gets a special impetus, and crystallizes a new form, and forges ahead. For the study of man, the great period in modern times extended over the thirty years from about 1840 to 1870. One might almost call it a "thirty years' war"—a war between two words, Ethnology and Anthropology; a war between those who were historians and philosophers on one side, and those who were for science, particularly biology (wherever it might lead one), on the other; a war between humanitarians whose science was related to their advocacy of a cause on one side and, on the other, pure scientists who would separate scientific truth from all other human concerns.

A good way to watch the thirty years' story unfold is to read the journals of the competing societies which sprang up during that time. A quick and especially interesting history is to be found in the Decennial Anniversary Address by the great French anthropologist, Paul Broca, to the Anthropological Society of Paris which he founded ten years earlier in 1859 (Broca 1871-72). The address was published in the society's journal and also

15

translated into English for publication by the Anthropological Institute of New York. Broca, himself an anatomist and human biologist, was the descendent of a long line which included Blumenbach, Cuvier, and many others. Imbued with the spirit of exact science, he strongly opposed mixing science and sentiment, or science and politics, and his little history, quoted extensively below, emphasizes the dangers.

In Paris in 1800 was founded the Society of the Observers of Man "by a union of naturalists and of medical men" to promote the study of natural history mainly by providing guidance to travelers and explorers of far places. The Society was deprived of new data by the long series of Napoleonic Wars which interrupted commerce and foreign travel and "turned its attention to questions of ethnology, historical and psychological. Natural history was neglected for philosophy, politics, and philanthropy."

"This abortive experiment had been long forgotten when some English philanthropists founded in London, in 1838, the 'Society for the Protection of Aborigines.'" Eminent scholars were among its members, but "its aims were rather political and social than scientific. It was at this time that the question of slavery, already solved by England, began to occupy the attention of the French government. In the session of 1839, the Chamber of Deputies . . . had appointed a commission to report upon this important subject; and the society in London, hoping that the pressure of public opinion might have a favorable influence on the decision of the chamber, resolved to establish in France a society for the emancipation of the Negroes. One of its leading members, Mr. Hodgkin, came to Paris, and put himself in communication with several distinguished persons, and more particularly with the eminent naturalist and anthropologist Milne-Edwards. But an association of this kind was not at that time possible in France. . . . Instead of a political association, Milne-Edwards and his friends resolved to found a scientific society, and thus sprang into existence the celebrated 'Ethnological Society of Paris,' . . . authorized on the 20th August, 1839."

When "the first volume of its *Memoirs* appeared, some English *savants* appreciated the usefulness of its work, and resolved to imitate it. Through their means, in May, 1844, a similar society was formed in London, and took, like it, the name of the

Ethnological Society, and a short time subsequently a third
society, founded in New York, adopted the same title."

In 1847 "the meetings of the society [i.e., the Ethnological
Society of Paris], hitherto peaceful, were agitated by the question
of slavery. The first thing was to determine the distinctive characteristics of the white and black races; but it was in vain that
the naturalists and anatomists, too few in number, tried to
restrain the discussion within the limits of natural history. . . .
The debate became more lively at each meeting; the outside
world began to be interested; . . . and the public willingly
believed that ethnology, of which it then heard for the first time,
was not a science, but something between politics and philanthropy. . . . This absorbing controversy lasted nearly a year"
when it was ended by the abolition of slavery. "But the Ethnological Society had been so completely absorbed by this question
that, deprived of it, its chief motive to action seemed no longer
to exist." The enfeebled society died—though weak sisters remained in London and New York.

In America (physical) anthropology was making great progress, according to Broca's lights. Then, "In 1851 . . . the United
States were agitated by the abolition question. . . . By one of
those confusions of ideas . . . it was imagined that slavery was
bound up with the polygenistic theory, while emancipation was
inseparable from the monogenistic." "A tremendous war absorbed
for many years the resources of the country. Science was lost
sight of amid the clash of arms, and when the victory of the
North had solved the question of slavery, anthropology . . .
suffered a period of eclipse. . . ."

Meanwhile, in Europe anthropology was going ahead, but
"When facts ran counter to popularly conceived opinions, they
were greeted with contempt. . . . It was then that the founders of
the Anthropological Society of Paris determined to form a
tribunal before which opposing views might obtain a hearing."
"After more than six months occupied in collecting subscriptions,
and in obtaining, not without difficulty, authority to hold its
meetings (under the control of the police), the new society
met for the first time on the 19th of May, 1859, and began work
on the 7th of July following."

Meanwhile, in Germany the anthropologists in the many scat-

18   SOL TAX

tered cities were unable to meet frequently, so they established
instead an annual congress. "The first session was held at
Gottenburg, in the month of September, 1861." Circumstances
interfered with well-laid plans, and the congress never actually
met again. But work continued through *The Germanic Archives
of Anthropology,* founded in 1865, and the *Journal of Ethnology,*
first published on January 1, 1869.

"The Ethnological Society of London was quietly pursuing
its labors when the perusal of our [the Anthropological Society
of Paris] publications excited in its midst the desire to add
modern anthropology to the old programme of ethnology. But
the most influential members . . . opposed the introduction of
anatomy and natural history. . . ." "On the 24th of February, 1863,
the dissenting members founded, under the presidency of Mr.
James Hunt, a new society, which took, like ours, the name of
the Anthropological Society." "The Ethnological Society, weak-
ened for a moment by this defection, increased its efforts, and
soon saw the necessity of enlarging, in its turn, its own sphere."
In 1868 Thomas Huxley was elected president. "Nothing could
be more significant than the choice of this gentleman, whose fame
rests on his works on zoölogy, comparative anatomy, and craniol-
ogy. . . . From this time forward the Ethnological Society and
the Anthropological Society differed only in name."

"While France, Germany, and England were contributing thus
powerfully to the progress of anthropology, the other countries of
Europe were not idle.—Everywhere, from Sweden to Sicily, from
the Volga to the Tagus, learned men were at work."

"In Moscow, in 1866, there was formed, in the 'Society of the
Friends of Nature,' . . . a special section of anthropology" which
became quickly productive and successful.

But Broca concludes this 1869 survey of progress with a
difficult case. "At Madrid, a Society of Anthropology was
founded in 1865." "The Minister of Progress . . . had been
pleased to honor with his presence (the 5th of June, 1865) the
ceremony of inauguration. It was only when the society wished
to set to work that its difficulties began. The first question sub-
mitted for discussion was that of the aboriginal races of the
peninsula—an inquiry offensive, imprudent, and savoring of
heresy—for the very name of aborigines was pregnant with

controversy. . . ." They stopped meeting until the revolution of September. "Last 21st February they held their second inauguration."

In addition to the formation of national societies, and of journals and periodicals, Broca could also report the founding of the International Congress of Anthropology and Prehistoric Archaeology, and its first sessions in 1866, 1867, and 1868, each in a different part of Europe.

In 1869 Broca could rightly entitle his Address "The Progress of Anthropology." Two years later the rival English societies joined to become the Anthropological Institute of Great Britain and Ireland. In 1873 there was again a split, this time based on personalities, and a new London Anthropological Society with its journal *Anthropologia* came into being; but it was short lived. The sciences settled down to work. International communication, research, and publication made great strides. The names anthropology, ethnology, ethnography, archaeology, prehistory, philology and linguistics became firmly established. They had different meanings from place to place, and from time to time. In some places these branches of the science of man became more unified than in others, and everywhere each has its different history. But on the whole the hope of Broca was realized in the years to come. He said in 1869 that on the pivotal base of anatomy and biology, anthropology could "extract, by means of a rigorous synthesis, the ultimate ideas of *general anthropology* which sooner or later will be the crown and glory of our science."

What Broca here referred to as general anthropology became soon the synthesis characteristic of the science in England and America. On the continent of Europe the separate words anthropology, ethnology, prehistory, and linguistics need still to be used to encompass the whole. But in all of America and most of Asia the word anthropology stands for the whole study of man. Cultural anthropology, social anthropology, economic anthropology, anthropological linguistics, are equally used with physical or biological anthropology. All of the specialists now use again the single word that Broca saw would unite the world in the synthesis of general anthropology.

Before Columbus, the American aborigines had their own ideas about the nature of man. From the point of view of the European tradition of science and scholarship, North and South America, like Africa and Oceania and much of Asia, were places to explore. The American Indians were one of the greatest new mysteries of the Age of Exploration. It is little wonder then that the Americas should one day become a center of anthropological study. The English, French, Germans, and other Europeans provided the traditions of scholarship, the books, the theories; but the Americas provided a laboratory close by.

This is true in different ways throughout the Americas, but I shall speak particularly of the United States. Thomas Jefferson, the third President of the United States, is sometimes also said to be its first anthropologist; he not only developed empirical research in archaeology, but he studied carefully the data on living Indian tribes and was a pioneer in the study of Indian languages. As A. I. Hallowell (1960a:15-16) puts it:

> Jefferson emerges as a significant figure in early anthropological thinking in this country not only because of his enduring interest in the Indian, his personal investigations, and expressed opinions. Through his attitude of rational inquiry, his active association with learned men of his time, and his role in our national government, he personifies, in a sense, the distinctive historical context in which anthropology in the United States was nourished in its infancy. . . .
> In a letter (1789) to Reverend Joseph Williard, President of Harvard, he said: "What a field have we at our doors to signalize ourselves in! The Botany of America is far from being exhausted, its Mineralogy is untouched, and its Natural History or Zoology, totally mistaken and misrepresented. . . . It is for such institutions as that over which you preside so worthily, Sir, to do justice to our country, its productions and its genius. It is the work to which the young men, whom you are forming should lay their hands."
> While Jefferson does not mention any discipline explicitly devoted to the study of man in his letter, his own pioneer work in the collection of Indian vocabularies, his descriptive and statistical data on Indian tribal groups tabulated in the Notes, his excavation of a mound, and the memorandum he prepared for the Lewis and Clark expedition concretely demonstrate, in principle, the kind of inquiry that he thought could be profitably carried on in America. Thus, without an academic label, he himself and others of his circle set an example by accumulating new knowledge regarding "Homo sapiens Americanus." This was anthropology, without portfolio, pursued on our own frontiers.

Jefferson set the pattern of the nineteenth century wherein statesmen-scholars investigated the American Indians for their own sake, even as history was pushing them into isolated corners of the country. The long series of students of the American Indian, of which the best-known names are Gallatin, Cass, and Schoolcraft, culminated in a sense with Lewis Henry Morgan, who was one of the first men in the world to combine personal intensive field work in a native culture with comparative work and general theory. Missionaries and others lived with Indians and occasionally published important observations; but of those who made firsthand observations, Morgan was the first who tried also to place his results in world-wide perspective. In doing so, he virtually founded one of the great branches of modern social anthropology—the comparative study of family and kinship structure.

Anthropology in America was thus never a simple offshoot of European thought; it was an independent center in which firsthand knowledge of a variety of cultures gave it both special opportunities and a particular character. Brinton, Powell, Holmes, Putnam, Bandalier and dozens of others were great names in the development of anthropology in the late nineteenth century. Europeans led in uncovering their own long prehistory; but they were required to go thousands of miles to experience in person non-European cultures. It was in America then that the theorists themselves also had close experience with a profusion of exotic languages, cultures, and peoples. It was not until the twentieth century that European anthropologists included empirical field work in their training and practice.

The divorce from actual peoples perhaps explains the great development of social theory in England in the last half of the nineteenth century. The names of Spencer, Tylor, Frazer are symbols. France during this period concentrated on prehistory and physical anthropology, and when at the turn of the twentieth century it picked up social theory where it had left off more than fifty years earlier, it was with a set of new empirical tools in Compte's sociological tradition; and Durkheim, Mauss, and others avoided a good deal of what has come to be called arm chair speculation.

In Germany, in this same period, there developed first a

psychological and then a geographical tradition of cultural anthropology. Theodore Waitz developed the basic physical anthropology of the peoples of all the world; Adolf Bastian surveyed their cultures and described what he thought were the basic psychological ideas of all men; and Freidrich Ratzel developed what has come to be called anthropogeography. All were in different ways empirical, and when Franz Boas came to America with a German education, it was also with a strictly empirical background. It was easy for him to fit into the established American tradition. It was easy for him to take advantage of the opportunities there for field research. Boas has been influential in American anthropology partly because American anthropology had already developed the tools and theories that suited his ways.

Nevertheless, the continuity of American anthropology appears to me to stem most directly from the British. The tradition of mixing philanthropic and scientific interests that came in the original combination of the anti-slavery movement and the formation of the Ethnological Societies around 1840 never ended in England; it carried over into America. The insistence on "pure science" which twenty years later caused "anthropologists" to split off from ethnologists was a reflection of confusion in knowledge about evolution and race. The "anthropologists" thought that the anti-slavery bias of many ethnologists interfered with the search for truth. They fought emotionally about this, and many of them were willing to justify slavery because they thought that Europeans probably were higher on the evolutionary scale than Africans and perhaps Asians. As time passed, it became evident that some races could not be shown to be inferior to others; but it also became clear that political and social policies had very little to do with such technical questions. After the Civil War in the United States, Broca complained about the foolish use of science, as we have seen.

Thomas Huxley had remained in the Ethnological Society in London, despite his biological orientation. He too, after the American Civil War, pointed out that if, indeed, the Negroes or any other race are inferior, it is reason to discriminate in their favor, rather than against them to redress the balance.

The fact is that the "ethnologists" in England, rather than the "anthropologists," became the leaders in the Anthropological Institute in which they combined. It is from the tradition of scholarship begun with the founding of the Ethnological Society of Paris in 1839 and continued by the Ethnological Society of London and the Anthropological Institute, that American Anthropology gets its major European continuity, particularly through the person of Edward Burnett Tylor who is known to most anthropologists in America as the Father of Modern Anthropology.

In the succeeding essays it will become evident that Americans, following in this tradition, are specialists but also generalists. Whether we are archaeologists or linguists, students of the arts or of geography, whether we study the behavior of baboons or the refinements of the human mind, we all call ourselves anthropologists. It will become evident also that we all carry with us the liberal tradition of the first ancestors. Humankind is one; we value all peoples and cultures; we abhor any kind of prejudice against peoples, and the use of power for the domination of one nation by another. We believe in the self-determination of free peoples. We particularly abhor the misuse by bigots or politicians of any of our knowledge. As scientists we never know all of the truth; we must grope and probe, and ever learn; but we know infinitely more than the glib racists —whether in the United States or in South Africa. We are equalitarians, not because we can prove absolute equality, but because we know absolutely that whatever differences there may be among large populations have no significance for the policies of nations. This comes from our knowledge as anthropologists; but it also pleases us as citizens of the world.

It is a pleasure to introduce now these chapters by a group of young North American anthropologists. They will not talk about anthropology very much, but rather about what anthropologists have learned in the hundred years since it became so well fixed among the sciences. They will speak about human evolution—how man became different from the other primates in behavior and in form; about the origin and nature of language, and how it makes us human; about the long history of human culture and society, and the theories that we have to account for the similarities and the differences that we find among communities of men. What do we know on a world-wide scale about society, economy, politics, law, religion, medicine, the arts? Nineteen young colleagues in the United States will describe much of the panorama of man as we know it in the 1960's, emphasizing the horizons that are open for us to explore.

BIBLIOGRAPHICAL NOTE

Interest among anthropologists in the history of the discipline is so recent that research is mainly either not published (eg., the papers of the Social Science Research Council's Conference on the History of Anthropology; see *Items*, 1962, Vol. 16, No. 3) or is widely scattered. There is, of course, a large literature on the histories of the subfields as parts of biology, linguistics, archeology, etc. Histories of cultural anthropology include Lowie's *History of Ethnological Theory* (1937) and such smaller pieces as Tax (1955). The development of the discipline as a whole is described in a few works as Haddon's *History of Anthropology* (1910), Penniman's *A Hundred Years of Anthropology* (1952), and Hays' *From Ape to Angel* (1958). The primary sources for the histories of the subfields and the manner in which they became integrated into the main field are the books and journals of the societies which began in the nineteenth century. A discussion of this literature can be found in Tax (1956). Particular national histories of the field are in Hallowell (1960) and Heine-Geldern (1962). There are biographies of anthropologists like Tylor and Boas; a recent biographical approach to the history of anthropology is Kardiner's *They Studied Man* (1961).

2.

THE EVOLUTION OF SOCIAL LIFE

Irven DeVore *

MAN HAS ALWAYS BEEN interested in the story of his own development. This curiosity extends beyond the few millennia of human history, for which we have the testament of the written word, to the hundreds of thousands of years of human prehistory. Most of the major events in the evolution of man's social life occurred during the past million and a half years in what geologists call the Pleistocene—a period when continental glaciers repeatedly covered large areas of the Northern Hemisphere. It will never be possible to reconstruct man's evolutionary past entirely, but three lines of evidence are particularly useful. The first of these is the evidence which the archeologist uncovers at the living sites of prehistoric men—the bones of the men themselves, together with the tools they made and the foods they ate. The interpretation of these archeological data is augmented by studies of contemporary hunting-and-gathering tribes, which constitute a second kind of evidence. The economic base and ecological adaptation of some of these living hunter-gatherers has changed very little in five hundred thousand years. The third is the study of the natural history of monkeys and apes. Because of their close biological kinship with man, monkeys and apes have always figured prominently in discussions of the origin of human behavior. The purpose of this paper is to discuss the social behavior of monkeys and apes for the purpose of re-

* The organization of the data for this article was supported by a National Science Foundation grant for the analysis of primate behavior, while the author was a Fellow of the Miller Institute for Basic Research in Science, University of California, Berkeley.

25

constructing man's development from a common primate ancestry to his uniquely human way of life.

Until recently very little could be said about the behavior
of monkeys and apes in a natural habitat. Prior to 1958 there
were only three long-term field studies of monkeys and apes in
the wild—studies by Carpenter on howling monkeys and gibbons,
and by Itani on Japanese macaques. In the past four years, however, the naturalistic study of the nonhuman primates has been
one of the most rapidly expanding fields in the behavioral
sciences. At the present time more than fifty persons from
eleven countries, including zoölogists, psychologists, and anthropologists, are engaged in such studies.

From these recent field studies of monkeys and apes, it is
now possible to describe, in a broad sense, a fundamental
primate way of life—one which is shared by monkeys, apes, and
man. This way of life is not found in most of the prosimians;
that is, the tree shrews, lorises, lemurs, and tarsiers. Among
these "primitive monkeys" there are many other variations on
the primate way of life, but these will be excluded from this
discussion, and "primate" in the following remarks refers only
to monkeys and apes. By comparison to other mammals, primate
social behavior has certain rare, almost unique, qualities. Essentially, primate life is group life. It is more than that, however, for
many animals live in herds or groups. It is the special characteristics of primate groups which set them apart in the mammalian
phylogeny. The primate group is relatively large; the average is
about twenty, but among baboons it may be as large as two
hundred. Membership in the group is persistent and stable;
unlike most mammals, there are no seasonal changes in group
composition. The group is highly organized; it includes both
sexes and all ages from birth until death. Individual differences
based on age, sex, and relative dominance result in a separation
of roles and statuses among the group members. These characteristics of primate groups—comparatively large size, stable membership, and role differentiation—lead to complex social relationships and special accommodations among the members of the
group. This is easiest to see in the socialization of the infant.
The infancy of primates is not only long by comparison to other
animals, but also, from the very outset, child rearing is a *group*

activity. This is in striking contrast to the situation found in many animals, where the mother is separated from others of her species during the birth period and lives alone with her offspring until they are able to support themselves. Even among mammals which live in herds, the "group" is usually a harem composed only of other females and their offspring, or has only one adult male attached to the herd. In the primates, on the other hand, the mother is neither separate from the group while her offspring are young, nor does she live in a female harem. On the contrary, she and her infant are surrounded by curious juveniles and adults of all ages, and she depends upon the adult males to protect the young infant from danger.

In considering the primate background to human social groupings, it is this organization of all the members of the group—young and old, male and female—into a functioning social system that is more striking than the presence or absence of a "family" within the group. Among the monkeys and apes, only the gibbon lives in what has been called a "family," that is, an adult male and female pair with their offspring. This resemblance with the human family, however, is fortuitous and is produced by entirely different behavior patterns. Except for a mating pair, adult gibbons are extremely antagonistic. As a result of this antagonism, gibbon pairs live apart from each other, and their offspring remain with them only until maturity, when they are old enough to seek mates and form a new mating pair. The gibbon group, then, is more comparable to a breeding pair of birds than it is to the human family. The human family never occurs in isolation, but always as a subgroup within a larger social unit, such as the tribe. It is significant that gibbons, whose physical adaptation to life in the trees is more extreme than any other ape's, are the least like man in their social organization as well. By contrast, the baboons and macaques, who are more specially adapted to life on the ground than any other primate except man, have a social organization that resembles that of humans in many fundamental respects. These are the only monkeys whose average group size, about fifty, is comparable to that of human hunter-gatherer groups. It is also among the baboon-macaques that the roles of adult males and adult females differ to the degree they do in human societies. The adult male

baboon, with powerful muscles, large canine teeth, and a body
weight twice that of the female, is specialized for defense of
the troop; the female is specialized for childbirth and child
rearing. These characteristics of sexual dimorphism are most
pronounced in ground-living monkeys and apes and least evident
in tree-living forms. The primates can be arranged along a continuum from the ground-living gorilla, baboon, macaque, and
man to the arboreal monkeys and apes. The arboreal gibbon
falls at one extreme, with the least amount of sexual dimorphism
—the two sexes being virtually indistinguishable. Ground-living
primates illustrate the other extreme. The sexual dimorphism
of adult baboons has a morphological basis; in humans, adult
male and female roles depend on cultural designations. This
comparison should not be pushed too far, however. Human behavior is significantly different from monkey and ape behavior.
The human family is based on a new biological system, including
loss of "heat" or estrus in the female; and human ideas of own-
ership, exogamy, and cooperation are as unique among the
primates as human language, tools, and war.

A brief description of the social organization of a baboon
troop will illustrate important differences and similarities between monkey behavior and human behavior. In 1959 Professor
Sherwood Washburn and I studied baboons living in the game
parks of Kenya, East Africa. Baboons are common all over
Africa, but it was only in these protected areas that we
could observe the undisturbed interrelationships of the baboons
with other animals and plants. We were interested not only in the
internal organization of the baboon troop, but also in the environment to which baboon social behavior has adapted. Behavioral observations had been made on baboons before, but
always of captive colonies. Under conditions of severe over-
crowding, social behavior in these colonies was seriously distorted and constant lethal fighting among the adult males
resulted in a very high death rate of females, juveniles, and other
males. As a result of these early studies, male dominance behavior in baboons and macaques has been viewed as egocentric,
vicious, and detrimental to the welfare of the group. In Kenya
we found precisely the opposite was true. In the wild, the relationships among the adult males of the baboon troop remain

stable over long periods. Each male knows the dominance status of every other male, and these statuses are rarely contested. The stability of the male hierarchy is reinforced by the fact that some of the older and more dominant males tend to stand together against the younger, maturing males, creating a subgroup or "central hierarchy" within the over-all adult male dominance hierarchy. If one of the males in the central hierarchy is threatened, the other males in it tend to back him up. Thus this central group of males outranks individuals, even though a young male outside the central hierarchy might be able to defeat any member of it separately. The stability of the male dominance hierarchy seems to derive from the fact that it is based on the combined strength of these clusters of males rather than on individual fighting ability. In troops where the rank order or dominance hierarchy is clearly defined, fighting is rare. In fact, the usual effect of male dominance, once relations among the males themselves are settled, is to *decrease* fighting and disruptions in the troop. The dominant males, particularly those in the central hierarchy, will not tolerate fighting among the other troop members. If bickering does break out they ordinarily run to the scene of the fight and stop it. Because the dominant males protect the weaker members of the troop from harm, females and juveniles are attracted to them. They come to the males to groom them or just to sit beside them. There is no need for the males to herd the troop members together; the others will not leave the vicinity of the males even for a few minutes. So, although dominance depends ultimately on force, it leads to peace, order, and popularity.

The most important function of the adult males, however, is protection of the other troop members from danger which originates outside the troop. In the Kenya game reserves where we studied baboons there are many large predators, including lions, leopards, cheetahs, wild dogs, hyenas, jackals and eagles. At night, when predators are most active, baboons sleep in a protected place—usually in the top of tall trees or on a steep cliff. During the day, however, the troop may wander several miles from a safe refuge, and it is when they are thus exposed on the open plains that the defensive functions of the males are most apparent. The troop moves across the savanna arranged in a particular order. Adult males and older juvenile males occupy the van, with other adult males along the edges and at the rear of the troop. The most dominant males of the central hierarchy walk in the center of the troop, surrounded by females with infants and a group of the youngest juveniles. This arrangement of the troop members places the females and young in the safest position, at the center of the troop, and any predator which approaches the troop will first encounter adult males. If a predator *does* try to attack, the females and juveniles hurry ahead while the adult males continue walking slowly. Within seconds the adult males are interposed between the predator and the rest of the troop. On one occasion a show of defiance by an adult male turned three hunting cheetahs away from the baboon troop. If predators prevent the baboons from returning to their usual sleeping place, the troop waits with the less dominant males while the males in the center move ahead and find an alternate route. Eventually the dominant males return and lead the troop to a safe sleeping place. From this brief description it is clear that baboons are well organized to cope with the dangers inherent in ground living. It is remarkable that a baboon troop can be so efficiently organized without the aid of language. Baboons actually exchange very few vocalizations, and these are largely expressions of danger, fear, anger, and contentment.

Just as in man, the social organization of monkeys and apes is based on the learning capacity of the infant during a long period of dependency on adult care. The infant baboon is born into a very protected social environment. The bond between the infant and its mother is intense, but all adults in the troop are solicitous of the infant's welfare, creating an atmosphere of security in which social contacts and early learning take place. By the time the mother weans her infant, it has joined a play group of other infants its own age. These young juveniles stay near the protective adult males. Through their constant association with each other in these play groups, the skills of adult life are practiced and developed, and by the time they reach adulthood the juveniles have established a relationship with every other member of the troop. One important result of this long period of accommodation by the troop members to each other is that each troop becomes a discrete social unit with

distinct social boundaries. Even when several troops are gathered
at the same waterhole, the members of different troops do not
mix. Females in estrus do not seek mates in adjoining troops,
nor do males try to shift to a new troop. This exclusiveness of
troop membership among East African baboons is not so apparent in all monkeys and apes. There is a constant turnover in the
membership of some gorilla groups, and the hamadryas (or
"sacred") baboons of northeast Africa do not remain in large
troops during the day. They split into small groups in the morning and come together again at a sleeping place in the evening. In
all monkey and ape groups which have been studied, however,
sexual behavior has not proved to be the primary determinant of
the social group, as it was long thought to be. On the contrary,
a female is receptive (or "in estrus") only a few weeks during a
one-to two year period. She is not receptive to males during
pregnancy or lactation, and because most female baboons and
macaques give birth at about the same time each year, many
months may pass with little or no sexual activity in the troop.
Nevertheless the troop retains its characteristic structure throughout the year. In fact, sexual behavior, when it does occur, tends
to be disruptive of otherwise close social bonds, while expressions
of peaceful, affectionate behavior are constant features of baboon
daily activity. At every stage of a baboon's life it is connected
to the other troop members by a complex series of relationships
which, in their totality, bind the troop together. These relationships include: the mutual support which adults find in the
dominance hierarchy; the attraction of the infant, the mother,
and the adult males for each other, as well as the attraction which
the males have for the other troop members; the bonds between
the juveniles in the play group; the pleasurable activity in
grooming groups; and a shared social tradition. And it is these
features of baboon life, rather than infrequent sexual activity,
which give the baboon troop its characteristic social organization.
In the evolution of baboon behavior, the conditions of life on
the ground favored *all* those behavioral patterns which make it
possible for individuals to live in the intimate association of the
troop.

From this brief description of baboon social life, what suggestions can be made about the evolution of human behavior? Al-

though every human group has an equally long history, our best clues for the reconstruction of the life of Pleistocene hominids are found in the way of life of stone age hunters living today. While the social customs, religion, and art of contemporary hunter-gatherers have surely undergone considerable change in the last half million years, the adaptation of the group to its environment has probably changed far less. Certainly a comparison of the simple tools made by African bushmen, pygmies, or Australian aborigines, with the tools of Middle Pleistocene men would indicate that some contemporary hunter-gatherer groups have continued to exploit their environment in much the same way. In any case, there is little to be gained by comparing baboon social behavior with modern civilization or with agricultural societies. Even when baboons are compared to hunter-gatherers living in a similar environment, the differences far outweigh the similarities. Except for certain fundamental similarities—a group size of about fifty, a stable organization with separation of male and female roles, and a prolonged period of infant dependency—human groups have little in common with baboons. There is, for example, no lasting bond between particular males and females in a baboon troop, and therefore no basis for the establishment of family units. The population structure of the small, inbred baboon troop contrasts with the exogamous mating patterns of human groups. Put another way, human groups are related to neighboring groups by ties of marriage and kinship. As a result, the shift of individuals from one human group to another is the rule rather than the exception.

Differences in diet alone between vegetarian baboons and carnivorous hunter-gatherers necessitate patterns of life which differ markedly. This contrast is even more striking when it is extended to other monkeys and apes. All monkeys and apes are vegetarians, eating the fruits, berries, buds, and leaves of the forest. Some, such as baboons, macaques, chimpanzees and gorillas find food on the ground as well. Baboons, for example, have extended their diet to include a wide variety of insects, underground roots, and, occasionally, a small animal. Diet is highly correlated with the distances primates travel. Tree-living monkeys forage in a small area, and many of them probably live their whole lives within a kilometer of the spot where they were born. By contrast, baboons range widely; a troop in savanna country moves over an area of about forty square kilometers during the course of a year. Although this area is the largest home range described for any nonhuman primate, it is tiny by comparison to the home range of a hunter-gatherer group. An entire baboon troop can live in an area which is too small to support even a single human hunter. The earliest known hominids, the australopithecines (or "man-apes") of a million years ago, were hunters, and as hunting became an important way of life, the minimum area which the group occupied must have increased in size at least tenfold over the home range of a baboon troop. In this respect humans are more like other group-living predators than they are like monkeys and apes. A pack of wolves, for example, covers a range which is about eighty kilometers in diameter. Although the size of the range of a human hunting group varies widely according to local conditions, many hunting and gathering tribes occupy an area of approximately this same size.

One important reason a human group can exploit so large an area is the existence of an improved home base, or camp. No monkey or ape has such a base; when a baboon troop leaves its sleeping place in the morning, all the troop members must move together. There is no assurance that the troop will return to the same sleeping place in the evening, and every individual, even though sick or injured, must keep up with the others or risk permanent separation from the troop. Because the whole troop moves together, it is not possible for baboons to hunt other animals effectively. Even more important, the absence of a home base makes it impossible for males to go in one direction in search of game while females and juveniles disperse to gather vegetable foods—a system of food-getting which seems universal among hunter-gatherers. Again, it is among wolves, not monkeys, that closer parallels are found. Wolves establish a den which they may use for several seasons, and adults in the pack aid a new mother by returning to the den and disgorging meat for the female and her pups. This kind of food-sharing at an established base has no counterpart in nonhuman primate groups. In fact, every individual in a monkey or ape group forages for himself;

monkey mothers do not share food even with their own infants. On the basis of diet alone, then, it is possible to predict many of the major contours of group life. From this point of view the emergence of consistent, effective hunting initiated revolutionary changes in the primate way of life. Fortunately the evidence of hunting habits is well preserved on the living floors of prehistoric men, and dramatic discoveries by archeologists in Africa are adding daily to our knowledge of the diet and way of life of these Pleistocene hominids.

To summarize: although it is true that man shares a basic social heritage with the other primates, this similarity is apparent only when monkeys, apes, and men are compared to the other vertebrates. Those features of social life which we recognize as distinctly human—the family; rules of incest and exogamy; hunting and food-sharing at a home base—seem to represent a sharp break between man and the other primates. In attempting to reconstruct how a human way of life might have developed from this basic primate pattern, it is possible to envision two stages: The first is represented by the small australopithecines of the Lower Pleistocene, who combine erect, bipedal locomotion with a small brain capacity. The second stage is represented by the taller, larger-brained men of the Middle Pleistocene. In succeeding papers, Geertz and Howell will discuss these stages of human evolution in detail; my purpose is merely to indicate these two levels in the evolution of human behavior as convenient points at which to compare human life with that of monkeys and apes.

At the earlier, australopithecine, stage there is little to suggest that social life was very different from that found in monkeys and apes. Although these creatures were bipedal toolmakers, their cranial capacity was scarcely larger than that of some living apes, and there are indications that they had not yet developed the striding walk which allows humans to cover long distances with minimum effort. The first australopithecines were probably still more vegetarian than carnivorous; their most important tools were most likely used for collecting vegetable foods rather than hunting. Like baboons, such a group may have stayed together while foraging through the day, and it seems unlikely that the group contained internal kinship divisions of the sort we would call a family. If these speculations are true, australopithecine behavior was only a step beyond chimpanzees'. In the wild, chimpanzees have recently been observed using sticks to get at insect nests, and, like baboons, occasionally killing and eating small animals.

Although the australopithecines are the earliest known hominids, the fact that their canine teeth were reduced to human proportions indicates that tool use was a habit of long standing; that is, tools had long since replaced canine teeth as weapons for hunting and defense. In essence, only the rudiments of the human mode of life were present in a pattern which may not have been very different from chimpanzees'. Yet erect posture and tool use had already started the trend which led to the emergence of a distinctively human way of life. The next stage of hominid development for which good evidence exists is the Middle Pleistocene of half a million years ago. By this time larger men with bigger brains had developed a recognizably human way of life. Tools and weapons were more complex and hunters were killing large animals. In the camps of these early men the habits and attitudes, the cultural heritage of the human group as we know it, must have developed rapidly. For five hundred thousand years this hunting-and-gathering way of life was the universal mode of economic organization. Although agriculture and settled communities have vastly complicated man's social life, as recently as ten thousand years ago all men were hunter-gatherers, and it is in this context that subsequent human history must be viewed.

At present the story of man's development through this long period of prehistory is still a great puzzle for which we have only scattered pieces. As new evidence accumulates—from the archeologist's spade, from the study of contemporary hunter-gatherers, and from the natural history of monkeys and apes—it will be increasingly possible to retrace man's passage from his common ancestry with the other primates to his uniquely human way of life.

BIBLIOGRAPHICAL NOTE

I have made no attempt to list all of the field reports and journal articles on which the preceding remarks are based, but the following references include the most pertinent and readily accessible. Schaller's book on the mountain gorilla (1963) is the most thorough study of the ecology and behavior of a nonhuman primate available. DeVore (in press) contains summaries of a series of recent field studies of monkeys and apes, as well as chapters on reproduction, communication, and social development. Petter (1962) has recently published the only substantial report on the behavior and ecology of a group of prosimians. Itani's (1954) book on the Japanese macaque is in Japanese, but Imanishi's (1960) article summarizes much of the Japan Monkey Center's research to that date. Background references for the reconstruction of human behavior in the Pleistocene include Roe and Simpson (1958), Tax (1960a), *Scientific American* (1960), and Clark (1959). The description of wolf behavior is based on Murie (1944) and on conference reports by Benson Ginsburg, who is directing a research project on wolves at the University of Chicago. Other references are contained in the general bibliography at the end of this book.

3.

THE TRANSITION TO HUMANITY

Clifford Geertz

THE QUESTION OF THE relationship of man to the other animals has been a persisting one in the human sciences. Since Darwin, it has hardly been doubted that there is such a relationship. But concerning its nature, and particularly its closeness, there has been very much more debate, not all of it enlightening. Some students, especially those in the biological sciences—zoölogy, palaeontology, anatomy and physiology—have tended to stress the kinship between man and what we are pleased to call the lower animals. They see evolution as a relatively unbroken flow of biological process, and they tend to view man as but one of the more interesting forms life has taken, along with dinosaurs, white mice and dolphins. What strikes them is continuity, the pervasive unity of the organic world, the unconditioned generality of the principles in terms of which it is formed. However, students in the social sciences—psychologists, sociologists, political scientists—while not denying man's animal nature have tended to view him as unique, as being different, as they often put it, not just in "degree" but in "kind." Man is the toolmaking, the talking, the symbolizing animal. Only he laughs; only he knows that we will die; only he disdains to mate with his mother and sister; only he contrives those visions of other worlds to live in which Santayana called religions, or bakes those mudpies of the mind which Cyril Connolly called art. He has, the argument continues, not just mentality but consciousness, not just needs but values, not just fears but conscience, not just a past but a history. Only he, it concludes in grand summation, has culture.

The reconciliation of these two points of view has not been easy, particularly in a field such as anthropology, which, in the United States at least, has always had a foot in both camps. On the one hand, anthropologists have been the main students of human physical evolution, tracing the stages by which modern man emerged out of a general primate background. On the other, they have been the students par excellence of culture, even when they were not entirely certain what they meant by that term. Unlike some biological scientists, they could not ignore man's cultural life as belonging "over on the Arts side," beyond the confines of Science altogether. Unlike some social scientists, they could not dismiss his physical history as irrelevant to an understanding of his present condition. As a result, the problem of the origin of culture, no matter how often ignored as unimportant or derided as insoluble, has continually come pressing back to the center of our attention as, piece by piece, the story of the physical evolution of *Homo sapiens* has been put together. It is the peculiar genius of such an eclectic discipline as American anthropology that the triumphs of one branch of it expose the failures of the others; and in such a way the science is built.

For the past half century or so, the reigning solution of the origin-of-culture problem has been what might be called the "critical point" theory. This term, which I take from the recently deceased dean of American anthropology, Alfred Kroeber, postulates that the development of the capacity for acquiring culture was a sudden, all-or-none, quantum-leap type of occurrence in the phylogeny of the primates. At some specific moment in the history of hominidization—i.e., the "humanization" of one branch of the primate line—a portentous, but in genetic or anatomical terms probably quite minor, organic alteration took place. This change, presumably in cortical structure, enabled an animal whose parents had not been competent, in Kroeber's words, "to communicate, to learn and to teach, to generalize from the endless chain of discrete feelings and attitudes" to become competent. With him culture began and, once begun, set upon its own course so as to grow wholly independently of the further organic evolution of man. The whole process of the creation of modern man's capacity for producing and using culture was conceptualized as one of a marginal quantitative change giving

rise to a radical qualitative difference. Kroeber used the simile of
the freezing of water, which can be reduced degree by degree
without any loss in fluidity until suddenly it solidifies at 0°C.
Another anthropologist compared the process to that of a taxiing
plane as it accelerates along the ground toward that tremulous
instant when it is launched into flight. A physical anthropologist,
critical of the notion, referred to it drily as the appointment to
rank view of the appearance of man, "as if he had suddenly
been promoted from colonel to brigadier general." Man's humanity, like the flare of a struck match, leaped into existence.

There were three major considerations which led to and
supported this general view. First, there was the tremendous
apparent gap between the mental abilities of man and his closest
living relatives, the great apes. Man can talk, can symbolize,
can fabricate tools, etc.; no other contemporary animal can
even approximate such accomplishments. One primatologist
couple even undertook the heroic experiment of raising a chim-
panzee in their household as though it were an adopted sibling
to their natural daughter, giving it, in a rough sort of way, the
same care and education given to the human child. But though
the chimp learned a good many rather unusual things for a
chimp to learn—how to operate a spray gun, how to pry the
lids off of tin cans with a screwdriver, and, at one glorious
point, how to pull an imaginary toy around by an imaginary
string—it never even began to learn to talk. And, unable to
talk, it was soon left far behind by its less agile but more
loquacious human sister who proceeded onward, one presumes,
to spin complicated theories about the uniqueness of the human
condition.

Second, language, symbolization, abstraction, etc., seemed,
on purely logical grounds, to be all-or-none, yes-or-no matters.
One either spoke or did not; made tools or did not; imagined
demons or did not. Half-religions, half-arts, half-languages did
not seem even conceivable, for the essential process which lay
behind them—i.e., the imposition of an arbitrary framework
of symbolic meaning upon reality—was not the sort of activity
of which there were partial versions. The progress from simple
reflex activity, through conditioned responses and complex
sign behavior, to symbolic thought was seen as a series of jumps,

not an ascending continuum. Between the perception of the
natural relationship of dark clouds to rain and the establishment
of the arbitrary relationship of dark clouds to hopelessness
there were, so it was thought, no intermediate stages.

And, third, there was the more delicate problem of what is
usually called "the psychic unity of mankind." This has reference to the proposition—today not seriously questioned by any
reputable anthropologist—which asserts that there are no important differences in the nature of the thought process among the
various living races of mankind. If one assumes that culture
appeared full-blown at some instant of time at a period before
racial differentiation began, then this proposition becomes true
virtually by deduction. To raise the question as to whether there
might be historical differences in the ability to acquire culture
among different species of hominids—i.e., among the various sorts
of "men," living and extinct—seemed to raise it with respect
to different races of modern men. And as the empirical evidence
against such differences among the various groups of *Homo
sapiens* was, and is, overwhelming, the hypothesis seemed dis-
proved on the face of it. Thus comparative psychology, semantics, and ethnology converged to support the critical point
theory of the origin of culture.

One branch of anthropology, however, did not so converge—
human palaeontology, i.e., the study of human evolution by
means of the discovery and analysis of fossil remains. Ever since
that strange Dutch physician, Eugene DuBois, found the skull
cap of *Pithecanthropus erectus,* the "erect ape-man," in a Javanese
river bed in 1891, historical physical anthropology has been
steadily piling up evidence that makes the drawing of a sharp
line between man and non-man on an anatomical basis increasingly difficult. Despite some halfhearted attempts to establish a
"cerebral Rubicon"—a critical brain size at which the ability to
behave in a properly human manner springs full-grown into
existence like Athena from the brow of Zeus—the findings of
human palaeontologists have, bit by fossil bit, smoothed the
curve of the descent of man to the point where flat assertions
about what is human and what is not human have come to have
a painfully arbitrary air about them. Whether or not human
minds or souls come in degrees, human bodies most assuredly do.

The most disturbing fossil finds in this connection have been the various sorts of australopithecine "man-apes" which have been coming out of southern and eastern Africa since Raymond Dart dug the first one up out of the Transvaal in 1924. Certainly the most momentous discoveries in the history of human palaeontology, these fossils, which date anywhere from three-quarters of a million to a million and three-quarters years ago, show a striking mosaic of primitive and advanced morphological characteristics, in which the most outstanding features are a pelvis and leg formation strikingly similar to that of modern man and a cranial capacity hardly larger than that of living apes. The initial tendency was to regard this puzzling conjunction in one animal of a "manlike" bipedal locomotive system and an "apelike" brain as indicating that the australopithecines represented an aberrant and ill-fated line of development separate from both the human and the great ape lines—better to be a thorough-going ape than half a man, as Ernest Hooton once put it. But the present consensus is that they represent the oldest known forms in the evolutionary process which eventually produced modern man out of some generally simian stock. In these bizarre half-men our own full humanity is rooted.

F. Clark Howell will discuss the significance of the australopithecines from the point of view of human phylogeny in the next chapter; my interest in them here is in their implications for the critical point theory of the origin of culture. These more or less erect, small-brained proto-men, their hands freed from locomotion, manufactured tools and probably hunted small animals—or at least some of them did so. But that they could have had a developed culture comparable to that of, say, the Australian aborigine or possessed language in the modern sense of the term with a brain about a third the size of our own seems wholly unlikely. In the australopithecine we seem to have, therefore, a kind of "man" who evidently was capable of acquiring some elements of culture—simple toolmaking, sporadic hunting, and perhaps some system of communication more advanced than that of contemporary apes and less advanced than that of true speech— but not others, a state of affairs which casts something of a shadow on the critical point theory. What seemed presumptively unlikely, or even logically impossible, turns out to have been empirically true—like man himself, the capacity for culture emerged gradually, continuously, step by step, over a quite extended period of time.

But the situation is even more desperate. Because if the australopithecines had an elementary form of culture (what one anthropologist has called "proto-culture") with a brain one-third the size of that of modern man, then it follows that the greater part of human cortical expansion has followed, *not* preceded, the "beginning" of culture. In the critical point view man was considered more or less complete, neurologically at least, before the growth of culture commenced, because the biological capacity for culture was an all-or-none thing. Once achieved it was achieved entirely; all else was a mere adding on of new customs and developing of older ones. Organic evolution proceeded up to a certain point and then, the cerebral Rubicon crossed, cultural evolution took over, a process in itself autonomous and not dependent upon or productive of further nervous system alterations. The fact that this is apparently not the case, that cultural development was underway well before organic development ceased, is of fundamental significance for our view of the nature of man. He becomes, now, not just the producer of culture but, in a specifically biological sense, its product.

√ This is true because the pattern-of-selection pressures during the terminal phases of the evolution of the human animal was partly determined by the initial phases of human cultural development, not simply by natural environmental factors alone. A reliance upon tool manufacture, for example, puts a premium on both manual dexterity and on foresight. Within a population of australopithecines an individual somewhat better endowed with these characteristics would have had a selective advantage over an individual somewhat less well endowed. Hunting small animals with primitive weapons involves, among other things, great patience and persistence. The individual with more of these sober virtues would have an advantage over a flightier individual with less of them. All these various abilities, skills, dispositions, or whatever, are, of course, dependent in turn upon nervous system development. And so the introduction of tool manufacture and hunting must have acted to shift selection pressures so as to favor the rapid growth of the forebrain, as, in all likelihood,

did the advances in social organization, communication, and
moral regulation which, there is reason to believe, also occurred
during this period of overlap between cultural and biological
change.

Much of the work in this area is, of course, still speculative,
and we are just beginning to ask the questions rather than to
answer them. The systematic study of primate behavior under
natural conditions which DeVore described, and which is having such an impact on our interpretations of the social life
of early man, is, save for a few isolated exceptions, scarcely
a decade old, for example. The fossil record itself is now expanding at such a fantastic rate and dating procedures are becoming
so rapidly refined that only the foolhardy would attempt to
set out definitive opinions on particular matters. But, details,
evidence, and specific hypotheses aside, the essential point is
that the innate, generic constitution of modern man (what, in a
simpler day, used to be called "human nature") now appears
to be both a cultural and a biological product. "It is probably
more correct," the physical anthropologist Sherwood Washburn
has written, "to think of much of our [physical] structure as a
result of culture rather than to think of men anatomically like
ourselves slowly discovering culture." The slogan "man makes
himself" now comes to have a more literal meaning than originally supposed.

The ice age, with its rapid and radical variations in climate,
land formations, and vegetation, has long been recognized to
be a period in which conditions were ideal for the speedy and
efficient evolutionary development of man. Now it seems also to
have been a period in which a cultural environment increasingly
supplemented the natural environment in the selection process
so as to further accelerate the rate of human evolution to an
unprecedented speed. It appears not to have been merely a time
of receding brow ridges and shrinking jaws, but a time in which
were forged nearly all those characteristics of man's existence
which are most graphically human: his thoroughly encephalated
nervous system, his incest-taboo-based social structure, and his
capacity to create and use symbols. The fact that these distinctive features of humanity emerged together in complex
interaction with one another rather than serially, as for so long

supposed, is a fact of exceptional importance in the interpretation of human mentality, because it suggests that man's nervous
system does not merely enable him to acquire culture, it positively demands that he do so if it is going to function at all.
Rather than culture acting only to supplement, develop, and
extend organically based capacities genetically prior to it, it
would seem to be ingredient to those capacities themselves. A
cultureless human being would probably turn out to be not an
intrinsically talented though unfulfilled ape, but a wholly mind-
less and consequently unworkable monstrosity. Like the cabbage
it so much resembles, the *Homo sapiens* brain, having arisen
within the framework of human culture, would not be viable
outside of it.

The general implications of this revised view of the transition
to humanity are many, only a few of which can be touched upon
here. On the one hand, it has forced a reinvestigation and re-
formulation of the theoretical considerations which supported
the critical point theory in the first place. The argument from
comparative primate psychology, for example, it is now apparent,
established not the uniqueness of modern man, but rather the
distinctiveness of the whole five- to twenty-five-million year
hominid line of which he is but the culminating and, it so
happens, the only living representative, but which includes a
large number of different kinds of extinct animals, all of them
much "closer" to man than is any living ape. The fact that
chimpanzees do not talk is both interesting and important, but
to draw from that fact the conclusion that speech is an all-or-
nothing phenomenon is rather like assuming that, since the
giraffe is the only living quadruped with such a long neck, he
must have achieved it by a sort of quantum stretch. The great
apes may be man's closest living relatives, but "close" is, to
commit a pun, a relative term. Given a realistic time scale they
are not actually so close at all, the last common ancestor being
at the very least fifty thousand centuries back in what geologists
call the Pliocene, and perhaps even further back than that.

As for the logical argument, that too has come to be questioned. The rapidly increasing interest in communication as a
general process which has marked disciplines from engineering to
ethology in the last decade or two has, on the one hand, reduced

speech to but one—admittedly highly flexible and efficient—mechanism for the transmission of meanings among many, and, on the other hand, provided a theoretical framework in terms of which series of graded steps leading up to true speech can be conceived. This work cannot be reviewed here, but as an example one linguist has compared eight different systems of communication ranging from bee dancing, fish courtship and bird singing through gibbon calls, instrumental music and human language. Rather than pivoting his entire analysis around the simple, and by now somewhat overburdened, sign-*vs.*- symbol distinction, he distinguishes thirteen design features of language and attempts in terms of them to analyze the difference between human and subhuman communication more precisely and to construct a possible course from the gradual development of true speech out of proto-speech during the ice age. This kind of work, too, is only in its infancy. But the day seems to be coming to an end when the only thing that could usefully be said about the origins of language was that all humans equally possess it and all non-humans equally do not.

Finally, the established fact that there are no significant differences in innate mental capacity among the living races of man is not contradicted, but if anything supported and deepened by the postulation of differences in the capacity to acquire culture among different forms of prosapiens men. The physical divergence of the human races is, of course, a very recent matter, beginning perhaps only fifty thousand years or so ago, or, by the most conservative estimates, less than one hundredth of the length of the whole hominid, i.e., man-forming, line. Thus mankind has not only spent the overwhelming proportion of its history in an altogether common evolutionary process, but this period now seems to have been precisely the one during which the fundamental features of its humanity were forged. Modern races are just that: modern. They represent very late, and very secondary, adaptation in skin color, facial structure, etc.—probably mainly to climatic differences—as *Homo sapiens* dispersed throughout the world toward the close of the glacial period. These adaptations are thus entirely subsequent to the basic formative processes of neural and anatomical development which occurred between the founding of the hominid line and

the emergence, fifty- to one hundred fifty millennia ago, of
Homo sapiens. Mentally, man was made in the ice age, and the
really decisive shaping force in producing his uniqueness—
the interaction of the initial phases of cultural development and
the culminating ones of biological transformation—is part of the
common background of all modern races. Thus, the view that the
capacity for carrying culture, rather than bursting into full
flower at a single point, was hammered out in old stone age tool-
shops over an extended period of time, far from undermining the
doctrine of psychic unity explains and specifies it. It gives it a
realistic historical grounding it previously rather lacked.

But even more important than the revision of reinterpretation
of older theories which the synchronous, rather than the sequential, view of the relationship between the evolution of human
anatomy and the birth of human culture necessitates, is its
implications for a novel way of thinking about culture itself. If
man grew up, so to speak, within the context of a developing
cultural environment, then that environment must needs be
viewed not as a mere extrasomatic extension, a sort of artificial amplification, of already given innate capacities, but as
ingredient to the existence of those capacities themselves. The
apparent fact that the final stages of the biological evolution
of man occurred after the initial stages of the growth of culture
implies, as I have already noted, that "basic," "pure," or "unconditioned" human nature, in the sense of the innate constitution of man, is so functionally incomplete as to be unworkable. Tools, hunting, family organization, and later, art, religion,
and a primitive form of "science," molded man somatically, and
they are therefore necessary not merely to his survival but to his
existential realization. It is true that without men there would
be no cultural forms. But it is also true that without cultural
forms there would be no men.

The symbolic network of belief, expression, and value within
which we live provides for us the mechanisms for ordered
behavior which in lower animals are genetically built in to their
bodies but which in ourselves are not. The uniqueness of man
has often been expressed in terms of how much and how many
different things he is capable of learning. And, although chimpanzees who learn to play with imaginary toys may give us some

pause, this is true enough. But what is of perhaps even more fundamental theoretical importance is how much there is for man to learn. Without the guiding patterns of human culture, man's intellectual life would be but the buzzing, blooming confusion that William James called it; cognition in man depends upon the existence of objective, external symbolic models of reality in a way no ape's does. Emotionally, the case is the same. Without the guidance of the public images of sentiment found in ritual, myth, and art we would, quite literally, not know how to feel. Like the expanded forebrain itself, ideas and emotions are cultural artifacts in man.

What this heralds, I think, is a fundamental revision in the theory of culture itself. We are going, in the next few decades, to look at culture patterns less and less in terms of the way in which they constrain human nature, and more and more in the way in which, for better or for worse, they actualize it; less and less as an accumulation of ingenious devices to extend pre-existing innate capacities, and more and more as part and parcel of those capacities themselves; less and less as a superorganic cake of custom, and more and more as, in a vivid phrase of the late Clyde Kluckhohn's, designs for living. Man is the only living animal who needs such designs for he is the only living animal whose evolutionary history has been such that his physical being has been significantly shaped by their existence and is, therefore, irrevocably predicated upon them. As the full import of this fact becomes recognized, the tension between the view of man as but a talented animal and the view of him as an unaccountably unique one should evaporate, along with the theoretical misconceptions which gave rise to it.

BIBLIOGRAPHICAL NOTE

Kroeber's statement of the "critical point" theory is to be found in his *Anthropology* (1958:71-72). A somewhat different, less cautious formulation of the theory, emphasizing the discontinuity between symbol using and other forms of thought, can be found in White (1949). For brief discussions of the australopithecinae and their significance, see the chapters by Leakey and by Washburn and Clark in Tax (1960b); some comments on australopithecine cultural achievements can be found in the chapter by Hallowell in the same book. Hallowell (1959) is also valuable in this connection. A good popular summary of the theory of the relationship between tool using and neurological change can be found in an article by Washburn in *Scientific American* (1960) and, in fact, this entire special issue on "The Human Species" is relevant. Finally, I have myself developed the above arguments at greater length and more technically in "The Growth of Culture and the Evolution of Mind" (1962), and have in fact adapted a number of passages from this paper into the above essay.

4.

THE HOMINIZATION PROCESS

F. Clark Howell

MODERN PALEOANTHROPOLOGICAL studies seek to understand, in both biological and cultural perspective, those factors which effected the evolution of man. The biologically-oriented anthropologist is especially concerned with the nature and adaptive significance of major anatomical and physiological transformations in the evolution of the body from an apelike higher primate to the single variable species, *Homo sapiens*. He must equally concern himself with the origin and evolution of distinctively human patterns of behavior, especially capabilities for culture and the manifestations of such capacities, and not only with their biological bases.

The fossil record of man and his higher primate relatives is still far from adequate. However, in the last several decades significant discoveries have been made which considerably expand our knowledge of ancient human and near-human populations. There is not now a single major range of Pleistocene time from which some one or more parts of the world has not at last yielded some hominid skeletal remains. Hence, there is now some pertinent evidence to suggest the general sequence and relative order of those bodily transformations during this process of hominization. In this process major changes were effected at quite unequal rates, in: the locomotor skeleton, the teeth and their supporting facial structures, the size and proportions of the brain, and the enveloping skull bones. And there were equally significant and accompanying changes in behavior. In the course of the last decade the earlier phases of this process have received considerable investigation. Some significant aspects of that work are to be considered here.

Man is a primate and within the order Primates is most closely related to the living African anthropoid apes. How immediate the relationship, or to put it another way, how far removed in time the point of common ancestry prior to divergence, is still unsettled. Except under special circumstances skeletal remains are not readily preserved in the acid soils of forested habitats; hence fossil remains of anthropoid apes from the requisite late Tertiary time range, some twenty- to a few million years ago, are uncommon, and when found are often very inadequately preserved. Nevertheless, apelike higher primates are known to have had a widespread Eurasiatic distribution (up until five to ten million years ago, by which time such creatures had disappeared from increasingly temperate Europe); they were presumably also common in parts of Africa, although there, fossiliferous beds of that age are singularly rare. Fragmentary jaws and teeth of such creatures indicate their higher primate—indeed, specifically ape—affinities. They also suggest substantial diversity in anatomical structure as well as in over-all size. The rare and fortunate occurrence of other skeletal parts (such as limb bones) indicate that some distinguishing characteristics of modern apes were later evolutionary "specializations" rather than the "primitive" ancestral condition. Several specimens of jaws and teeth, from regions as widely separate as northern India and eastern Africa, and some ten- to fourteen million years in age, show some hominid resemblances. Until more adequately preserved skeletal remains are recovered, these few provocative fragments will remain enigmatic. The antecedents of the hominids, the so-called proto-hominids, are still really unknown, and one can only speculate about the very early formative phases in the process of hominid emergence.

The anatomical-physiological basis of the radiation of the hominids is generally acknowledged to have been a major transformation in structure and function of the locomotor system. The lower limb skeleton and associated musculature were modified under selection pressures eventually to permit a fully erect posture and efficient, habitual bipedal gait. The changes effected in the lower limb were extensive and revolutionary. The characteristic curvature of the loins, the short, broad and backwardly shifted hip bones and their displaced and strengthened articulation with the sacrum, their sinuous distortion to form a basin-like structure about the lower abdomen, as well as the shortened ischial region, were all part of a complex of largely interrelated modifications adaptive for terrestrial bipedalism. There were related changes in the musculature of the hip and thigh, in relative proportions and in structure and function of specific muscle groups, all to afford power to run and to step off in walking, to maintain the equilibrium of the upright trunk during the stride, and to extend fully and to stabilize the elongated lower limb at hip and knee—an impossible stance for any ape. And the foot was fully inverted, with the lateral toes shortened and the hallux enlarged and immobilized, the rigidity of the tarsus enhanced through the angularity of joints and strengthened ligaments, with the development of prominent longitudinal and transverse arches, and the heel broadened to become fully weight-bearing.

The singularity of the erect posture was long ago recognized from comparative anatomical studies of man and the nonhuman primates. Its priority in the hominization process has been fully confirmed by the discovery in Africa of the still earliest known hominids, the australopithecines (genus *Australopithecus*), creatures with small brains, but with lower limbs adapted to the erect posture and bipedal gait, or at least for upright running. Some evidence suggests that the full-fledged adaptation to bipedalism, that which permitted leisurely and prolonged walking, was not yet wholly perfected. The hominid type of dental structure, with small incisor teeth, reduced and spatulate-shaped canines, and noninterlocking canines and anterior premolar teeth all set in a parabolic-shaped dental arch, was also fully differentiated. Brain size, as estimated from skull capacities, was only about a third to two-fifths that of the size range of anatomically modern man. There are several distinct forms of the genus *Australopithecus*, surely distinct species (and probably valid subgenera), with consistent differences in skeletal anatomy as well as in body size. One larger form attained a body weight of some one hundred twenty to one hundred fifty pounds, whereas another was much smaller with a body weight of only some sixty to seventy-five pounds.

Although thus far restricted to Africa, these earliest known hominids were nonetheless fairly widely distributed over sub-

stantial portions of that continent. Their ecological adjustments
are now known in some measure and can even be paralleled
among certain present-day African environments within the same
regions. One small South African species is recorded under rainfall conditions some 50 per cent less than that of the present-day
(now twenty-eight to thirty inches) in the same region—a rolling,
high veld country of low relief and little surface water. Other
occurrences testify to more favorable climatic and environmental
situations. Generally speaking, the environments were relatively
open savanna. In southern Africa remains of these creatures,
along with other animals, occur in caves in a limestone plateau
landscape where caverns, fissures, and sink holes probably
afforded fairly permanent sources of water which was otherwise
scarce. But there, and also in eastern Africa, sites were in
proximity to more wooded habitats fringing shallow water
courses, or mantling the slopes of adjacent volcanic highlands. It
is just such transitional zones, the "ecotones" of the ecologist,
which afford the greatest abundance and diversity of animal and
plant life.

The absolute age of some of these creatures can now be as-
certained as a consequence of refinements in the measurement
of radioactivity (potassium/argon or K/A) in some constituent
minerals of volcanic rocks. Their temporal range extends back
nearly two million years with some representatives apparently
having persisted until less than a million years ago. Their discovery has therefore tripled the time range previously known
for the evolution of the hominids.

Culturally-patterned behavior appears concurrently with these
creatures. In several instances there is direct association with
some of their skeletal remains. The field investigation of undisturbed occupation places, maximizing the possibility for the
recovery of evidence in archeological context, has culminated
in these significant discoveries. Traditional prehistoric archeological studies, on the other hand, were largely preoccupied with
the sequential relationships of relics of past human endeavors,
often in secondary contexts. The careful exposure of undisturbed
occupation places has permitted wholly new inferences into
the nature of past hominid adaptations and patterns of behavior.
This work has broader implications for it forces complete re-

jection of the traditional viewpoint of some anthropologists which envisioned the sudden appearance of human behavior and culture at a "critical point" in man's phylogeny, a matter discussed earlier by Geertz.

This most primitive cultural behavior is manifest in several ways. There was a limited capability to fashion simple tools and weapons from stone (and presumably in other media, although perishable materials are not preserved). These objects, the raw material of which was not infrequently brought from sources some distance away, include deliberately collected, sometimes fractured or battered, natural stones or more substantially modified core (nodular) and flake pieces fashioned to produce chopping, cutting, or piercing edges. Several undisturbed occupation places with associated animal bones attest also to the acquisition of a meat-eating diet. It was limited, however, to the exploitation of only a narrow range of the broad spectrum of a rich savanna and woodland fauna. It comprised predominantly various freshwater fish, numerous sorts of small amphibians, reptiles (mostly tortoises and lizards), and birds, many small mammals (rodents and insectivores), and some infants (or the very young) of a few moderate-sized herbivorous ungulates. Vegetal products doubtless constituted a very substantial part of the diet of these predaceous-foragers, but the conditions of preservation prohibit other than inferences as to what these may have been. At any rate carnivorous behavior of these earliest hominids contrasts markedly with the essentially vegetarian proclivities of recent apes (and monkeys).

Such food remains and associated stone artifacts are concentrated over occupation surfaces of restricted extent—in part at least seasonally exposed mud flats around ephemeral lakes adjacent to periodically active volcanoes. These occupational concentrations have a nonuniform distribution over the occupation surfaces; there are dense central clusters of tools and much broken-up and crushed bones (presumably to extract the marrow), and peripherally more sparse occurrences of natural or only battered stones and different, largely unbroken skeletal parts of their prey. In one case a large ovoid-shaped pattern of concentrated and heaped-up stony rubble, with adjacent irregular piles of stone, suggests a structural feature on the occupation surface. These uniquely preserved sites in eastern Africa, sealed in quickly by primary falls of volcanic ash, afford some tantalizing glimpses into the activities of these primitive creatures. Such occupation places may well represent an ancient manifestation of the adjustment to a "home base" within the range, a unique development within the hominid adaptation.

We can now delineate some of the basic features of the early radiation of the hominids to include: (1) differentiation and reduction of the anterior dentition; (2) skeletal and muscular modifications to permit postural uprightness and erect cursorial bipedalism; (3) effective adjustment to, and exploitation of a terrestrial habitat; (4) probably a relatively expanded brain; (5) extensive manipulation of natural objects and development of motor habits to facilitate toolmaking; and (6) carnivorous predation adding meat protein to a largely vegetal diet.

The adaptation was essentially that of erectly bipedal higher primates adjusting to a predaceous-foraging existence. These adaptations permitted or perhaps were conditioned by the dispersal into a terrestrial environment and the exploitation of grassland or parkland habitats. The African apes (and also the Asiatic gibbon), especially the juvenile individuals, show occasional though unsustained efforts at bipedalism; it is highly probable that this preadaptive tendency, which developed as a consequence of the overhand arboreal climbing adaptation of semierect apes, was pronounced in the still unknown proto-hominids of the Pliocene. Wild chimpanzees are now recognized sometimes to eat meat from kills they have made, and also to manipulate inanimate objects, and even to use and occasionally to shape them for aid in the food quest. This would surely suggest that such tendencies were at least equally well developed among the closely related proto-hominids.

Terrestrial environments were, of course, successfully colonized long previously by other primates. These are certain cercopithecoid monkeys, the secondarily ground-dwelling quadrupedal patas monkeys and baboons of Africa and the macaques of Asia (and formerly Europe). Hence their adaptations, social behavior, and troop organization provide a useful analogy for inferences into the radiation of the proto-hominids. Comparative investigations of the nonhuman primates, including the increasingly numerous and thorough behavioral and ecological studies of monkeys and apes in natural habitats mentioned by DeVore, have substantially broadened our understanding of the primate background to human evolution. These studies serve to emphasize those particular uniquenesses of the human adaptation.

A half million or probably nearly a million years ago, hominids were in the process of dispersal outside the primary ecological zone exploited by the australopithecines. In part, this dispersal can be understood only in respect to the opportunities for faunal exchange between the African and Eurasiatic continents, and the prevailing paleogeographic and paleoecological conditions of the earlier Pleistocene. The diverse Saharan zone failed to constitute a barrier to this dispersal, or to that of Pliocene and early Pleistocene mammal faunas for that matter. Moreover the extensive seas of the Pliocene and earliest Pleistocene were sufficiently lowered, either due to continental uplift, or, less likely, as a consequence of the incorporation of oceanic waters in extensive arctic-subarctic ice caps, so as to afford substantial intercontinental connections.

Probably within a hundred thousand years, or less, representatives of the genus *Homo* were dispersed throughout most of the Eurasian subtropics and had even penetrated northward well into temperate latitudes in both Europe and eastern Asia. This dispersal involved adjustment to a diverse new variety of habitats. Cultural and perhaps physiological adaptations permitted, for the first time, man's existence outside the tropics under new and rigorous climatic conditions, characterized by long and inclement winters. It was unquestionably facilitated by anatomical-physiological modifications to produce the genus *Homo* including prolongation of growth and delayed maturation, and behavioral changes favoring educability, communication, and over-all capabilities for culture.

The fully human pattern of locomotion was probably perfected by this time. These final transformations in the hip, thigh, and foot permitted a fully relaxed standing posture, with the body at rest, as well as sustained walking over long distances. The skeletal evidence is unfortunately still incomplete, but some four to six hundred thousand years ago the lower limb skeleton appears not to have differed in any important respect from that of anatomically modern man. Brain size, and especially the relative proportions of the temporal-parietal and frontal association areas, were notably increased to some one-half to two-thirds that of *Homo sapiens* (and to well within that range which permits normal behavior in the latter species). And some further reduction and simplification also occurred in the molar (and premolar) teeth and the supporting bony structures of the face and lower jaw.

Hunting was important as a basis for subsistence. Meat-eating doubtless formed a much increased and stable portion of the normal diet. Much of the mammalian faunal spectrum was exploited, and the prey included some or all of the largest of herbivorous species, including gregarious "herd" forms as well as more solitary species, and a variety of small mammals. Several occupation places of these early and primitive hunters, some of which are quite undisturbed, are preserved and have been excavated in eastern Africa and now also in Europe. These localities preserve prodigious quantities of skeletal remains of slaughtered and butchered mammals. The famous and enormous cave locality (Locality I) of Choukoutien (near Peking) in eastern Asia is a unique occurrence of occupation of a site of this type at such an early time. At Choukoutien, although other ungulate and carnivorous mammals are also present, about 70 per cent of the animal remains are represented by only two species of deer. In Africa the impressive quarry included a number of gigantic herbivorous species, as well as other extinct forms. In two such occupation sites in eastern Africa, over five hundred thousand years old, the very abundant fauna included species of three simians, two carnivores, two rhinos, eight pigs, two to three elephants, sheep and buffalo, two hippos, three giraffids, a chalicothere, six horses, as well as numerous antelopes and gazelles, and other remains of small mammals (rodents), birds, and some reptiles (tortoises). Preferential hunting of certain herd species is recognized at several somewhat younger occupation sites in Europe. At one of two sites in central Spain recently worked by the writer only five large mammalian species are represented, and of these a woodland elephant and wild horse are most numerous, with infrequent wild oxen (aurochs) and stag (red deer), and very rare rhinoceros. The remains of some thirty individual elephants, many of which were immature, are represented in an area of approximately *three hundred* square meters! At another such open-air site, on the edge of the Tyrrhenian sea north of Rome, remains of horse predominated over all other species. Some indication of the level of cultural capability and adaptation, as well as requisite plasticity for local ecological adjustment is afforded by the diversity of game species which were exploited and the corresponding distinctions in occurrence, habitat preference, size of aggregation, and their species-specific patterns of behavior.

Toolmaking capabilities are notably improved along with the establishment of persistent habits of manufacture. These reflect, in part at least, more dexterous and effective control of manual skills. Corresponding evolutionary changes in the structure and function of the hand, especially development of the fully and powerfully opposable thumb, with expansion and complication of the corresponding sector of the cerebral motor cortex and interrelated association areas, were all effected under the action of natural selection.

Not only was the over-all quantity and quality of the stone tools increased. New techniques were developed for the initial preparation as well as for the subsequent fashioning of diverse and selected sorts of stone into tools (and weapons). New types of stone tools make their appearance, including in particular sharply pointed and cutting-edged tools of several sorts, seemingly most appropriate for butchery of tough-skinned game. Certain stones already of favorable form were deliberately trimmed into a spheroidal shape, it is thought, as offensive missiles. These and other forms of tools subsequently become remarkably standardized. This fact, and the very broad pattern of geographic distribution throughout Africa, southern and western Europe, and through western into southern Asia and the Indian subcontinent, suggest also a sophisticated level of communication and conceivably even the capability of symbolization.

More perishable stuffs, such as wood and fiber, are unfortunately very rarely preserved. However, several such early sites in Europe attest the utilization and working of wood, fashioned into elongate, pointed, and spatulate shapes. The discovery had doubtless been made of the thrusting spear, a major offensive weapon in the pursuit of large, thick-skinned mammals. Again, although traces of the utilization of fire are nearly equally as rarely preserved, there is incontrovertible evidence of its discovery and utilization (whether for heat or cookery is uncertain), both in Europe and in eastern Asia.

The development of a hunting way of life, even at a very unsophisticated level of adaptation, it has been argued, set very different requirements on early human populations. It led to markedly altered selection pressures and was, in fact, responsible for profound changes in human biology and culture. Many workers regard this adaptation as a critical factor in the emergence of fundamentally human institutions. Some of those changes which represent the human (*Homo*) way of life would include: (1) greatly increased size of the home range with defense of territorial boundaries to prevent infringement upon the food sources; (2) band organization of interdependent and affiliated human groups of variable but relatively small size; (3) (extended) family groupings with prolonged male-female relationships, incest prohibition, rules of exogamy for mates, and subgroups based on kinship; (4) sexual division of labor; (5) altruistic behavior with food-sharing, mutual aid, and cooperation; and (6) linguistic communities based on speech.

It may appear impossible ever to obtain direct evidence of this sort from the fossil and archeological record. Yet an approach which combines the field and laboratory study of the behavior of living nonhuman primates with analysis of basic patterns of adaptation and behavior of human hunter-gatherer populations can enhance enormously the sorts of inferences usually drawn from the imperfect evidence of paleoanthropological investigations. The favorable consequences of active coöperation between students concerned with the origin and evolution of human behavior, however diverse in background and orientation, is already evident and has considerably advanced understanding of the process of hominization. In the coming years it may be comparable with those advances in paleoanthropological studies effected through the fullest cooperation with colleagues in the natural sciences.

BIBLIOGRAPHICAL NOTE

The point of view expressed here is also discussed by Washburn and Howell (in Tax 1960a) and at greater length in Howell (1961) where pertinent references may be found. A colloquium volume (Coloques Internationaux 1958, Centre National de la Recherches Scientifiques, Paris, 1958), with chapters by various authorities, provided the title for my own essay, and is rewarding reading for anyone seriously interested in the subject. Much basic information, as well as ecological viewpoints which will surely provide the basis for much further research, will be found in the recently published symposium volume (Howell and Bourlière, eds., 1963). Much of the research work from which I have drawn conclusions and generalizations is still in progress, in both field and laboratory, and only preliminary reports are available at most. Many of my colleagues have shared with me their field experiences, basic data and preliminary interpretations, and to each of them I am deeply grateful.

5.

HUMAN POPULATIONS

Frank B. Livingstone

THE STUDY, BY anthropologists, of the biological characteristics of the human species has been marked by significant changes in the postwar years. The basic change is reflected in the title of my essay: "Human Populations." Now we are attempting to describe human variability, or at least that of interest to anthropologists, in terms of the population as the unit of study. Previously the individual had been the unit of study, and human genetic variability was described in terms of races. In racial analysis the individual was the unit which was classified as belonging to this or that race or mixture of races. Of course, one still has to study individuals; but the basic datum which is the anthropologist's major concern refers to populations. One can blood type individuals as belonging to either blood group O, A, B, or AB, but it is the variability in the frequencies of the O, A, and B genes in the populations of the world which is our major concern. I have used this example because it was the discovery of such genes as the ABO blood groups that are found in all human populations but in different frequencies which necessitated this change to the study of the population and its characteristics.

In the postwar years the application of relatively simple biochemical techniques to the analysis of human proteins has resulted in the discovery of a great deal of human genetic variability which was heretofore undreamed of. Since the basic techniques of paper electrophoresis and paper chromatography are relatively inexpensive and easy to run, they have been widely

60

used and great numbers of human populations have been studied. One of the most studied of human proteins is hemoglobin, and in the short space of ten years some twenty different varieties of adult hemoglobin have been discovered in the human species. Most of these hemoglobins appear to be due to the presence of a single gene. But while some of these genes are quite widespread among human populations, others seem to be restricted to a few groups.

In addition to simply bringing about an increase in our knowledge of the genetic variability of the human species, the studies of human hemoglobin genes have great theoretical significance and have played a major role in changing our thinking about the nature of human genetic variability and its explanation. The first of these hemoglobin genes to be discovered was the sickle cell gene. When the distribution of this gene in the populations of the world was first beginning to be known, the sickle cell gene was thought to have great anthropological significance, which means in other words that it was considered to be a racial trait or restricted to one so-called primary race, the Negroids. Even today one can read in the newspapers and national magazines that the sickle cell gene is only found in Negroes. But this is simply not true; appreciable frequencies of this gene have been found in Portugal, Italy, Greece, Turkey, Arabia, Kuwait, and India, in addition to Africa. Attempts were made to explain these occurrences of the sickle cell gene by Negro admixture, but some of these populations would then have to be 150 per cent Negro. Thus, racial analysis could not explain this particular bit of human genetic variability. Prior to the discovery of the sickle cell gene, there were other known human traits which varied considerably in the populations of the world but which were unrelated to race, so that the sickle cell gene was only the last of a great number of traits which were not "useful" in anthropology. However, the sickle cell gene raised some disturbing questions about the nature of human genetic variability and in addition suggested an explanation of this variability other than that of race.

Since persons who are homozygous for the sickle cell gene have a very serious disease, sickle cell anemia, there is a constant loss of genes in each generation. With random mating, one can

calculate for a given gene frequency how many individuals
will die each generation from sickle cell anemia and hence
how much the frequency of the sickle cell gene will decrease in
the population. The presence of high frequencies of the sickle
cell gene in many countries of the Old World thus raised the
question of how they could be maintained in the presence of this
adverse selection. As Dr. James V. Neel, who first worked out the
mode of inheritance of the phenomenon, pointed out (1950),
there were two outstanding possibilities for explaining these high
frequencies: either a high mutation rate to the sickle cell gene
from its normal alleles, or selection in favor of heterozygotes for
the sickle cell gene. Although a high mutation rate could possibly
explain the high frequencies, it would raise the further question
of why the mutation rate seemed to vary so considerably in the
populations of the world. Hence this possibility was scarcely considered, particularly since there was also no evidence in its favor.
Despite many other attempts to explain the high frequencies of
the sickle cell gene by race mixture, random gene drift, or meiotic
drive, the most plausible explanation was natural selection in
favor of heterozygotes for the sickle cell gene. And if this was the
explanation of the distribution of the sickle cell gene, was it the
explanation of much of the rest of human genetic variability? The
demonstration by Dr. Anthony C. Allison and others (1955) that
heterozygotes for this gene had a greater resistance to falciparum
malaria showed that, indeed, natural selection and not race explained the high frequencies of the sickle cell gene. Thus,
these discoveries concerning the sickle cell gene began a trend
toward examining each gene or trait of human variability in-
dividually in an attempt to investigate the role of natural
selection.

Previously human genetic variability had been used for taxonomic purposes in anthropology. Individual traits or genes were
considered to have anthropological value or be useful to anthropology only if their variability could be used to divide the
human populations of the world into races or if a particular trait
was considered to be a marker of the racial origins of some
groups.

When the world distribution of the ABO blood groups began
to become fairly well mapped out, these genes were used in the

same way, as tools in racial analysis. The blood groups were the first set of genes not concerned with external morphological characteristics to have their world distribution well known. The races which were discovered by examining their distributions were somewhat different than those based on morphology; but although the genes and races discovered were different, the concepts and methods of analysis were the same. With the discovery in the postwar years of many more genes which varied in their frequencies in the populations of the world, it was thought that the solution to the problem of race was near at hand. This followed from the idea that when we knew enough human genetic variability we would finally be in a position to discover how many races of man there really are. Genetic variability was conceived of in terms of races which were not human conceptions of reality but which actually existed out there. So that the question of how many races was quite legitimate. But the increases in knowledge did not seem to solve the problem, but only to confound it. For each new gene, a new set of races was discovered, and thus the amount of human genetic variability which could not be explained in terms of the usually accepted races increased enormously. The situation became discouraging; so much so that a recent reappraisal of the value of these newer blood group and hemoglobin genes for taxonomic purposes has labeled them worthless. This means that their distributions are not related to the morphological characteristics by which races are usually constructed. But this does not mean that the genes are worthless; the racial classifications are.

Although genetic characteristics were used to discover the races of man, these races were also thought to explain the distribution of genetic traits in an historical way. Thus, populations were similar or different in several genetic characters according to whether or not they were members of the same race. Coupled with this use of race to explain similarities and differences was the widespread use of migration as an explanatory concept. The analysis of any particular group consequently consisted in separating out the racial elements in it and then postulating how these elements migrated into the area inhabited by the group from the race's original homeland. The group would be labeled di- or tri-hybrids or a primary race according to how many races were thought to have contributed to their ancestry. Most of human variability was thus explained by associating each trait with some primary race and its subsequent migrations. I think it is easily seen that this is an historical explanation. It does not attempt to explain why some people are dark-skinned or light-skinned, but only how dark and light skinned peoples got distributed the way they are. However, race and migration were considered to be the causes of human variability. But migration is not a principle or cause of anything, but just a simple fact; either it happened or it did not.

This type of racial analysis was not practiced in a vacuum but had many conceptual similarities to the cultural anthropology of the day. Independent invention, centers of civilization, and diffusion were the concepts then in vogue in cultural anthropology, and these concepts were utilized in both limited historical studies like Spier's study of the sun dance among the Plains Indians and grander historical schemes such as Elliot-Smith's diffusion of everything from Egypt, or the culture circle theory of Graebner and Schmidt. Thus, in all fields of anthropology cultural or biological variability was being explained by such postulated historical timetables.

At the same time there was an almost complete rejection of any determinism. Perhaps the reason for this rejection is the incompatibility between determinism and racial analysis. One of the assumptions of racial analysis was that the traits or genes used to trace racial heritage were nonadaptive, which means, in other words, that the trait was not related to any environmental factor. If such traits were related to some selective factor in the environment, then the geographical distribution of this environmental variable would to a great extent explain the distribution of the trait, which would thereby not be an indication of common ancestry. In most racial analysis this alternative explanation was not even considered, or if so, dismissed as not proven. When the sickle cell gene was proven to most scientists' satisfaction to have a selective advantage in a malarious environment, it raised the question of how many others were also related to some selective factor in the environment.

While impossible canons of proof were required to show the presence of natural selection, the postulated migrations or diffusions did not require proof in the same sense. The observed similarities themselves were evidence for connections and hence proof. Usually migrations were attributed to the inner urgings of individuals, or man's eternal desire to see the other side of the mountain; but people do not migrate; they get pushed— and usually by their own overbreeding. Migrations, invasions, and expansions by animals other than man also occur and are explainable in terms of the ecology of the animal. Whether an animal population is increasing or decreasing its numbers or territory are functions of the availability of its ecological niche. When the population size is far below that which the niche can support, it will increase at an enormous rate which will at least double the population every generation.

This process of filling an ecological niche is extremely rapid in terms of geological time. In the past few centuries the filling of the Australian continent by the rabbit, or of practically the entire world by the brown rat are examples of this phenomenon among other mammals, while in the human species the recent Japanese expansion or the Irish expansion of the eighteenth- and early nineteenth centuries are examples. However, such population explosions are not characteristic of most animal populations most of the time, but instead these populations tend to remain fairly stable or fluctuate around some mean or optimum value. Of course as a result of the great technological advances during the last few hundred years, the human populations of the world have been far from either ecological or populational stability.

On the other hand, during the long paleolithic period of human history the hominids were undoubtedly part of a much more stable ecological community. Hence they occupied completely the available ecological niche—which appears to have been the tropical and temperate regions of the Old World—for much of the paleolithic period, and their populations were relatively stable. Although the fossil finds are sparse for much of this time, this does not mean that there were wide-open spaces which were inhabitable and accessible but unoccupied. The Australian aborigines, the last remaining people with a paleolithic culture, seem to accord with this view of the ecology of early man. Joseph B. Birdsell has demonstrated (1957) that it might take two thousand years to fill up the continent of Australia. Since the aborigines have lived there for much longer, their populations must have been comparatively stable and in biological equilibrium for a considerable length of time. Birdsell has also shown that the population density is significantly correlated with rainfall and hence with the food supply. This indicates that the food supply was the major determinant of population density, but it does not mean that the process by which the population size was controlled was starvation. Although disease, predators, starvation, and fighting mediated by territorialism control the populations of other animals, the Australian aborigines illustrate that even at their rudimentary level of culture, man is totally different from other animals in this respect. There is a famous quote from Spencer and Gillin that the Australian pulls in his belt and starves philosophically, but the ethnographic evidence clearly indicates that the major factor controlling aboriginal population size was infanticide. Thus, in man, cultural control has now superseded biological control. It is interesting to speculate how long this has been the case. In paleolithic sites many infant bones have been found—some even purposeful burials. Usually these are considered evidence of a high infant mortality rate due to other causes such as disease, but I think the Australian evidence indicates that they may more likely be cases of infanticide.

Among recent more developed societies, Ireland is a good example of the cultural control of population size. Prior to the potato famines of the mid-nineteenth century the population of Ireland rose from about one million to eight million in two hundred fifty years; however, for the last fifty to one hundred years the population of Ireland has been stable at about four million. After the famines the old practices of retaining the farm intact for the eldest son, dowry, and late marriage by males, which had been abandoned, were reinstituted. These have been the major factors determining the lower reproduction rate and hence population stability, but the "cause" of this stability has often been given as the food supply.

In preceding examples I have dealt with the demographic or ecological characteristics of human populations and attempted to show that culture was a major factor determining these biological variables in human populations. Since culture determines the sizes, densities, and reproduction rates of human populations, whether or not these populations expand, contract, survive, or migrate, are in turn determined to a large extent by their culture as it adapts to its environment. The next task is to consider the genetic variability among human populations in terms of this approach. Since the genetic variability, which we now express in terms of gene frequencies, is determined to a large extent by the ecological characteristics of human population, it too can be explained by cultural differences. It is the result of culture and not the other way around as is usually supposed.

Modern population genetics attempts to explain gene frequency differences in terms of the factors which can change gene frequencies. These factors are: mutation, natural selection, gene flow, and gene drift. It should be noted that this is a very general theory which is capable of explaining *all* gene frequencies although, of course, for any particular gene the exact magnitudes of these factors which control gene frequencies are not known. All genes mutate, drift, flow, and for a given environment have fitnesses associated with their various genotypes. Hence differences in the frequency of any gene can be explained by these general factors. Thus, the problem becomes that of ascertaining how culture can influence these general factors and in this way determine to a great extent human genetic variability.

The first factor, mutation, is the source of all genetic variation. But since mutation tends to be repetitive and there is no good evidence for qualitative differences in mutation among the world's populations, this factor by itself cannot explain human genetic variation. In the past few years human cultural activity ranging from x-ray to nuclear bomb production may well have greatly affected human mutation rates. This may be a significant determinant of future human variation, but culturally determined differences in mutation rates do not appear to have affected present or past human genetic variability to any great extent.

Gene flow, which is defined to include the dispersal of genes among human populations by either migration or admixture, has certainly been an important factor determining the present-day distribution of gene frequencies. On the other hand, the role of gene drift, which is the tendency of gene frequencies to fluctuate from generation to generation in small populations, is much more difficult to ascertain. Today there is considerable disagreement among anthropologists and geneticists as to the extent gene drift has been important, but this controversy is beyond the scope of this essay. In any case, I think it can be seen that gene flow is a function of the demographic variables—population size, expansion rate, and density; and the amount of gene drift which can occur is also dependent on population size. Thus, culture plays an important role in determining these factors—gene flow and gene drift—which control gene frequencies.

Finally I want to consider the cultural determinants of the major factor controlling gene frequencies, natural selection. Up until a few years ago natural selection was not considered to have played an important role in determining human genetic variability, and even Darwin had abandoned his brainchild when it came to the human species. But the demonstration of the overwhelming importance of natural selection in determining the distribution of the sickle cell gene has changed our thinking. Now we do not speculate about how many races there are or where they migrated, but instead about the possible means by which natural selection could have produced the observable human differences.

Natural selection operates in any population in two ways: through either differential mortality or differential fertility. Thus, the direction and amount of natural selection which is occurring in any population is determined by the amount and causes of mortality and fertility. Again I think it is obvious that the variability in the causes of death among the human societies of the world are determined to a very considerable extent by cultural differences. Some causes of death such as infanticide, accidents, or warfare are the direct result of cultural activity, but even others, like measles, influenza, or the common cold, require the huge host population which is the result of the agricultural and industrial revolutions. When man was a hunter with the sparse population which is characteristic of large carnivores, the kinds and number of endemic diseases were undoubtedly very different from the present when he is the most populous large animal.

Natural selection can also be considered from another aspect as two different kinds of competition: first, as the competition between individuals within a single population; and second, as the competition between populations. Within a single population the amount of natural selection which is occurring is expressed by the relative fitnesses of the genotypes, while the average fitnesses of the populations are measures of the competition between populations. The classical model of population genetics was concerned with the first or intrapopulational aspect. When the concepts of population genetics first began to influence anthropology, cultural influences on biological variability were examined in terms of this model; however, culture is the property of a population, so that it is the competition between populations in which culture is the major determinant. The outcome of this competition between populations is determined by the ecological potentials of the cultures of the respective populations and not by their respective genes. For example the replacement of Bushman genes by Bantu genes over most of East and South Africa was not due to the superiority of Bantu genes, but to their association with a culture which could support higher population densities. In the competition with Bushman hunting-and-gathering culture, the agricultural-pastoral Bantu culture simply swamped the hunters, and the population density of the area increased at least tenfold. The fact that it was the ecological potentials of the respective cultures which determined this replacement is obvious since the Bantu have not replaced the Bushman in the Kalahari Desert where agriculture is impossible with the Bantu technology. Of course, the agricultural populations have adapted to the new selective factors which are characteristic of their ecological niche while the Bushman has not.

Perhaps the greatest change in the direction of natural selection is the great increase in infectious disease which has followed the development of agriculture with its more sedentary way of life. An increased resistance to infectious disease is one of the more important adaptations among agriculturalists, but this increased resistance is not the reason for agriculturalists replacing hunters in Africa or anywhere else. However, differential susceptibility to infectious disease has frequently been cited as the reason for the replacement of one culture or people by another. But this is simply one or more example of biological determinism as an explanation of culture change. Unfortunately, this way of thinking is ubiquitous in Western thought. Even the evolution of culture itself has been considered to be the result of the peculiar biology of Homo sapiens. For example, the usual explanation of the development of blade cultures in the upper paleolithic period and for the glorious art of this same period has held that Homo sapiens' "restless creativity" is the cause. This point of view—that man is responsible for culture and hence that man precedes culture—has led to the rejection of just about every well-defined fossil hominid population as our ancestors since such brutes could not possibly have had the brains or intellect to create culture. More recently the exactly reverse position is gaining acceptance; now culture and tools are regarded as responsible for man. For the upper paleolithic period instead of Homo sapiens being responsible for blade cultures, blade cultures are now thought responsible for Homo sapiens. Such an approach is more in accord with our newer concepts of the process of human biological evolution and the role of natural selection in that process. Man's genetic constitution, whether it is his brains, brawn, or blood, is the product of natural selection, and this natural selection is in turn the result of his environment and his way of life, which for man can be called his cultural ecology. Hence his genes are the result of his culture. Like other animals, man is what man does, and the fact that he has been doing cultural and intellectual things for the past millennia has resulted in his present proficiency in these activities.

BIBLIOGRAPHICAL NOTE

P. B. Medawar's little book, The Future of Man (1961), is an excellent introduction to the methodology and philosophy of the modern approach to human biology. S. M. Garn (1961), or the relevant chapters of T. Dobzhansky (1962) are good summaries of our knowledge of human genetic variability. For more detailed studies of specific genes or traits see G. A. Harrison (1961) or S. M. Garn (1959). Marston Bates (1955) is a good introduction to the biology and control of human populations, while A. Montagu (1962) contains specific studies of the interrelationships of man's biology and culture.

6.

THE PSYCHOLOGICAL APPROACH IN ANTHROPOLOGY

Edward M. Bruner 9/17/79

THE FIELD THAT I AM reporting upon here, culture and personality, is one of the most controversial in contemporary American anthropology. The reasons usually offered in explanation of the controversy are that the field is relatively new—systematic studies by psychologically oriented anthropologists were not initiated until the late 1920's—and that the early work of some of these scholars was lacking in scientific rigor. But this explanation is not entirely satisfactory.

The more fundamental reason is that culture and personality presents a seemingly irreconcilable impasse to some social and cultural anthropologists, such as A. R. Radcliffe-Brown and Leslie White, who take the position that we should study only social and cultural systems. They say that anthropologists should not be concerned with either psychology, personality, or individuals, even in a cross-cultural framework. They fear that the psychological anthropologist will offer naïve explanations of social institutions and events in terms of individual motivation— for example, that war is caused by man's aggressive instinct— without reference to the complex historical, political, and economic factors which precipitate warfare in any given instance.

The modern student of culture and personality, on the other hand, well aware of the excesses of his predecessors and of the cautions of his critics, contends that the psychological dimension is an essential component of human existence, and further, that adequate understanding of relationships among men or their cultural institutions must include statements about

71

what goes on within an individual's mind—about what he thinks
and feels—with due attention to irrational, unconscious, processes as well as to the rational, conscious ones. It is the acknowl-
edgment of the importance of unconscious and cognitive processes
which characterizes culture and personality research.

Psychiatrists also study unconscious processes, and it was, in
fact, "the encounter of anthropology . . . with psychoanalysis
that gave rise to culture and personality studies" (Singer
1961:10). Many contemporary workers in the field today do rely
upon one or another variant of the Freudian psychoanalytic
model. But there are basic differences in objective and approach
between psychiatry, and culture and personality. Our discipline
is not a mere extension of psychology applied cross-culturally,
and we are not clinically oriented, in that no attempt is made
to help or cure the mentally ill. Nor are we primarily interested in any particular person in all his uniqueness; individuals
are studied for the light they shed on regularities in the social
process. Indeed, psychological anthropology takes as its field
of investigation the study of culture as such, only it does so
from a special point of view and with reference to a limited
number of problems.

In this paper we shall examine some of the premises of the
psychological approach starting with universal aspects of the
human condition and ending with the analysis of specific cultures. Let us begin by viewing the origins of man and culture in
evolutionary perspective. As Clifford Geertz and Clark Howell
have pointed out in earlier papers in this series, the emergence
of modern man from the lower animals did not occur all at once,
as if by divine or legislative act, but was a slow, gradual, possibly painful process that took place over many hundreds of centuries during and even before the ice ages. In some respects,
the hominization of our species is relived, or recapitulated, by
every one of us and our children, as each newborn infant is
slowly, gradually, and painfully transformed from an animal-like
being into a more or less fully socialized adult member of some
particular human society. For at birth, children have much in
common with our primate ancestors in that neither can talk,
love, laugh, believe in ghosts or gods, nor reflect upon themselves in relation to the larger environment that surrounds them.

The frustrations and joys of childhood are, in a very real sense, the residue and inheritance of man's imperfect and incomplete biological and cultural development in the past.

I do not wish to push too far the analogy between the hominization of our species and the socialization of children, as the mechanisms involved, the time depth, and other aspects of the two processes are certainly different. A basic difference is that the genetic potential for humanization, acquired over the last few hundreds of thousands of years, is immediately present in every human infant, and the infant is ready and eager to actualize this potential in the family context. The essential similarity, however, is that culture made us human phylogenetically and culture makes us human ontogenetically. But culture was not a gift from the gods, nor did it just grow by itself. It was achieved at great psychic cost. All of us, all humanity, past, present, and future, pay the price of civilization.

Let us be more specific about those universal aspects of a cultural mode of adaptation which exact this psychic cost. Infants are helpless at birth and immature for a relatively long period; and they are born with or soon develop aggressive, sexual, and acquisitive desires which must be controlled in the socialization process (Freedman and Roe 1958). There is no known human society in which men can kill, rape, or rob at will, and there is no known human society in which children and adults, at one time or another, and in one way or another, have not experienced such desires. Every culture must control the expression of aggression; otherwise society would be disrupted. And every culture must regulate the allocation of women and property, simply because there are never enough of these scarce commodities to satisfy everyone. Individuals who cannot adequately control their aggressive, sexual and acquisitive needs can never adjust to any human society. Persons who approach this extreme are either killed, ostracized, or placed in mental or penal institutions.

On the other hand, it is difficult to imagine a society in which all personal desires of all individuals were gratified. Such a hypothetical society would probably be without suicide, or neurosis, or crime as we know it, but it would also lack passion, creativity, and change. Our imaginary culture would, I think, be a rather dull place, inhabited by fully satisfied vegetable-like beings instead of by human beings. But to return to this, the real, world: if all the aggressive, sexual, and acquisitive needs of an individual were immediately and completely gratified, then that individual would never become fully human. We develop ego strength, self-awareness, and a sense of reality as a consequence of external controls and inhibitions. Some degree of frustration is necessary for survival and maturity.

The psychic cost to which we have referred, the inherent frustration associated with the socialization process, is even more specific. There is a necessary delay between wish and gratification, the wishes and desires themselves may be ambivalent, and cultural goals are often contradictory. Children are universally reared in a nuclear family unit or in some culturally stipulated substitute, and the transition from complete dependence upon the parents or parental surrogates to independence in the larger community is often difficult and awkward. This is so because prolonged intimate association in the family context leads to extremely complicated interpersonal bonds. From the point of view of the child, "the beloved person is the frustrating agent, and the pleasure-giving object inflicts pain" (Freedman and Roe 1958: 465). The child develops strong sexual and aggressive feelings toward one or both parents, feelings which are frequently reciprocated and which are only partially controlled by the incest taboo. Further, family units are never exact duplicates of one another. Thus what the child learns at an early age from his parents may be in conflict with what he learns at a later age from his peers.

The inherent conflict between personal desires and cultural demands is resolved in slightly different ways by each individual and by each society, although there are some universally human regularities in the process and in the techniques of resolution. One means is by a variety of unconscious defensive mechanisms. We repress culturally unacceptable desires by banning them from consciousness; we project and displace some by attributing our own desires to outsiders or to scapegoats in our own society; we deny the existence of other desires or sublimate them, thereby placing the released energy to work for the benefit of society. We may reverse incompatible wishes, for example, by expressing approval when we really feel hate, or we may direct an aggressive impulse against ourselves with a consequent loss of self-esteem.

Society provides disguised means of gratification in fantasy, literature, drama, folk tales, play, or religious ritual. Such forms of fantasy have a variety of social and individual functions, but by directing potentially harmful impulses into approved or at least acceptable channels, some measure of vicarious satisfaction is provided for the participants. Satire, cartoons, and jokes almost universally perform similar functions. For the individual, the content of dreams both reflects and expresses culturally patterned stress.

Society must, of course, directly fulfill some personal needs, but in every instance it rigidly defines the appropriate objects, goals, and techniques of gratification. Most societies carefully define those persons whom it is proper to hate, precisely specify approved sexual objects, and develop a complex series of rules regulating the acquisition of wealth and property. It is indeed remarkable how elaborate are cultural norms governing aggressive, sexual, and acquisitive aspects of human behavior.

We have some comments to make about the means of resolving the basic human conflict between personal and cultural needs. The first is that these varied mechanisms, taken together, must be investigated on the individual and on the societal level simultaneously. The nature of the problem is such that it cannot be adequately studied entirely from the perspective of individual psychology, without regard for the socio-cultural context in which the individual develops and in which his needs are expressed, nor can it be studied entirely from the perspective of the cultural system, without regard for the individual and the mechanisms he employs to adjust to his society. Neither the psychiatrist nor the cultural anthropologist alone can satisfactorily handle all dimensions of the problem within the framework of one single discipline. It is such problems that give rise to psychological anthropology, to anthropologically-oriented psychology, and to coöperative inter-disciplinary research.

Our second comment merely gives emphasis to what has already been implied. We have seen that a major function of the emergence of culture was to direct, channel, and prescribe how our aggressive, sexual, acquisitive, and other needs were to be gratified. From the point of view of our species, man is more flexible than any other animal in that his behavior is more dependent upon learning than upon biology or inherited predisposition. But this potential variability is never allowed free spontaneous expression within the boundaries of any given society. Human behavior is universally patterned by cultural norms and prohibitions. Man may be infinitely plastic but particular cultures are not. Each culture has its own special variant of what it means to be fully human and civilized, its unique ways of handling children and of socializing them, and its own model of the good life. This variety of present-day cultures and social structure proves that the human experiment is a continuing process.

The members of a society do not, of course, reconstruct or recreate their culture every generation. They are born into an existing system and they inherit a cultural tradition from their parents and elders. Psychological anthropologists are very much interested in the process by which culture is transmitted from one generation to the next. One means by which this is accomplished is through the application of social and supernatural sanctions. Children who conform to their culture are rewarded and those who do not are punished. The agents of punishment in addition to the parents may include other relatives, neighbors, peers, teachers, or political authorities. They may utilize a variety of techniques including beatings and other forms of physical punishment, threats of bodily harm by supernatural beings, the withdrawal of food or love, and the inculcation of guilt or anxiety. As a consequence of these and other techniques the child internalizes some, but not all, cultural norms; he develops a conscience which serves as a constant reminder of parental and cultural prohibitions. In the later years it is the internalized anticipation of punishment which serves as a substitute for sanctions applied by the real parents or other authority figures.

This process is not completely negative, however, in that it is not dependent entirely upon frustration, sanction, and punishment. In the course of growing up children come to identify with their parents or with others who serve as models of the cultural ideal. They emulate the behavior of these models, and they evaluate themselves with reference to the standards established by them. To paraphrase Erich Fromm (1944), eventually the members of a society want to act as they have to act; they come to desire what is socially necessary. Most people in most societies most of the time strive to achieve their particular culture's definition of the good life, because they find it personally and socially rewarding.

But not all people do so. Thus far in this paper we have dealt with particular cultures as if they were constant monolithic entities, and we have talked as if the personality structures of all members of a given society were relatively uniform. These are obvious oversimplifications, and it is now time to correct them. Many of us, in popular speech, commit a similar error when we say, for example, that Americans are materialistic, Englishmen are formal, or Italians volatile. Irrespective of whatever element of truth there may be to these stereotypes, it is perfectly clear that not all Americans are equally materialistic, and undoubtedly there are informal Englishmen and passive Italians. The problem we have raised is this: how can we make statements about those aspects of personality shared by an entire group or nation in view of the personality differences that exist between individuals and subgroups within the society? The more fundamental question here concerns the nature of the correspondence between culture on the one hand and personality on the other.

In a short but incisive book, Anthony F. C. Wallace (1961) has contributed to our understanding of this problem. He does so by contrasting two different points of view which he calls the replication of uniformity and the organization of diversity. In the first view, the aim is to describe how the character structure of one group differs from that of another, and the emphasis is on the uniqueness of each. The members of a society are considered to have learned the "same things" because of similar early experiences and because of common participation in the same cultural system. The culture is considered relatively homogeneous, individuals are thought to share a uniform personality organization, and one expects to find a nearly perfect correspondence between culture type and personality type. Industrialization, urbanization, revolution, and other forms of rapid culture change are seen as leading to personal breakdown and social disorganization. It is assumed that each new generation becomes a replica of the preceding one in both cultural tradition and character structure. The research problem is to investigate the mechanisms of socialization by which this is accomplished.

In the second view, which is Wallace's own, culture is, in fact, characterized by diversity of individuals and groups, each acting to further their own interests, and socialization is not considered to be a perfect mechanism for ensuring the replication of either culture or character from one generation to the next. Individuals differ because of variations in genetic constitution and because of unique experiences in the life career. Society is stratified, regimented, and diversified due to age-sex differences, occupational specialization, the necessary inequality in social life, and differential participation in the total culture. Rapid culture change does not necessarily lead to disintegration; as Wallace says, it is the natural condition of man. In view of the above, the research problem is to investigate the basis of orderly social life. How do diverse individuals organize themselves so as to maintain a cultural system which is itself constantly changing, shifting, and oscillating?

The crucial distinction is between behavior and motivation. To take an example from my own profession, the students who attend my lectures behave in strikingly similar ways. All are dressed more or less alike, all arrive and leave at approximately the same time, most prepare their reading assignments, and unfortunately, even their answers to the examination questions are quite similar. But it is a commonplace of university life in America and probably elsewhere that the underlying motivations of the students are highly variable. One man comes to the university because of an inner compulsion to learn; another because of parental pressure; a third out of expediency—he hopes to make contacts which eventually will be beneficial in his later business or political life; and a fourth, because of social expectation, comes to college because his friends do. Of course, the motivation in any given case would be much more complex than I have indicated, but the general point should be clear; common participation in a social institution does not imply psychological uniformity among the participants. Individuals may conform to their culture because of a wide variety of different motives. In other words, the same behavior may satisfy different personal needs, and the same needs may be satisfied by different behavior.

In Wallace's view, the basis of societal functioning is complementarity, not uniformity. In any social interaction it is not necessary that motivation be shared or even that one party understands the motives of the other; it is only necessary that the behavior of each be more or less predictable. To paraphrase Wallace, the relationship between professor and student does not depend on mutual conformity to one role, but on a complementarity of different roles. Complex human social systems are able to function precisely because each person is relieved of the burden of understanding the motivations of others and of acquiring the appropriate skills and knowledge necessary for the performance of others' roles. Nor is it necessary for him to reveal many aspects of his own personality to those with whom he interacts. To some extent, each of us lives in our own private world.

As we have seen, it cannot be assumed that the members of a society share a common social character. But does this imply that each individual is unique? Certainly not. In the words of Clyde Kluckhohn and Henry A. Murray (1954), every man is in certain respects like all other men, like some other men, like no other man. There may not be a perfect one-to-one correspondence between the culture of a society and the personality of its members, but some correspondences do exist. In order to study them, as well as the areas in which no correspondences occur, we must make detailed analyses of subgroups within a society and of the primary social units which have significance in personality formation and cultural transmission. We cannot infer personality from social institutions or overt behavior alone, but must investigate the shared aspects of emotional and cognitive patterning based upon detailed study of individuals and of their significant social relationships. We must continue to study the varied means by which culture structures and channels the expression of universal human needs, and we must turn our attention to the bases of conformity and change in social life (Kaplan 1961; Wallace 1961; Spiro 1961). These are complex problems, but they are among those that will be of crucial importance for psychological anthropology in the next decade.

BIBLIOGRAPHICAL NOTE

Culture and personality is generally associated with such early studies as the trilogy by Margaret Mead, *Coming of Age in Samoa* (1928), *Growing Up in New Guinea* (1930), and *Sex and Temperament in Three Primitive Societies* (1935), and with Ruth Benedict's *Patterns of Culture* (1934). These books may be obtained in paperback editions at almost every campus bookstore.

More recent developments are described in the following surveys: Singer (1961), Spiro (1961), and Wallace (1962). Each of these papers appears in volumes that contain other important articles and extensive bibliographies.

Although almost all modern anthropologists would disagree with one or another aspect of Freud's culture and personality writings, two of his books in particular, *Totem and Taboo* (1918) and *Civilization and Its Discontents* (1930), are most suggestive treatments of problems that have retained their significance. Another highly original thinker is A. I. Hallowell; see his *Culture and Experience* (1955).

The best brief introduction to psychological anthropology is Wallace, *Cuture and Personality* (1961).

LANGUAGE AND THOUGHT

Susan M. Ervin

LANGUAGE HAS LONG been viewed as the chief differentiator of man from beast. Yet there has been increasing evidence that species other than man have both highly developed intelligence and systems of communication. Does man alone have language? The question is a tantalizing one, for we find many features of human language in other species. Bees can give information about distant food sources to other bees. Other primates can warn about hazards, gesture to induce action in their fellows, develop new sounds in new situations. But here we must hesitate, for as far as we know, primate communication refers only to the here and now, and neither bees nor primates nor any other species but man can discuss kinship, or justice, or emotion recalled in tranquillity.

Human language is unique not in its particular features, but in its combination of them. Three of these features of human language are paramount: it combines and recombines limited elements, it creates arbitrary meanings for combinations, conventional in a social group; and it refers to distant objects and events and to intangible concepts. The first property, the creation of new combinations, makes human language flexible and expandable in form. We can always invent new sentences which can be immediately understood. The other properties make it expandable in meaning. We can eventually talk about space exploration and the United Nations in any human language. There are a few who expect to find that dolphin language has equal versatility, but as far as we know now, human language is indeed unique.

81

Broca's center

We do not know when human language emerged with this combination of features. Language itself, and many of its effects, are nonmaterial and leave no clues for the archaeologist. What, so far as we can tell, were the consequences of this evolutionary innovation? Much of what we call human culture—religion and oral literature, for instance—consists in largely verbal products. Further, it is clear that language must have made possible more flexible and complex social organization. If you have ever arrived alone in a foreign country with no knowledge of its language, you can feel how powerless a creature is when reduced to the use of gesture and force.

Social organization is certainly possible without language, just as culture can be transmitted without language. We are not driven back to instinct nor even to learning anew all the experience of our elders if we are mute. Any animal which imitates by instinct or by learning can also learn the use of tools, appropriate reactions to danger, and social responses to his fellows. In fact, it is still true of humans that we acquire most of our face-to-face social skills and our physical and manipulatory skills this way. What does language add? It adds efficiency in time and space. It is hard to conceive of large political systems without language. Even today writing and radio transmission continue to alter political possibilities. Language also adds the possibility of certain complex categories of social organization regardless of technological level. Even in the isolated village where transmission through time and space is restricted, social organization may include such units as the paternal uncle, a unit difficult or impossible to convey without speech.

To view language as a tool or as a channel like a telephone wire designed for transmission is too simple. Our utterances are only in part influenced by what we know and feel. The point to be examined more thoroughly is that what we know and feel may be influenced by what we say. Here we glimpse an unexpected and pervasive effect of language.

The idea that language is formative as well as formed is not a new one. Von Humboldt, and more recently, Sapir and Whorf, have expressed this notion forcefully. Since they wrote, there has appeared a variety of experimental evidence on the place of verbal skills in human behavior, which puts the problem they defined into a different perspective.

In its most extreme form, this view states that man can only think what he can say, that the categories of his language provide the categories of his perception, memory, metaphor, and imagination. This view implies that the categories of language make man radically different from other species in his intellectual processes, and make the infant different from the child. This view would lead to the conclusion that speakers of different languages cannot think alike since there is a difference in categories and modes of thought which no translation can bridge.

Of course there is some truth in all these statements. But are the differences we see due to language? Perhaps it is impossible to isolate the effects of language from all the other sources of different behavior. Species differ in thousands of ways besides language, both in structure and in experience; a child inevitably has learned more than an infant; speakers from different language communities vary in social organization, values, and cultural traditions. None of these comparisons can answer the question we have asked—what is the effect of a contrast in language itself, when everything else remains the same?

Let us go to the simplest of actions, comparison. Species differ a good deal in their sensitivity to fine contrasts in various physical dimensions. Speech has given man no superiority to the dog in discriminating odors, or to owls in detecting objects in the dark. We can compare people from various linguistic communities with differing detail in their systems of labeling colors, and we find that they can all match and compare colors equally well, whether their labels are refined or crude. For example, Zuñi Indians have a single term for the hues that English speakers call "yellow" and "orange." This doesn't lead them to confuse the two colors—they can still see the differences.

There is one dimension however that we know is affected by training in a language. That is the discrimination of speech sounds themselves. We hear best those differences our own language employs. That's one reason we have trouble learning to pronounce the words in a new language. Why does language improve our hearing of speech sounds but not our sensitivity to colors? We discriminate colors all day, in judging distances, picking out objects by their contours, and so on, but we employ speech sounds only in hearing speech. In our transactions with the physical world, we learn to make discriminations whether or not our language provides categories to talk about them. Judgments about the physical world are often probabilistic because the human, or the animal, cannot test all the dimensions of concern to him. He learns that it is economical to make use of the correlations in the physical world—for instance, that what is large tends also to be heavy. There is evidence that some fundamental dimensions—in this case a dimension of size, strength, and weight—permeate the judgments made by various people, regardless of language. Children, in fact, only gradually learn to distinguish these logically distinct but empirically correlated dimensions. In a large program of cross-cultural studies, Charles Osgood has found that dimensions based on these natural correlations underlie many systems of metaphor. Anyone who judges the United States to be large is also likely to judge it to be heavy though it has never been weighed. While these correlations show up in verbal reports, they do not seem usually to be caused by them, but rather to reflect direct experience. It is possible that similar probabilistic judgments would be made by other species if appropriate tests were devised.

In any ordinary situation, a great many things are present at once. What determines what we notice first? Experience, of course. We are likely to notice the unfamiliar, and we are likely to notice those things that have been helpful in the past, if we must act. Does language and its categories influence us? Evidently, yes. Let me describe a relevant experiment.

The largest tribe of American Indians in the United States is the Navaho tribe, living on and near an area in Arizona reserved for their use. The typical occupations there are sheepherding and a little agriculture. The Navaho often live in isolated clusters of dwellings, speaking little or no English. It is possible to find Navaho children varying in their degree of knowledge of Navaho or English, but living in similar circumstances. The Navaho language has an interesting set of verb categories. In many European languages, if I say "hand it to me," I must specify the gender of the object. But the gender, for inanimate objects, may be arbitrary. In Navaho, the verb categories are also different according to the object whenever I say "hand it to me." But the categories are semantically consistent and predictable. All flat flexible objects like paper and rugs require the same category, and long rigid objects like pencils and sticks, a different category. There are about eleven of these categories. The Navaho child must learn the categories very early, since they apply to all verbs concerning handling of objects. It may be expected that children who speak Navaho might learn to notice the physical form of objects especially early.

In an experiment, two groups of Indian children were compared, one speaking primarily Navaho and the other English. The children were shown a painted block and asked to pick another like it. The choice they were given was between a block similar only in color and one similar only in form. In fact, the English-speaking children matched the blocks by color and the Navaho-speaking children by form.

Thus we might conclude that language has determined what the children noticed. However, in another experiment, the Indian children were compared to Boston nursery school children with very different surroundings and training. These children matched by form, like the Navaho-speaking children, though they did not speak Navaho. Why? Perhaps because they had used form-board puzzles, or any of the numerous commercial toys in the United States requiring choices according to form. At any rate, we can see here that language is only one of many factors which determine which basis of matching is chosen, and which aspects of the situation seem dominant.

There is another point to be observed in this experiment. The children did not say anything. The differences in their choices were based on past emphasis on observing the features of their environment. The effects may occur whether or not people speak or even think verbally.

The evidence presented so far may be summarized in this way: language has little importance where direct comparison of simple sensory dimensions is involved, but it begins to matter when more complicated choices are required.

There have been many attempts to compare species in complex problem-solving. Any differences between man and other species

SUSAN M. ERVIN

might of course be based on other factors, such as greater intelligence, and not merely on verbal skill. For the most part, experimenters have given up such comparisons in the past decade or so, because the great variety of differences between species makes interpretations of behavioral contrasts difficult. Some of the procedures used with animals have been tried with children. In this case, verbal training could be used experimentally, to see if verbal habits alter problem solutions.

Delayed response experiments have been used for many years. They require that the subject watch the experimenter hide a reward—often food—and then wait before responding. Duration of delays before successful responding differs in various species. For some the longest possible delay is only a few seconds. It has been found that the children who have been taught verbal descriptions of the various alternatives rehearse the description of the correct cue during the delay. Thus they are able to bridge the time gap. Of course we know that adult humans can retain such information over very long periods of time, but it is still a puzzle how they do this without constant verbal rehearsal. At any rate it does seem that verbal skills aid in the delay of response.

In another type of experiment, an animal might be required to choose the left-hand side twice, the right-hand side twice, and so on. The rules are always stated in terms of number. We know that primates perform better than rats in this procedure, and that in humans, performance is related to mental age. Before deaf children have learned to count, this procedure is more difficult for them than for normal children.

Suppose a child has to behave differently toward different people. This is a common social fact—he must bow to one and not to the other, and so on. It has been found that children who were taught labels for the classes to which distinctive behavior was necessary learned that behavior much faster. The category, of course, was established in learning the names. The rest was easy. It may be that the child merely has to say the name to himself to remember the correct behavior.

Another case when verbal habits most clearly aid in a difficult problem is in a procedure in which the rules are shifted after a solution is learned. For example, suppose you are given four blocks differing both in size and color. You learn first that you are correct whenever you choose the black one. Then the rules shift. There are two shifts possible. One might be that the white one is correct, the black always wrong. The other simply is a shift to the size dimension, ignoring color. It is quite clear that rats and people differ in this problem. For rats, the shift to a different dimension is easier then reversing the rules. For people this is not so. It seems clear to an adult that he would simply note that "black is right" becomes "black is wrong" or "white is right." Opposites are always close verbal associates. But what happens with children? Before they are fluent verbally, they behave like rats in this experiment. But if they are taught to mention the color when choosing, the reversal of the rule becomes easier for them than switching to a new dimension. This experiment is a good one because it has shown clearly that it is the verbal training and nothing else which makes for differences in performance.

In this group of problem-solving experiments, the benefits from verbal skill derive from what may be called verbal mediation. During exposure to the materials, the subject comes to talk—or think about them verbally—and the categories available in his language are appropriate to the behavior that he must perform subsequently. In all of these experiments, there is some interspecies difference, and an advantage to verbal training that is small but consistent. The ability to delay choices while retaining the relevant information, the ability to generalize new behavior to a category defined by a label, the ability to solve more complex problems by using labels, all have practical implications both for man's technology and his social organization.

The evolution of covert responses which help performance has actually been observed in young children. At around one or two, children do not use language as an aid in choosing between actions. Speech serves more as a trigger than as a differential one. For the young child one word in a given situation may be as good as another. Soon we find that a child who must press a button twice can do better if he counts "one, two" than if he says "press two times." Eventually, he does not have to speak aloud. Here we see the self-directive role of language in the process of evolution in the child. At first it comes from outside as a communicated direction; then it is spoken aloud by the child as self-direction; and finally it becomes silent thought. Presumably further abbreviations occur with training as the quick and efficient mental processes of the adult are developed.

Is it always more efficient to have verbal training? No. In some forms of activity language gets in the way. In aiming at a target, in the manipulation of tools, in solving mechanical puzzles, in learning physical skills, practice may be of more use than talk. Occasionally, if it distracts or misdirects observation, speech may hinder learning.

For the retention of information, the evidence suggests that language is important, since it supplies ready categories. The price of efficient codification, however, is some distortion. Suppose you are shown a chip of color. If you are asked to select it again a few minutes later from a larger assortment, performance will be good. But if a longer time lapse occurs, your performance will deteriorate and will come to depend increasingly on the appropriateness of the categories for color which your language supplies. Suppose you labeled the color as "blue." If in fact the color was the one you most often call blue you may choose it again, but if it was a pale lavender blue you will probably select a hue that is bluer than the original. There have been many experiments with more complex materials than color, showing that memory can be distorted by the categories available.

Speech and verbal thought imply codification of the complex and infinitely varying stimuli of experience into the finite categories supplied by the grammar and vocabulary of a particular language. Codification simplifies greatly the task of organizing and retaining information. Any scholar in a new field knows that he retains more information as a consistent framework of categories is acquired. The codification made possible by language permits man to solve many problems more easily than other species, and when he has solved a problem once, he may generalize to problems similar only in the most abstract way and solve them quickly too.

It would be a mistake to suppose that other species are completely incapable of solving any of the complex problems it has been reasonable to try with them. With clever training, primates have solved some astonishingly complicated problems. It sometimes seems as if the test really examined the experimenter, for it takes great ingenuity to devise suitable training methods and to go beyond the biases of one's own thinking to discover how other species reason. Such experiments clearly show that language is not necessary for all kinds of complicated thinking. They have also shown that verbal responses do shorten training time and hasten certain solutions. What we do not know is the point where it is possible to draw a sharp qualitative line beyond which it is impossible for an animal without language to go. For example, we do not know what mathematical processes are impossible for some primates.

Thus far only cognitive organization has been considered. We can only speculate about the role of language in the internalization of social categories and values. Man can label his own behavior and react to it as an object, and can compare his own acts to those of others and to an idealized norm and thereby make moral judgments about himself. This objectivity about the self may be compared to a change in logical thinking. The great Swiss psychologist, Piaget, has studied the growth of logical and moral thinking in children. As they grow older, children's judgments of the world take on a changed perspective, away from the self. For example, a child learns early that he has a brother, but it is a more difficult achievement to recognize that he himself is a brother to his brother. Modern astronomy is the extreme in the evolution away from a self-centered view. While the labels of language may be, and often are, applied differently to others and to the self, to outsiders and to insiders, they are potentially neutral. G. H. Mead, a philosopher-sociologist, has said that language helps one to "take the role of the other," to place one's self, one's social position, and one's behavior in the same perspective as others'. Piaget has implied a parallel evolution in children's concepts of natural science. But as yet we do not have experimental evidence of the role that language actually plays in this evolution.

The effects discussed earlier depend on the provision of categories by languages for classification and evaluation of experience, but languages differ. A child who learns a language learns a system of categories—those categories signalled by the grammar of that language and those codified by its vocabulary.

In addition, he learns the probabilities of what different things will be said in that language. Normal individuals know what the listener expects, though they may not always say just that. For example, the French talk more often about verbal disputation than Americans, and the Japanese more often about filial duty. These are differences in the actual usage of speech which reflect contrasts in values. Anyone brought up in a society learns not only the language but what its speakers are likely to say. Consequently, as has been demonstrated, bilinguals shift language and content together. This does not mean that speakers of different languages are not *able* to say the same things, but that languages differ in what it is easy to talk about. Psychiatrists have found that under special conditions people will say things they have never said before. The fact that they do not ordinarily say them is of more interest than the fact that they can say them now. Societies differ in the aspects of culture which they transmit by verbal means rather than by other methods of direct reward or imitation. In some societies the voice of conscience may not be a voice at all.

We may conclude that the existence of a formalized and conventional system of symbols in man has had important consequences. It affects not only what we ordinarily consider social life, but also the processes of thought, memory, and feeling which we ordinarily consider private. The importance of a symbol system increases the farther the situation is from direct sensory or motor experience. Those activities which involve comparing simple stimuli, aiming at a target, and manipulating tools show least dependence on symbolic behavior. But if complex choices and observations are necessary or if much information must be processed and retained through time, the codification made possible by language has more pronounced effects. It often makes man more flexible and efficient than other species, and it helps make people from different language communities different in their nonverbal behavior. While we need more evidence on this point, it may be that the development of certain kinds of thinking in the domain of logic, morality, and social organization are so difficult as to be virtually impossible without language. Today, scientists do not all agree that the development of language necessarily has affected man's inner experience as profoundly as it has changed his social and cultural behavior. It still remains an open issue what the limits of these effects may be.

BIBLIOGRAPHICAL NOTE

Tests for higher mental processes in animals have been discussed in Stone (1951). Some examples of animal communication are presented by Brown (1958: ch. 5), and a comparison of the common features of communication in man and various animals was made by Hockett (1960). A more advanced treatment of this subject is available in Lanyon and Tavolga (1960). The thesis that language and thought are related to each other was developed by Edward Sapir, whose *Language* (1921) has become a classic. A widely-read elaboration of this idea with many examples appears in Whorf's writings, edited by J. B. Carroll in *Language, Thought and Reality* (1956: 207-45). R. W. Brown also considers this issue (1958: ch. 7), and some relevant experiments are described in Saporta (1961: sec. 8) and in Maccoby et al. (1958: sec. 1). Some related Soviet research on language and thought is reported by Luria (1961). A philosophical view of the role of language in social development is provided by G. H. Mead (1934).

8.

A PERSPECTIVE FOR LINGUISTIC ANTHROPOLOGY

Dell H. Hymes

I SHOULD LIKE TO BEGIN with a prediction. The salient trait of linguistics, in the first half of the twentieth century, from the standpoint of anthropolgy, has been its quest for *autonomy*. Its noted accomplishments have been in the analysis of self-contained *structure*. In the second half of this century, the salient trait will be a quest for *integration*, and the noted accomplishments will concern the engaging of linguistic structures in social contexts—in short, in the analysis of *function*.

I oversimplify, but not unduly. Of course there are many lines of linguistic work in which advances have been, and will continue to be made, apart from the change just stated. But the oversimplification focuses attention where it belongs in an overview such as this, on the questions that take the center of the stage.

For some while, the leading questions in linguistics have concerned: How best describe the system that constitutes a particular language? How identify and explain the uniformities and differences of internal structure among languages? For linguistics, certainly for linguistics associated with anthropology, the leading questions increasingly concern: How best describe the workings of a language in a particular social context? How identify and explain the uniformities and differences between languages in social function?

The study of functions is being developed in two main ways: through interest in semantics and through interest in social variation in speech. I shall discuss each in turn, and then argue

92

that both imply an approach that fits into an evolutionary perspective.

But first, since I am discussing linguistics from an anthropological point of view, let me say something about the relation of the two disciplines in the United States, and the terms by which the relationship is known.

American anthropology has always recognized the study of language as a branch of its activity, partly because of the exigencies of American Indian studies (so important in its formative years), partly because of the theoretical outlook of such shaping spirits as John Wesley Powell, Daniel Garrison Brinton, Franz Boas, Alfred Kroeber, and Edward Sapir. When linguistics and anthropology are conducted in intimate association with each other, as in the United States, there often results an activity and product that has a distinctive character, and the need is sometimes felt for a distinctive name. The nineteenth century saw mostly such terms as "ethnological philology" and "linguistic ethnology." Since the Second World War a variety of terms have flourished in the United States—"ethnolinguistics," "metalinguistics," "anthropological linguistics," as well as "sociolinguistics" and "psycholinguistics." Each of the terms has been associated, uniquely or varyingly, with particular concerns, all of value, but each tending to emphasize one aspect of the place of linguistic research in anthropology. Recently I have proposed "linguistic anthropology" as a general term, defining it, simply and broadly, as the study of language in an anthropological context (Hymes 1963 and 1964a). (Broca, indeed, did use it to name one of the branches of a general science of anthropology just over one hundred years ago.) The term, and its definition, reflect the historical fact that anthropology and linguistics, as distinct disciplines, overlap in practice, rather than coincide. (Nor does either subsume the other.) Anthropology's concerns with language may lead it to draw on a variety of disciplines and studies pertaining to language besides linguistics proper, and in ways different than linguistics proper.

To put the matter in a formula: whereas it is the task of linguistics to coördinate knowledge about language from the viewpoint of *language,* it is anthropology's task to coördinate knowledge about language from the viewpoint of *man.*

There is thus a point of view implicit in the general name, an implicit criterion of relevance: the scope of linguistic anthropology is defined by the vocation of anthropology itself. It designates a branch of anthropology coördinate with physical (or biological), archeological, and sociocultural anthropology in the conventional American scheme of the profession.

The point of terminology goes hand in hand with the change of focus stated at the outset, and forms part of the context for the discussion to follow. Acceptance of "linguistic anthropology" as a name and subdiscipline entails recognition that anthropology must itself assume responsibility for some of the crucial questions concerning the functions and evolution of languages. These questions go beyond what need be asked or handled by descriptive and historical linguistics in their usual scope, for such questions have an ineradicable and explicit extralinguistic, social component. If I am right, the recent flurry of hybrid terms ending in "-linguistics" will be seen in retrospect as having marked the highpoint of prestige for a self-sufficient descriptive linguistics as focus for the major questions about language. My prediction is that the coming period belongs to a descriptive method conceived in the service of a broad functional approach, requiring as much ethnography as linguistics proper. The focus will be upon language as first of all an activity, not a product—in Wilhelm von Humboldt's terms, upon language as not so much *ergon,* as *energeia.*

Let me take up, as first of the two routes by which function is being approached, *semantics.* Structural description of a language is based upon the function of reference—the phonological and grammatical relevance of features depends upon it, no matter how the question is phrased—and it is in terms of the referential function that a number of younger American anthropologists are extending structural description to all of ethnography. The extension has a novelty, not only in the renewal of widespread interest in semantic description as part of ethnography in the United States, but also in the conception of the task.

The ethnographic task has sometimes been designated "mere" description. A new generation of ethnographers rejects the "mere," and sees in the formulation of an adequate ethnographic description a truly theoretical task, the development of a theory adequate to a particular case. Inference, hypothesis, prediction, are equally involved in accounting for a body of behavior, whether the universe is all communities or one. Rather than conceiving theory as only comparative, and their descriptive task as limited to recording and classifying, such ethnographers consider their role a more active one, involving the formulation of hypotheses and theories to account for appropriate or customary behavior of the group in question, and the testing of the formulations for their ability to do so.

This may only make more explicit and detailed something long implied by ethnographic work, a tradition of seeing things relative to context and "from the native point of view" that goes back at least to the roots of the Romantic movement in Herder. But because of its linguistic starting point, the work of making predictions explicit carries with it two important contributions: the devising of improved techniques for tapping, through linguistically expressed categories, the cognitive worlds of participants in the culture, and the thoroughgoing avoidance, through command of verbal detail, of the imposition of alien descriptive categories on those worlds.

The new approach gives special attention to the clues contained in native terminological systems. As Conklin puts it, "For the ethnographer, the semantic structure of such folk classification is of paramount importance. Upon his analysis of it depends the accuracy of many crucial statements about the culture being described" (1962:120).

In discovering the often complex patterns of semantic features involved in such systems, the ethnographer employs the fundamental technique of structural description, that of determining contrastive relevance within a frame. (This is what the much discussed subject of componential analysis is, or should be, all about.) Within a relevant context, one asks: What elements can be substituted for one another, and with what effect? And by extending techniques for finding relevant frames, the new approach helps solve a crux of which some had despaired: How carry a structural semantics beyond such obvious paradigmatic sets as inflexional endings?

At the same time, the approach does not stop with linguis-

tically codified systems, nor does it identify the theory of a
culture with verbal formulations of such a theory by natives.
Analysis is extended to all aspects of the culture, including
those aspects which may not be verbalized or those verbalized
inaccurately. The crucialness of control of linguistic data and
method lies in the fact that native lexical sets and statements
contain the evidence needed to discover and validate many,
perhaps most, of the principles the ethnographer must formulate
to account for native cultural behavior.

The main thing is that analysis be anchored in criteria (verbalized or not) that members of the culture use as they act—the
questions, so to speak, that they implicitly ask. The goal is an
old one, but failures to achieve it continue to appear. The conception of ethnography as the active formulation of a theory,
proceeding through control of linguistic detail, helps ensure
against such mistakes. An essential part of the conception is the
realization that cultures may differ not only in the ways they
categorize and segment some aspect of experience, but also in
the very aspects of experience they select and group together
for categorization. The general terms that translate our "red,"
"green," etc., for example, may be organized into a system governed jointly by two dimensions of experience, one colorimetric
(light : dark), one not (moist : dry), as among the Hanunóo of
the Philippines. The principles by which people choose where
to reside may involve considerations not only of genealogical
tie (which underlie our conventional ethnological categories
of patrilocal, matrilocal, etc.), but also features of ecology, social role, and other expectations and obligations. From the
point of view of this approach, then, it is essential to resist the
temptation to assign an aspect of a native culture too easily to
a familiar category, by either not investigating its full range,
or by explaining discrepancies away as due to confusion, or ig-
norance, or breakdown of an old system, or intrusion of a new
one. Such may be the case, but often enough the difficulty is
failure to discern a principle or system actually in use, one
which makes the full range of variation intelligible.

The familiar but incorrect category may, of course, come
either from a native or ethnological source. The new approach
avoids the Scylla and Charybdis of identifying valid theory

and scientific relevance with either native formulations or existing ethnological concepts. In a given case both have to be validated by the same criterion, predictive ability. The new approach does not reject native formulations, which are of great heuristic value; nor does it reject comparative study and the general concepts such study demands; but it insists on refining the empirical basis of comparative study, by providing more surely valid descriptions of the individual systems on which comparative study must depend.

By the integration of semantics with ethnography, the new work can help provide a better base for understanding two long-standing problems about the role of language in human life: (1) the extent to which the cognitive categories of a people find overt expression in linguistic forms, and, (2) to quote an essay by Brinton, "reciprocally, the reaction exerted by those forms on the later intellectual growth of those who are taught them as their only means of articulate expression."

To achieve the goal of mapping a people's cognitive world, however, one must map also the *speech economy* within which the linguistically mediated rules operate. Here's the rub. One must study not only the structure of the code (or codes), but also the patterning and distribution of its (or their) use. Let me specify three reasons for this. Two concern semantic description itself, and the third, the evaluation of its results.

(1) As is widely recognized, a term's meaning depends upon interaction between its own semantic properties and those recognized in the context in which it occurs. A term can indicate a range of meanings, and a context can support a range of meanings. In a given case the term does not so much positively name, as does the intersection of term and context eliminate from consideration most, or all but one, of the possible competing meanings. Hence some knowledge of the properties of the situations in which terms may be used is necessary.

(2) The frames within which terms contrast, and so yield to structural statement, are not all linguistic. Behavioral contexts of situation often unite in function linguistic elements that otherwise are heterogeneous. (E.g., the set of greetings may range from a minimal "Hi!" to the syntactically complex, "Well, I'll be a son of a gun, if it isn't Sid Mintz!".) The fact that the

elements contrast within some frame does not appear from their overt linguistic makeup, nor do the dimensions underlying the contrast (e.g., the twin dimensions of solidarity [intimacy: formality] and power [relative status] that often underlie the structuring of terms of address). The fact of contrast, and the dimensions, can be determined only by knowing the context of situation, and discovering what expressions have functional unity through being mutually substitutable for a given end within it. To be consistent, of course, the structural relevance of the context itself in relation to other contexts of situation should be determined. Hence, if the goal of a structural description of usage is to be achieved, there must be an analysis of contexts of situation to provide the frames of contrast needed to recognize part of the structure that exists.

(3) The situations in which language is used, and the importance of language in those situations differs among different groups. Among some peoples, language acts as the central medium for transmission of adult roles and skills, while among others, situations of training contain little or no explicit verbal instruction. The situations are ones of nonverbal observation and practice. Such differences may affect the import of linguistic categories for other behavior. So may differences in the functions to which speech predominantly is put, as when reference dominates in one group, and expression, or phatic communion, in another. The point is true *a fortiori* for the numerous groups in which more than one linguistic code is used. The semantic rules expressed in a code are less likely to affect activities in which the code has no part. In a multilingual community one must thus discover the uses and situations to which each code is specialized, if one is to assess the importance of its semantic patterns in the daily round. And of course some aspects of life are intrinsically more susceptible to the influence of linguistic categories. Philosophy and literature, for example, whose mode of existence is language, are more likely to show linguistic influence than technology. In other words, languages differ not only in the structuring of their categories, but also in the engagement of their categories in social life. Hence the study of such differences of function becomes part of the task of an ethnography concerned with meaning. Such differences may

also inhere importantly in the differential modes of use of one and the same language among different social groups.

In sum, when structural description is extended outward via the referential function of language, it leads from analysis of linguistic form into analysis of patterns of use in contexts of situation.

The same holds true when the scope of structural description is extended along the lines of the renewed interest in social variation in speech.

Such renewed interest in social variation shows several foci. One is linguistic structure itself. Such a focus leads to investigation of situations of coexistence of two or more codes, concerning itself with consequent changes, including loss of an existing code or crystallization of a new one; interference in the speech of bilingual individuals; adaptation of whole languages, including introduction of literacy in programs of fundamental education; and so on. Such studies may appear under many headings —bilingualism, linguistic acculturation, sociolinguistics, dialectology—as may studies with another focus, that of the matching of linguistic and social features. Studies of the second sort may investigate the linguistic correlates of role, status, reference group, and the like; determine how well members of a community can place each other socially from linguistic cues; determine the number and kind of functional varieties of speech in a community; and so on.

As the body of modern studies of such sorts grows, comparative analysis based on them will add much to our understanding of the social functions of language. Some increase will come from increased knowledge of structural detail, for the development of structural linguistics has added precision to the linguistic side. And now that ethnographers trained in structural linguistics, as well as linguists conversant with ethnography, are taking the problems to the field, precision may be added on the social side. But increased understanding will come from increased depth of perspective also. In the long history of relevant studies, attention has gone mostly to the *products* of change, generic correlates and functions of language being assumed. Modern ethnographic study of the social aspects of language, if it is close grained, must quickly find itself discriminating

contexts of situation and specific types of function, as it seeks
to explain change and covariation, as well as to record them.
And with the opportunity for testing theories of change at hand,
the field worker can hardly not turn attention from product
to *process*, from correlations of features to their interaction.
Observing the participants in linguistic encounters make use of
the functional variation in speech available to them as they actively conduct and judge what has been called "the presentation
of self in everyday life," one finds that the perspective of the
new ethnography applies here as well: there are patterns of use
to be formulated.

With such a focus on *acts* of speech, and the patterns implicit
in them, a threshold is passed. One enters the structural analysis
of the gamut of factors in acts of speech, and of the full range
of functions served. One comes to see the linguistic code as
but one factor of speech events among several, e.g. addressor,
addressee, channel, the form of the message, its topic, the context
of situation, to name major types. Frames of analysis, previously
conceived only in reference to features of the verbal text and
code, are found, when explored in a thoroughgoing way, to
comprise in one structural matrix features both of text and context, of code and situation, together. And the referential function, primary to analysis of the code, takes its place among a
roster of functions. (Here I can merely allude to some major
types—expressive, directive, phatic, metalinguistic, poetic—each
with resources, and rules of use and interpretation, specialized in
its service.) The patterning of grammar becomes a phase of
the patterning of speech activity in general, and the conceptual
starting point of analysis becomes, not the structure of a particular code, but the total structure of the totality of speech
habits of a particular group.

In sum, analysis of the conditions under which interference
and change take place, and of the ways in which linguistic
features co-vary with other factors of speech events, shows that
more than interference, change and variation are to be found.
There is a new realm of structure to be discerned and a new,
second descriptive science of language, beyond that of the linguistic code, to be constituted.

What is the nature of such a discipline? I can only project

it summarily here. It begins, as stated, by defining its object of study as the totality of speech habits of a community, rather than as the structure of a particular code. (Let "speech" here stand for all manifestations of language.) It assumes that all the speech activity of the linguistic community is subject to patterning, not just the code (or codes). It proceeds by discovering for the particular community the relevant *classes* of speech events, the relevant *factors* of speech events, and the range of *functions* served by speech. It then discovers the relations existing among them. It does for speech activity what the new ethnography, discussed above, does for any aspect of social life: it discovers and states the rules implicit in appropriate, or ordinary behavior.

Let me use this concept, rules of appropriate behavior, to make a little clearer what this second linguistic science, which may be called *the ethnography of speaking*, or *of communication*, involves. Think of any stranger to a community wishing to understand, to anticipate and interpret the ordinary behavior of its members, and wishing to learn how to observe the norms which govern that behavior. Think perhaps of a stranger entering the community by being born into it as a child. Suppose the child to have learned the rules of the community's language or languages. It now has the ability for which the first descriptive science of language at most seeks to account, the ability to produce and interpret grammatical utterances, and to judge grammaticalness. Yet with this ability alone, the child remains a partial stranger. It can produce all grammatical utterances, but yet it does not know *which* grammatical utterance to choose at a given time. Such a child would lack the ability for which the ethnography of speaking can be said to seek to account, and which children do in fact normally acquire—the ability to produce and understand utterances as appropriate to a situation, and, to judge appropriateness. In acquiring this ability, the child learns what the ethnographer of communication seeks to discover and state explicitly, the classes of speech events recognized in the community, and the rules governing the relations among them, their constitutive factors, and the functions subserved.

A monograph would be needed to outline the kinds of speech events, factors, and functions whose relations may make up the speech economy of a group, and to set forth ways in which they and their relations may be identified. Let me say only that existence of a rule is often shown by the response to its breaking. And the fact that not everything can co-occur, that it is not the case that anyone can say anything, by any means, in any way, to anyone else, on any occasion, to any purpose, is one of the ways in which a community's speech activity constitutes a system.

One further point: one must consider not only the makeup of acts of speech, but also the general role of speech activity. As noted regarding semantic analysis, speech is but one mode of activity among others, and one important way in which groups differ is in the ways the resource of speech is utilized. The fact that some societies hang onto a language as a symbol of identity at any cost, while others blithely exchange one language for another, is indication that the functional involvements of languages are not everywhere the same. Ethnographically, one must begin, not with the function of language in culture, but with the functions of languages in cultures.

So much for the content of a second, peculiarly anthropological, descriptive science of language. Aspects of it have been recognized before, but treated anecdotally. The question now is one of systematic, scientific treatment, both by individual descriptions and comparative studies. I have predicted that the renewed interest in semantics, and in social variation in speech, will lead to this. Other considerations might be advanced which lead into such a discipline, not least of which is the problem of misunderstanding between groups due to interference between differing patternings of speech activity. But let me now draw out the implications of such an ethnography of communication for an evolutionary perspective.

The main point is that such a descriptive science of communication is needed if the renewal of an evolutionary perspective on culture is to articulate with culture's part, language.

An evolutionary theory of language has again become a respectable scholarly topic, in the form of comparing the generic features of human language with those of communication in other species. Comparative study of the ethnography of speaking can contribute here, for the proper comparison is between whole systems of communication in environmental context.

Obviously human language did not spring forth full blown, but acquired its generic traits by selective adaptation within the communicative habits of definite prehistoric groups. The advantage of the oral-auditory channel over others is patent enough to explain its selection as the central medium of expression. Further retrospective unraveling of the complex interaction between an evolving brain, evolving code, and evolving society will be difficult, but two things are clear. First, with regard to *what* emerged, it is inadequate to ask merely: How did vocal sound become associated with meaning? No amount of vocabulary alone can add up to the chief property of true language —the productivity or adaptiveness inherent in its nature as an open-ended system, as a system not merely of words, but of paradigms and syntax as well. Second, with regard to *how* and *when* true language emerged, it is inadequate to ask: When did social coöperation, or traditions of toolmaking, or symbolic art, first appear? A number of such social and cultural traits can apparently exist and be transmitted without the intervention of language.

Our knowledge of linguistic systems provides a basis for postulating what formal features, if present, would require us to say of a system of communication, "yes, here is true language." We are far from having a knowledge of sociolinguistic systems adequate to postulate what sociocultural features, if present, would require us to say, "Yes, true language was here." There have been assertions that one or another feature of the prehistoric record must have involved the compresence of language, but we need to know, before such assertions can be judged, how *unnecessary* true language can be, by determining the range of functions served in various groups without its aid, or by means of some less developed system. We know that the more that people share an understanding of the context of communication, the simpler their means of communication can be and remain effective. Just how complex a means of communication, then, would have been required by our earliest manlike forebears in the small, tightly-knit hunting groups which they probably shared? Would a rudimentary system of a few phonemes have served? There exist today auxiliary systems of great communicative power, such as Mazatec (Mexico) whistle-talk, based on but four tones. Would a repertoire of independent interjection-like expressions, without system, have sufficed? If boys in some modern tribes learn to hunt without explicit verbal instruction, presumably boys in early prehistoric groups could also; and adult Siriono (Bolivia) rely on whistling while hunting, talking so little that they were once impugned as having no language at all.

Social coöperation does imply some form of communication; a tool tradition does imply the transmission of skills; recognizable art does imply the making of symbolic connections. But at what level of development do these, or other sociocultural phenomena, make necessary or inevitable the use of the systematic properties of true language? A comparative ethnography of speaking can help tell us.

Beyond the question of language's origin, there remains the task of reconstituting the question of its continuing evolution. The question has two main parts, *progress* (or evolutionary advance), and *process*.

The idea of progress in language has been associated with a variety of notions. There have been ideas of "primitive" languages, impoverished in vocabulary, rapidly changing, lacking definite systems of sounds and grammar. Languages have been ranged in sequences according to grammatical type, such as isolating, agglutinating, inflecting. Processes of efficiency and economy have been said to be general and at work in particular directions with determinable results. But no known languages are "primitive" in the sense of the stereotypes; neither the evolutionary typology nor the evolutionary sequence have held up under critical analysis; neither the generality nor the direction of the processes have been well demonstrated. For these and other reasons, the idea of evolutionary advance has been widely repudiated in linguistics. Even so, many linguists could be persuaded to grant it a limited validity. Its appropriateness is clearest in the comparison of earlier and later stages of an individual line of development, as when a language over time becomes better adapted to a new natural or cultural environment. It also seems clear that one language can be said to be more advanced than some other language with respect to a particular use or function. Most linguists would deny, however, perhaps on principle, that some languages can be said to be more advanced than others *in general*, whatever criteria might be used.

I myself believe that a reasonable case can be made that some languages are evolutionarily more advanced than others, *in general*, with respect to features and functions that define two general types or poles. Such a conclusion seems inescapable, if one accepts a biologist's criterion of advance as "change in the direction of and increase in the range and variety of adjustments to environment" (including, for language, sociocultural environment), and if one admits that the oft-mentioned *potential* equivalence of languages ("anything can be said in any language") is not the same as *actual* equivalence. Mostly what gets said in a language is what fits its grooves of habitual expression, and to make some things sayable easily and commonly may take decades of effort. (Witness the slow development of technical philosophical vocabulary and syntax in Latin.) But I shall not try to argue the point further, for unless the details are presented at painstaking length, the argument may be confused with prejudiced stereotypes about "primitive" languages, and the like, that still persist. Moreover, the primary scientific problem now is the analysis of specific lines of sociolinguistic development on the level of historical process known as microevolution.

The importance here of an ethnography of speaking is that by taking as its starting point the totality of speech habits of a population, it facilitates microevolutionary linguistic studies. The adaptation and differential retention of speech habits can be analyzed in a natural way, for one examines a natural totality of speech habits, seen as an integral part of the whole sociocultural adaptation of the community, in whatever size social field proves pertinent. In particular, by subsuming and integrating the formal structure of the code among other aspects of the patterning of speech, one avoids the artificial barrier raised between language and the rest of culture which allows language and culture to be described—and this is so often the case—as disjunct abstractions in disparate frames of reference. The ethnography of speaking keeps in view phenomena that frequently are not taken up into either frame of reference. By holding on to the whole range of elements and structures, the varied functions they serve, and the complex and changing interdependence between the two, an ethnography of speaking can provide the descriptive anatomy for the microevolutionary analysis that must underlie any adequate general theory of linguistic evolution.

The approach of an ethnography of speaking, moreover, also serves the needs of historical linguistics proper, as it turns toward explication of change in terms of function. There are many modes of study of linguistic variation and change, but a socio-evolutionary approach can, by its generality and integration of structural with functional perspective, integrate them. In large part, this turns on the fact that every type of linguistic change involves an interaction between structure and sociocultural context of use. Even the changes most immediately motivated by structural factors depend for their realization, and what regularity and spread they achieve, on considerations that are not purely linguistic, but sociolinguistic. Hence an explanation of change that refers only to structure, or to context of use, is partial. An adequate explanation relates structure and context of use to each other; and an adequate account of structure in social context is precisely the goal of an ethnography of speaking. Conversely, by its attention to adaptive variation within and between communities, an ethnography of speaking cries out for interpretation in terms of processes of change; and an adequate perspective on such change can only be evolutionary.

If consistently carried out, then the perspective of an ethnography of speaking can integrate the concerns with the functioning of language that are now coming to the fore, as well as help establish the basis for a broader integration of anthropology's concerns with language, an integration within a general evolutionary framework.

BIBLIOGRAPHICAL NOTE

The range and sources of anthropological interest in the study of language are represented in Hymes (1964a), including general considerations by Boas, Greenberg, Goodenough, Levi-Strauss, Pike, Malinowski, and Firth in Part I. There is a mid-century survey by Olmsted (1950), and recent ones by Hoijer (1962) and Leach (1965). The chapters on "Language" in the *Biennial Review of Anthropology* (1959-   ), edited by Bernard Siegel, provide a continuing account with somewhat different emphases each two years (Lounsbury, 1959, 1961; Bright, 1963; Gumperz, 1965). For historical analysis, see the General Introduction and Part X of Hymes (1964a), and Hymes (1963).

On ethnographic semantics, see, beside work of Goodenough (1956a, 1956b, 1957), Conklin (1955, 1962, 1964) and Frake (1962a, 1962b, 1964a), Sturtevant (1964), which has a good bibliography; especially the work of Lounsbury (1964a, 1964b); Romney and D'Andrade (1964); and the forthcoming Special Publication of the *American Anthropologist* on componential analysis and structural semantics, edited by Eugene Hammel.

On sociolinguistics, see, for important aspects of past and recent work, Weinreich (1953; new edition in preparation), Haugen (1956), Ferguson and Gumperz (1960) (reviewed by Friedrich (1961)), Friedrich (1962), and Parts V-IX of Hymes (1964a). For current work and trends, see Gumperz and Hymes (1964); the forthcoming volume from the Conference on Sociolinguistics, held at UCLA in May 1964, edited with introduction by William Bright; the forthcoming volume from the summer seminar on sociolinguistics, sponsored by the Social Science Research Council's Committee on Sociolinguistics, and edited by Charles Ferguson; and the reader in sociolinguistics, now in press, edited by Joshua Fishman.

On evolution of language, see Brosnahan (1960); Greenberg (1957: 56-65); Hockett (1960); Hockett and Ascher (1964); Hymes (1961); Lenneberg (1960); and Sebeok (1962).

9.

THE STUDY OF EVOLUTION

Eric R. Wolf

EVEN TO THE CASUAL observer it will be apparent that the development of anthropological theory has been characterized by fits and starts rather than by orderly accretion and continuity. We shall need a sociologist of knowledge to tell us why this should have been so; but the fact is indisputable. The theoretical structure erected by the evolutionists of the nineteenth century fell under the axe of diffusionist criticism; but the pieces of the old house were not used in the construction of the new theoretical edifice. The diffusionists built anew, disregarding the problems and answers of their predecessors, only to suffer a similar fate at the hands of the functionalists.

The problems of the past were neither answered nor remembered; new problems and new answers simply replaced the old. Thus it is not surprising that the old problems should return now to concern us. In the recent past, American anthropologists have again become interested in the problems posed by the early evolutionists. Sometimes this interest is eclectic, seeing equal but separate "good" in evolutionism, diffusionism and functionalism; but there has also been a striving towards a new, integrated approach in which the theoretical contributions of the past would form a new and exciting synthesis.

The early evolutionists believed that the world in which they lived could be illuminated by the hypothesis that human culture had undergone progressive and cumulative growth; and they labored to show the lawful nature of this growth. The categories they used in their demonstration proved unhappily clumsy, and

108

their assumption that clusters of these categories, taken together, would serve to define unequivocal stages of cultural development, proved oversimplified and unwarranted. The diffusionists demonstrated the limitations of these categories when they showed that possession of the bow and arrow did not automatically raise the Bushmen to the level of barbarism, while its absence did not condemn the Polynesians to a state of savagery. Concepts like matriarchy or totemism, regarded as universal or near-universal, and therefore useful in building the evolutionary perspective, were dismembered into separate components which demonstrably did not always occur together.

Yet in performing their tasks of criticism and testing, the diffusionists did not return to the basic question that had exercised the minds of their antagonists. Rather they set aside altogether the problem of cumulation in culture, and sought instead greater knowledge of how the traits that made up a given culture had come together in one place at one time. There emerged a picture of culture as a congeries of unrelated, inherently separable components, "a thing of shreds and patches," a view which among American anthropologists was tempered only by the realization that in moving through space, culture traits, and the temporary aggregates of traits they called cultures, bore some relation to the nature of the physical environment and to the presence or absence of other neighboring societies. The first of these interests was to develop later into the culture-ecological approach of Julian Steward who came to inquire into the specific relationships of a particular technology to a particular environment, and into the resulting limitations on the borrowing of other traits; the other gave rise to the many interesting acculturation studies of the thirties and forties in which groups of Indians were seen in their multiple relationships to other cultural groups surrounding them.

Both of these approaches are now components of the new evolutionist perspective. But the diffusionists proper were in turn assailed by the functionalists who derided the diffusionist perspective of history as a Brownian movement of traits, and drew attention instead to the meshing of traits, their interrelationships and interpenetrations in real life as lived by Trobriand Islanders or Tallensi. We now know that they, too, overstressed

the internal fit of traits and overplayed the analogy of culture
to an organism in which every part contributes to the maintenance of every other. Their marvelously detailed studies of internal linkages in culture have led them to ascribe to their cultural
bodies a "wisdom" *sui generis,* much as Walter Cannon, the
physiologist, came to speak of the "wisdom of the body."

The new evolutionism that is arising in America wishes to
make these various approaches relevant to each other, to synthesize their positive contributions and to supplement the short-
comings of one by using the insights of the other.

From the evolutionists of the nineteenth century, we take,
first of all, the notion of cumulative development in human
culture, its movement towards the maximization of certain
values. This approach emphasizes quantitative differences and
implies that cultures can be ranked along some scale ranging
from small to large numbers. Such quantitative scaling is implied, for instance, in general propositions such as those made
by Leslie White to the effect that "culture evolves as the amount
of energy harnessed per capita per year is increased, or as the
efficiency of the instrumental means of putting the energy to
work is increased." In actuality, this measurement of energy
conversion presents many problems, problems that engage the
attention of anthropologists like Richard Adams and Marvin
Harris, and of sociologists like Fred Cottrell and Alfred Ubbe-
lohde. Another formulation holds that culture evolves as the
ability to use different natural resources expands, or as culture
is able to control more and different environments. A number of
rough schemata for the classification of environments in relation
to culture are now available, as for instance those developed by
Chapple and Coon or Philip Wagner, but much greater refinement in scoring environmental variables is possible, for example,
on the basis of the Köppen system of classification.

Another index of evolutionary cumulation in culture is the
increase of population since the Palaeolithic, used by V. Gordon
Childe to mark off major evolutionary advances; but here again
greater refinement is possible through the techniques utilized
by demographers to establish the comparative viability of populations. Raoull Narroll has used the number of people in the most
populous building cluster of the ethnic unit studied as an

index of social development, and has shown that this measure can be related systematically in a mathematical formula to the number of occupational specialties and to the number of organizational types. Morton Fried's study of the evolution of social stratification also implied two measures: a ratio between positions of prestige available for any given age-sex grade and the number of persons capable of filling them, on the one hand, and a ratio between strategic resources and persons possessing impeded or unimpeded access to them, on the other. Hornell Hart has drawn up logistic curves to demonstrate the ever increasing size of territorial and political units since palaeolithic times and has demonstrated the accelerated rate of growth in the development of these units. Various indices developed by Karl Deutsch to gauge the intensity of communication between social units await application to the measurement of cumulation in communication over the course of cultural evolution; and in a paper on folk medicine in Latin America, Charles Erasmus has related amounts and varieties of probable kinds of knowledge to the degree of specialization available to the society. It is furthermore not impossible that the movement towards componential analysis, such as Charles Frake's work on levels of terminological contrasts in the diagnosis of disease by a Philippine tribe, may ultimately yield a measure of the relative complexity of cognitive systems. Since environmental variables, energy conversion, division of labor, population, access to resources and prestige, intensity of communication and cognitive complexity appear to be mutually dependent, the possibility of establishing a master formula relating all or several of these terms seems within our grasp.

But evolution is not characterized merely by quantitative cumulation, it is also characterized by qualitative changes in organization. Such qualitative changes result in the emergence of new cultural components which subsume and integrate pre-existing components in a new way. Thus the invention of the sailing ship represents the integration of the boat with a particular technique for harnessing wind power, together with the minimum tackle for holding the two components in the proper relationship. The state represents a coördination of specialized social groups through the development of an apparatus capable of wielding power. The emergence of new qualitative levels is often followed by further attempts to develop and integrate the component parts. The development of the sailing ship depended upon the ever greater improvement in the design of hull, sails and rigging, and their more careful integration. The development of the state depended upon the standardization and specialization of component units, and their ever more complete subordination to the governing authority.

It is possible to observe the emergence of new levels of organization in many series of culture growths, but one major qualitative change has engaged the attention of anthropologists since the beginning. This may be called the qualitative shift from unspecialized or totipotent cultures, to cultures which rely for their operation on the specialization of parts. Unspecialized cultures —and most early hunting-and-gathering cultures belong to this type—are totipotent in the sense that each group had at its command all the cultural components necessary to relate man to environment, man to man, and man to universe. Such groups were capable of replicating the entire gamut of components when fissioning into two or more separate units. Birdsell has indicated that the population of such groups could be expected to double each generation, and that fission was likely to occur when such a population rose to 60 to 80 per cent of its carrying capacity. Such rapid fission and replication was therefore accompanied by an equally rapid movement into a wide variety of ecological niches, and a resulting adaptive differentiation of the various cultural sets to their different life situations.

This proliferation of totipotent units encountered a double limitation. First, differentiation and adaptation to different environmental variables favored a degree of complementary specialization and mutual interchange. Second, occupation of free niches by fissioning groups reduced the size of available territory to which their energy potential gave them access. With increased complementarity and limitations on free movement, there came increased interdependence and a correlative decline in the ability to fission freely. Social groups were ever less able to duplicate the entire range of needed cultural components in a new medium.

The characteristic bearer of such totipotent cultural sets was the kin group, ranging in forms from the nuclear family to the localized descent group embracing a number of nuclear families. The kin group, small or large, appears to be the ideal unspecialized unit, capable of providing all the services needed to sustain an individual while at the same time able to absorb maximal tensions and stresses which would sunder a more complex, specialized unit not similarly cemented together by the sexual division of labor and the bonds of emotional intimacy. Hence we witness throughout this stage, and indeed up to the very threshold of the industrial revolution, a proliferation of kin-based units, each oriented towards the maintenance of its particular membership, and hence often in opposition to other similar units or to the more specialized components of culture which characterize the next qualitative level of cultural evolution.

In the course of evolution, totipotent and specialized cultures have given way many times over to cultures which favor the growth of differentiation and specialization. In such cultures we witness the development of privileged positions, organized largely around the concentration of goods and labor from the different units and their subsequent redistribution. Such concentrations and distributions could be largely peaceful in character, as in the give-aways of Melanesians and British Columbian Indians, or in the intergroup exchanges of the Massim Island kula. But it could be based also on predatory activities in which the predators concentrated and distributed goods and labor originally produced by another group of people. Differentiation of roles between the pivotal position of chief, or war leader, or organizer of trade expeditions and the supporting positions of followers and applauding public polarized also the respective particularistic kin groups of these social actors. We witness not merely a differentiation in the power orbit of individuals, but a differentiation of their dependents into social classes. The result has been the emergence of social asymmetry in the place of equivalent, symmetrical relations. This asymmetry has grown steadily with the increase in surpluses made available by increased energy conversion and further specialization of labor.

Increasing social asymmetry in a more differentiated social order required the development of specialized machinery needed both to maintain and widen it, and thus prompted the emergence of the apparatus we call the state. It is important that the state emerged as a wide-ranging peak organization capable of maintaining order, of maximizing division of labor, and of concentrating and distributing surpluses produced, in competition with the particularistic kin groups of the past. To this day the success of any particular state depends on the respective competitive strength of its component units. Peak organizations may have to relinquish large areas of social control to such units, traditional or other, because their apparatus for maximizing administrative benefits is weak, or because the costs of administration stand in no relation to the benefits to be derived. Within these interstitial areas in the network of control, therefore, competitive units forever proliferate, especially when they offer their members goods and services not offered or delivered by the state. Anthropologists study such competitive relations when they examine the competition between the organization of the Chinese state and the kin groups of its gentry; the competitive orbits of particularistic caste and state-centered guild in India; the tug and pull of lineages in African kingdoms. Such problems are also studied by sociologists who appraise the bargaining power of organized sodalities like businessmen's associations or trade unions, or the powers of organized crime, or the networks of personal influence (called *blat*) developed by Soviet industrial managers.

Implicit in the approach of the old-line evolutionists, though not spelled out in these terms, was also the notion that a given feature of culture possessed a certain potential or capacity. This concept, when applied to cultural components, implies not only a range of capabilities, but also a lower and an upper limit. The upper or lower limit may be established quantitatively, in terms of energy converted, numbers of people coördinated, or in terms of cognition yield. Further qualitative analysis will tell us whether it could be lower or higher; whether it possesses inherent limits, or whether its operation produces side-effects which inhibit its intended impact. Thus we can measure the relative capacity of a hoe made of the shoulder bone of a bison and a steel plow in the breaking of tough prairie soil. We can gauge the relative carrying capacity of a territory as exploited by slash-and-burn cultivation or irrigated agriculture. We can look at kinship systems, and take note of the fact that the

Kariera system of Australia requires for its operation two inter-marrying groups, the Arunta system four, the system of the Ambryms six. We may note that the mutual aid and security set involved in the Latin American *compadrazgo* relation, based on ceremonial sponsorship in life crisis ceremonials, is limited in scope by the number of children available for sponsorship, while a savings-and-loan association in a Midwestern town can accommodate thousands of members. We are enabled to see how a Kachin chief attracts followers through the operations of the marriage system and the give-away, but how he cannot increase the exploitation of his sons-in-law without setting off a movement in the direction of egalitarian revolt (Leach 1954), or how the Melanesian big-man is forced to pile feast on feast to achieve and maintain prestige, but is prevented from maximizing his role by the danger of incurring the wrath of his overtaxed followers (Sahlins 1963). We grow aware of how an ancestor cult builds the solidarity of men descended from a common ancestor, but simultaneously how such adherence splits society into a series of narrow-range descent groups, each set off by its own ancestors, while a universalistic religion like Islam or Christianity possesses a wide range applicable to anyone wishing to enter the fold. The concept of capacity thus implies performance, but also limits and contradictions, a balance of gains and costs, to be used in a new kind of social cost accounting, both more important and more promising than the economic cost accounting with which we are already familiar from our own cultural experience.

Not all aspects of culture are, however, equally characterized by cumulative development towards a maximal value. It has long been realized that such cumulation is most characteristic of what has been called "the technical order," the energy converters of a society and the organization required by it. Harvey Moore (1954) has attempted to show why this should be so. According to him, only the technical order is capable of division of labor. Division of labor in turn involves specialization in skills and knowledge, and specialization in skills and knowledge renders more probable that increase in apparatus, skills, and know-how which results in the cumulative growth of the technical order.

In contrast, there are components of culture which are not cumulative in this sense. Their capacity is not measurable on a unidimensional scale, graded from low to high numbers; rather, they exhibit a capacity for multiple combinations. The technique for measuring this multivalence is the one first employed by E. B. Tylor (1889). It involves the application of the statistical method to ascertain the frequency of existing combinations, as well as the use of deductive reasoning to explain the resulting patterning of cases.

All attempts, for instance, to depict forms of descent reckoning as undergoing a progressive cumulation from primitive promiscuity through matriliny and patriliny to bilaterality have failed. Forms of filiation are not cumulative; they occur at very different levels of complexity in the technical order. Thus the horticultural Orokaiva of New Guinea are as patrilineal in form of descent reckoning as the pre-1946 Chinese, but both are clearly not at the same level of technical development. Forms of filiation and forms of marriage constitute some of the limited number of possible components through which groups of people can be related to the components of the technical order. Since their number is limited, they are recurrent rather than cumulative. No matter what the demands of the technical order, the forms of marriage will be limited still to polygyny, polyandry and monogamy.

Such recurrent components must be linked to the cumulative components of the technical order, but the linkage is often minimal and incomplete. "Perfect" combinations of matridominant division of labor, matrilineal kinship and matrilocal residence at marriage, for instance, have been shown to be rare among North American Indians, as have their patridominant opposite. Most groups show partial and incomplete combinations, due to a variety of interference in linkage. Similarly, there exist other sets in which apparently incompatible components are hooked together through the mediation of a third component which neutralizes the effects of their incompatibility. The Mundurucu of the South American tropical forest, for instance, are characterized by the apparently incompatible combination of patrilineal descent and movement to the wife's residential group upon marriage, a combination which brings together in one settlement a number of otherwise unrelated males, a difficult situation in a warlike society which demands continuous male coöperation. The required solidarity is here obtained through the introduction of a third component, the man's house, where the unrelated males sleep away from their wives and carry on in common their male-oriented tasks. Anthropological studies gain much of their importance precisely from the study of such unexpected third components that allow an otherwise unmanageable or poorly connected cultural set to operate and to survive.

Such third components also frequently govern the relation of a cultural set to conditions influencing it from outside. Here they act as regulators of cultural sets which would otherwise fall prey to disruption. Thus the potlatch, the great give-aways of the Northwest Coast Indians of British Columbia, regulated an otherwise incompatible relation between the native arrangements of kinship and status and the powerful flow of wealth emanating from the outside world as a result of the fur trade. Thus, too, in many Indian communities of Middle America enforced expenditures in religious ceremonial ensures an economic and social leveling that inhibits the growth of differential power within the community capable of delivering the community to its enemies.

Forms of marriage or descent are not cumulative; they may be substituted for each other or exist as alternative components in the same set. The same is true of other cultural components, for instance forms of burial, or magical beliefs, or ego-referent kinship terminology. The reason for this is probably that such components admit of no specialization, and that even in complex cultural sets they refer to the individual quae individual, the family quae family, the two least specialized groupings even in an industrial order. We have learned, for example, how magic —or religion akin to magic—persists on this level, even where science has made the behavior of statistical aggregates of people quite predictable and comprehensible. We may know how many people are struck down each year by cancer of the lung, or how many children are killed in automobile accidents; but the individual can take little comfort from this knowledge. For he must still come to terms with his unique personal fate if he discovers that he has cancer of the lung or if his child is run over by a car. Moreover, such existential realities and the responses to them remain remarkably similar among all human beings, no matter what their culture and the complexity of its specialized components. In this regard, there is little difference between the Dayak and the inhabitant of Kalamazoo.

The distinction between cumulative and noncumulative aspects of culture yields a new perspective in the study of particular cultures, a perspective which allows us to go beyond the organic models of culture postulated by the functionalists, and the mechanical models of culture possessed by the diffusionists, and yet make use of both. We are enabled to see any given culture as a set—an arrangement—of components coupled in a particular way, always located in an environment—a context—constituted by other cultural sets or arrangements. We recognize that cumulation in the technical order, actual or virtual, always poses an implicit or explicit threat to such a set. Put in another way, we can come to understand how a culture struggles against its past and towards it future. Similarly, any cultural set is forever under challenge from its neighbors, from the alternative components and alternative couplings of components present in its intercultural environment. In the end, we aim at an evaluation of how a cultural set maximizes the values we have selected as criteria for our linear scale and how it manages its internal and external schismogenesis to achieve this maximization; that is, we evaluate its capacity to contribute to cultural cumulation. In this evaluation, we are not debarred from considering, too, the existential values of the cultural set we are studying. Indeed, we need no longer shrink from the study of the particular and unique, for we have become aware that while our statistical treatments deal in frequencies and averages, in cultural evolution —as in other processes—it may be the unusual combination of components which can effect the transition to the next higher level of cultural cumulation.

BIBLIOGRAPHICAL NOTE

Significant statements of the renewed interest in evolutionism within American anthropology are in White (1949), Steward (1955), and Sahlins and Service (1960). The distinction between cumulative and non-cumulative aspects of culture is elegantly drawn by Moore (1954). Naroll (1956) represents a notable attempt to quantify aspects of evolutionary cumulation. A paper by Erasmus (1955) appears to me to open up new perspectives on the study of evolutionary cumulation in ideology. The distinctions used in this paper, between totipotent and specialized cultures, between symmetrical and asymmetrical social orders, are based on conceptual distinctions familiar to anthropologists. The concept of "capacity" of a given cultural component seems to me novel; it is illustrated in Leach (1954) and in Sahlins (1963). The technique for measuring the capacity of cultural components to combine with each other was first employed by Tylor (1889a), and forms the basis of the comparative work using the resources of the Human Relations Area File, which attempts to inventory and codify our knowledge of human cultures all over the world.

10.

THE ORIGINS OF AGRICULTURE

Robert M. Adams

THE IMPORTANCE OF agriculture for all that we know of a full and secure life hardly needs to be described. Great as are the cultural differences between peoples today who are dependent upon agriculture for subsistence, all of them have more in common than they share with the few surviving groups of independent hunters and collectors. Man's first acquisition of domesticated plants and animals not long after the end of the Pleistocene ice age, accordingly, has long been recognized as a great turning point or "revolution," perhaps comparable in importance only with the Industrial Revolution in which we are still engaged. Yet the direct, empirical study of this great transformation is still very young, hardly antedating the Second World War.

Not surprisingly, our understanding of the origins and early spread of agriculture is still very insecure and fragmentary. In fact, there is no area of the world for which the transition to food production can be traced step by step in adequate detail. But if general formulations about agricultural origins are thus somewhat hazardous, there is a corresponding advantage in discussing them here. The study of the rise of food production has been able to flourish only as a consequence of new conditions —the "explosion" of scientific manpower and research support which the postwar years have brought. Hence this problem perhaps can exemplify at least some of the anthropological work which these new conditions make possible, above all the crystallization of a group of major problems upon which the interests of many scholars, and even many disciplines, are focused intensively.

The problem of the early development of agriculture is rooted in the environmental and cultural conditions obtaining at the end of the Pleistocene, and we may begin by summarizing these very briefly. By this time, men whose skeletal remains were anatomically modern in type had made their appearance, and it can only be assumed that they were essentially modern in their capacities for cultural innovation as well. Although little survives other than material equipment devoted to the food quest, purposive human burials attended by a modicum of ritual hint at customs and preoccupations extending well beyond the realm of immediate subsistence requirements. Moreover, although most of the astonishing cave art of France and Spain during this period depicts animals to whom the hunt was devoted, both the technical quality of these paintings and the circumstances surrounding their execution clearly indicate that they were meant to symbolize and convey a world of conventionalized belief outside the practical requirements of the small bands who were responsible for them.

Relative at least to their predecessors in the Lower and Middle Pleistocene, these hunter-collectors during the last few millennia of the ice age were more specialized and better equipped, more numerous and widely distributed. In Western Europe, where the sequence is best known, groups not only successfully hunted great herds of reindeer, wild horse, and bison, but also harpooned salmon and caught rabbits and grouse with snares. Caves and rock-shelters in many cases seem to have been occupied fairly continuously over long periods. The finding of bone needles, together with suggestions of skin costumes in the Magdalenian art, implies that sewn clothing had been evolved which was well adapted to the cold climate. Hunters in Eastern Europe displayed comparable efficiency in the pursuit of the mammoth, and had developed earth houses as shelters in the absence of caves.

Increasingly able to adapt through cultural specialization to such challenges as the harsh subarctic environment around the fringes of the great European glaciers, man was able to increase the range of his occupation enormously. His first entrance into the New World, probably having occurred from twenty- to thirty thousand years ago, was one apparent consequence since it must have involved exposure to comparable climatic conditions in the crossing of a now-submerged land bridge from eastern Siberia to Alaska. Australia, too, first may have been occupied during the terminal phases of the Pleistocene, possibly involving at least modest and accidental marine crossings by raft.

The end of the Pleistocene, marked by the gradual onset of modern climatic conditions, is usually agreed to have occurred about eleven thousand years ago. While the causes for the shrinkage and disappearance of the enormous ice sheets covering Europe and North America are still disputed, at least there is full agreement that the effects were dramatic. The concentric zones of treeless arctic tundra, boreal forest, and deciduous forest, successively more distant from the ice, marched north in the wake of the retreating glaciers, while the melting of the great weight of ice induced complementary changes in land and sea levels which substantially altered the continental margins. With the northward progression of climatic and floral zones came new fauna—generally smaller, less gregarious, less migratory animals—appropriate to the dense forests which now began to extend well into the northern latitudes. But even where open plains remained, as in western North America and large parts of Eurasia, many of the larger Pleistocene species failed to survive. Among those which disappeared altogether were the mammoth and mastodon, and the American camel, horse, and sloth—all within a relatively short time, and all under circumstances which leave little doubt that man's increasing proficiency as a hunter was a major contributing cause. This very proficiency may have served, in other words, to exterminate major resources of game and thus to help pave the way for radically changed patterns of subsistence.

As a general account of the end of the Pleistocene, what has just been said is incomplete or misleading in two respects. Firstly, most of the world open to human occupation lay at great distances from the main glaciated regions centering on the poles, and the climatic changes associated with the end of the Pleistocene in more equitorial latitudes involved decreases in precipitation more prominently than increases in temperature. Moreover, the whole problem of whether or not climatic changes in all latitudes took place closely in phase with one another is still not fully resolved. Secondly, it must be noted that the Pleistocene as a whole was not a time of continuous glaciation but rather of almost continuous climatic changes, changes whose sequence and correlations long have been a major theme of research. Shifting climatic, floral, and faunal boundaries at the end of the Pleistocene thus were not a new phenomenon but one which had gone on repeatedly through all of man's biological evolution as a separate species. What was new was neither the fact of an ameliorating environment nor the consequent enlargement of life-zones favorable for man's existence, but rather the increased exploitative efficiency and adaptability with which he took advantage of these conditions.

Compared with Europe and the United States, much less is known of the new subsistence patterns which emerged at the end of the Pleistocene in areas like the Near East and Middle America where the wild progenitors of our major domestic plants and animals flourished. To generalize from the more northerly areas, perhaps the dominant character of the post-Pleistocene response was its diversity. Faced with habitats whose differences were amplified as the ice receded, and with the extinction of many species of great herbivores upon which he formerly had relied heavily, man rapidly worked out a whole series of specialized adaptations based on a bewildering variety of new local resources. We find groups like the Tardenoisans, Azilians, and Maglemosians in Western Europe, for example, coexisting within short distances of one another and yet utilizing entirely different types of habitat. There is evidence that nuts, seeds, and wild fruits were relied on more heavily as sources of food than they had been in Pleistocene times, and that this increased emphasis on the gathering or collecting of vegetal products also was characteristic of roughly contemporary assemblages in Mexico and the western United States. Of course, this shift required the development of ground stone tools for pounding or milling in order to remove husks and render the tough kernels digestible—tools which later would be necessary for the processing of domesticated grains.

The increasingly intensive and localized, even semisedentary, character of these post-Pleistocene subsistence patterns is evident also in the faunal resources they sought to exploit. The bow and arrow came into use in northern Europe, and, perhaps as a consequence, much greater numbers and varieties of bird bones turn up in refuse deposits than previously. Especially rapid technological developments took place in fishing, with gorges, nets, fish-spears, weirs, and even boats and paddles, all employed already in preagricultural times. Among land animals, most of the common smaller species of the forest were hunted or snared, implying less reliance on collective drives and greater stress on the individual stalking of prey within a restricted territory. Here the dog played a crucial role, perhaps first becoming a scavenger around the hunting camps but before long being fully domesticated. Particularly along the rivers and sea coasts, where land marine resources supplemented one another, relatively permanent settlements made their appearance upon great heads of discarded shellfish. These characterizations apply first and most directly to Europe, but by 3- or 4,000 B.C. they also become applicable to subsistence trends in North America.

The potentialities of an agricultural mode of subsistence for transforming man's way of life do not remove the *origins* of agriculture from this early postglacial milieu that I have sketched, nor do they establish the appearance of agriculture as an inexplicable historical "accident." Instead we have here a series of broad cultural and environmental trends, alongside of which the introduction of agriculture in certain favored areas seems a consistent and harmonious development. The widespread diversification of food resources after the Pleistocene, the numerous corresponding elaborations in technology, the increasing sedentarism—these are circumstances which alone can explain the tide of still largely unknown innovations which led to the domestication of plants and animals.

At least on present evidence, the earliest agricultural hearth lay in the Near East. Recent studies there suggest the domestication of the sheep by perhaps as early as 9,000 B.C. While the age of domestication of the goat is somewhat more obscure, it is probably of comparable antiquity. Domestic pigs, on the other hand, do not appear in the archeological record, as it is available at present, until around 2,500 years later, while the earliest domestic cattle yet known date from around 5,000 B.C. Meanwhile the domestic cereals, at first principally emmer wheat, einkorn and two-row barley, can be firmly traced to at least 7,000 B.C.; increases in cereal pollen suggest that they may have been in use considerably earlier.

While the material now available from which to generalize is admittedly fragmentary, we may infer from the long span suggested by these dates that the development of even a rudimentary subsistence agriculture probably did not take place as a single chain of events in a single small region. Instead it seems to have been a complex process which involved a prolonged period and consisted of many episodes not always closely dependent upon one another. The same conclusion emerges from a comparison of the substantially different life-zones in which our earliest known agricultural sequences occur.

One such zone is represented by the lowland Palestinian valley in which biblical Jericho later was situated, an oasis, where man and his potential domesticates gradually may have evolved a set of symbiotic relationships under hot, arid conditions. By not long after 8,000 B.C. the spring at Jericho and other neighboring Natufian sites had been occupied by small groups of hunter-collectors who also may have practiced some cultivation. At any rate, the presence of stone hoes and flint sickle-blades polished with use suggests that cereals were being reaped if not necessarily sown. Such are the accidents of archeological discovery and preservation that this ambiguity as to the presence of purposeful agriculture at Jericho continues until much later. Before the end of the eighth millennium B.C. a substantial walled village apparently had grown up on the site, but even from these levels domestic plants and animals have not been surely identified.

By way of contrast with Jericho, the site of Sarab in a cool Persian mountain valley near Kermanshah possibly was only the summer encampment of herdsmen-cultivators who had adapted their own patterns of winter and summer movement to those of the flocks of wild sheep and goats which they must have domesticated by the early seventh millennium if not earlier. And between the environmental extremes of Jericho and Sarab at opposite ends of the Fertile Crescent, we find roughly contemporary sequences of incipient agriculturalists and settled

villagers at sites like Karim Shahir, Jarmo, and others as distant
as Çatal Hüyük in southwestern Turkey. In general, village life
seems to have been fully established on an agricultural basis by
the late eighth- or early seventh millennium B.C., with settlements
having sprung up on the Anatolian plateau and all along the
foothills of the Zagros, Taurus, Lebanon and Anti-Lebanon
Mountains wherever local circumstances were favorable. However, just as in the early post-glacial cultural adaptations of
Northern and Western Europe, the most impressive features
of these early agricultural manifestations are their apparent lack
of contact with one another and the diversity of their responses
to differing local resources and opportunities.

The picture which emerges from recent research in the New
World is broadly similar. Taken in the aggregate, there is little
doubt that the food crops upon which the Indians of the Americas relied prior to European colonization had been independently domesticated from wild forms native in the Western
Hemisphere. Maize, by far the most widespread and most
important crop, was derived from a wild progenitor which
had flourished in Mexico and perhaps Central America. On
present archeological evidence its domestication probably occurred during the fifth millennium B.C., but preserved specimens
from cave deposits as late as the mid-third millennium were
still so small that they must have furnished only a very limited
contribution to the diet. Even the earliest maize yet found, it
may be noted, appears to have been derived from wild forms
already divergently adapted to the pronounced regional differences in soils and climate which make Middle America what has
been called "a geographical, cultural, and ecological mosaic."
And this same observation applies to the even more numerous
varieties of beans and mellons or squashes (Cucurbita), the
other members of a trinity of food plants which eventually
provided the basis for a nutritionally adequate diet even without meat or dairy products from domesticated animals. Beans
and the Cucurbita are also thought to have been of Middle
American origin, first having been domesticated by 7,000 B.C. or
even earlier. Yet a fully developed agricultural regime in which
the cultivation of maize, beans, and squash provided a sufficiently assured level of subsistence to support the formation of

settled villages apparently does not antedate 2,000 B.C. or so, anywhere in the New World.

The domestication of these crops reflects, in other words, the same kind of prolonged, independent experimentation in many diverse centers as that which I have suggested earlier for the Old World cereals. Moreover, the same process of many divergent, local derivations of food crops probably could be documented elsewhere in the New World. For example, the potato-oca-quinoa complex began in, and always was restricted to, the high plateaus of the Central Andean region of South America. We still await a concentration of archeological attention on those areas and time-ranges of the prehistoric past in southern and eastern Asia (and sub-Saharan Africa) which will explain the rise of food production in those vast regions.

Thus the formation of settled village communities relying mainly on agriculture probably had taken place by 7,000 B.C. in the Near East and then, essentially independently, by 2,000 B.C. in Middle America. While the process of selecting suitable domesticates and developing the techniques for their cultivation and consumption had extended over several thousand years in both cases, the consequences of the new mode of subsistence were immediate and profound. To begin with, it permitted a substantial enlargement of the residence group which could be sustained by a given area of land. With the introduction of storage facilities for agricultural products (here the invention of pottery played a vital role), it also gave far greater assurance of secure, continuous occupation than was possible with the fluctuating returns from hunting and collecting. Further, agriculture created new opportunities for trade and for the growth of specialized craft skills, for it demanded the farmer's labor only during periods of sowing, weeding, and harvesting and left unprecedentedly long periods free for activities not directly concerned with subsistence. As V. Gordon Childe has argued, it must have stimulated population growth not only by expanding food resources but also by creating a new economic importance for children who became productively employed at an earlier age than was possible in hunting. Finally, the agricultural cycle itself, the yearly renewal of the plants and herds, furnished a stronger, more integrative focus of group belief than ever had

existed previously. Perhaps for this reason small shrines or
temples appear very early in the archeological record of agricultural villages in all of the great nuclear areas of the Old and
New Worlds. These temples, gradually evolving from small
cults into great specialized hierarchies, in turn played a central
organizing role in the subsequent growth of larger, progressively
more complex and stratified societies that became the earliest
urban civilizations. But our emerging understanding of that
further evolution is another story and cannot be dealt with here.

From what I have tried to outline of present knowledge as it
emerges from ongoing research, the study of the origins of food
production is a pre-eminently interdisciplinary problem. Yet
at the same time it also remains a problem in which the role
of the anthropologist is central. The first of these interrelated
points is evident from the kinds of empirical work which have
proved to be necessary. They include, for example, the laboratory analysis of soils and refuse from archeological excavations
in order to reconstruct the environmental milieu in which early
steps toward agriculture took place. This may involve a botanist
in the identification of woody flora from lumps of charcoal, or a
soil chemist concerned with the climatic implications of ancient
leaching. Another line of approach begins with carefully plotted
present distributions of wild species thought to be antecedent
to the early domesticates. From a comparison of these with
the zones of archeological incidence of the same species, a plant
ecologist then may seek to infer differences in climate or other
natural conditions between the original period of domestication
and the present. Still a third type of inquiry involves the direct
study of the changing morphology of archeological remains of
early domesticated plants and animals in the attempt to understand the process of domestication itself. Turning from the
domain of the natural sciences, studies of contemporary agricultural technology, village organization, or modes of land use
by ethnologists have furnished useful leads to the interpretation of archeological findings from the same areas. Or again,
the historical geographer working with documentary materials
sometimes can help in assessing the importance of long-continued
activities like overgrazing or deforestation which make extra-
polation from present conditions back to the past more difficult.

Finally, the determination of the rate and time of different aspects of the process of domestication depends increasingly on a wide range of new physical and chemical techniques, of which radiocarbon dating is the best known example.

From these examples it is clear that geologists, zoölogists, botanists, and representatives of other disciplines frequently assume essential roles in the investigation of early food production, roles often at least as important as that of the archeologist in the collection of primary data. Herein lies the interdisciplinary aspect of research on the problem. But the role of the anthropologically-oriented archeologist still remains a crucial one. In the first place, data from excavations or distributional studies do not provide a mirror image of an ancient environment, nor even of a particular mode of prehistoric subsistence. Instead they are the very incomplete remains of an extinct culture which maintained certain patterned relations with its environment, and it requires an interpreter who is cognizant of cultural problems to determine what these patterns probably were. Furthermore, the rise of food production as a new mode of subsistence is an episode only in the human career, involving the transformation of specifically human institutions and behavior. Not suprisingly then, it generally falls to an anthropologically-oriented archeologist to direct, coördinate, and synthesize the various lines of research into the nature of this episode so that they converge on what is a pre-eminently anthropological problem.

To generalize further, the emergence of the food-producing revolution as an important focus of research exemplifies a shift that is underway in archeology toward the delineation of *processes* of change. Of course, what sometimes is called "space-time systematics"—the formulation of archeological time-units and the determination of their geographical extent and interconnections—continues as an essential component of research. But even the working out of such sequences and correlations is seen more and more as merely preliminary to intensive studies of the causes and content of particular cultural transitions. Moreover, these processes of transition or transformation increasingly tend to be viewed as affecting an interrelated system of cultural and environmental variables, rather than as detached typological trends which can be studied and understood in isolation.

With this newer approach, slight differences in local adaptations at a given period in the prehistoric past cease to be minor details and become the basic source for understanding how cultural and environmental variables interact with one another. In fact, much of the effort of specialists on the flora and fauna is devoted precisely to the fuller analysis of what local variations may signify. This implies that an increasing empiricism characterizes the common effort on problems like agricultural origins, and that there is a tendency to utilize comparative materials from modern ethnographic studies of groups under somewhat different conditions only with considerable scepticism. More important still, it implies a concentration of archeological attention on demonstrable basic trends, above all in the subsistence economy, instead of on intuitive reconstructions of ancient cultures as wholes.

In one relatively small area of research, then, this is the consequence that the great postwar increases in foundation support and scientific manpower have brought: Groups of specialists now collaborate much more frequently and effectively, across both disciplinary and institutional lines. Differences tend to emerge between the accepted limits of academic fields on the one hand, and the more rapidly shifting problems generated by this evolving team approach on the other. As a result, the over-all structure of research is more fluid, the pace is more rapid, and the emphasis on a rigorously inductive, preferably quantifiable, mode of analysis is more pronounced. To argue, as I have done earlier, that this is a time when processes of change or transformation have become the central focus of study is only part of the story. The other, and perhaps ultimately more important, part is that the structure of our discipline and our methods of study are themselves undergoing rapid transformation. The end to this process is not yet in sight.

BIBLIOGRAPHICAL NOTE

The best single point of departure for further consideration of this theme is a recently published international symposium which surveys what is known of the transition from food-gathering to food-production in many world regions (Braidwood and Willey 1962). While the contributions of the individual specialists differ considerably as to approach and are uneven in areal coverage, their joint effort is successful not only in displaying the varying substance of this transition under differing environmental circumstances but also some of the important threads of continuity in the processes by which it took place.

Other than this volume, most general treatments of what V. Gordon Childe first described as the "Neolithic Revolution" (cf. his *Man Makes Himself* [1951] and numerous other publications) are less encompassing in geographical scope. In fact, most tend to be confined to the course of that "revolution" in the New World or the Old World alone, and often within only limited regions of either. Among these might be mentioned a survey by Pedro Armillas on "Land use in Pre-Columbian America" in Stamp 1961), J. L. Lorenzo's "La revolución neolítica en Mesoamerica" (1961), and the account by Sonia Cole centering on the Near East and Europe (1959). The case for an early origin of root and fruit crop cultivation under tropical conditions, while not supported by the archeological evidence currently available, has been strongly put forward by Carl O. Sauer (1952).

Representative examples of the interdisciplinary teamwork upon which the study of the development of food production increasingly has come to depend are provided by the preliminary reports of the Tehuacan Archeological-Botanical Project in Mexico (MacNeish 1961—) and in Western Asia by the account of Robert J. Braidwood and Bruce Howe of their "Prehistoric investigations in Iraqi Kurdistan" (1960). A recent brief overview of climatological factors which contributed to the environmental framework for this transition has been given by R. F. Flint and F. Brandtner (1961).

11.
CULTURE AND ENVIRONMENT: THE STUDY OF CULTURAL ECOLOGY

Marshall D. Sahlins

"THE STERILITY OF THE soil in Attica," wrote Montesquieu, "established a popular government there, and the fertility of Lacedaemon an aristocratic one." We are not convinced. Yet the statement is characteristic of a main intellectual legacy in the ecological study of culture, environmental determinism, that ancient idea of "a mechanical action of natural forces upon a purely receptive humanity." From more recent forebears, notably including American field anthropologists of this century, we are heir to an opposed position, environmental possibilism, which holds that cultures act selectively, if not capriciously, upon their environments, exploiting some possibilities while ignoring others; that it is environment that is passive, an inert configuration of possibilities and limits to development, the deciding forces of which lie in culture itself and in the history of culture.

Another outlook appears. At first it was only as an offhand remark, a critical argument. Now it informs some of the best work in American archaeology and ethnology: It is an idea of reciprocity, of a dialogue between cultures and their environments. The truism that cultures are *ways of life*, taken in a new light, is the ground premise—cultures are human *adaptations*. Culture, as a design for society's continuity, stipulates its environment. By its mode of production, by the material requirements of its social structure, in its standardized perceptions, a culture assigns relevance to particular external conditions. Even its his-

132

toric movement is movement along the ecologic seam it is organized to exploit. Yet a culture is shaped by these, its own, commitments: it molds itself to significant external conditions to maximize the life chances. There is an interchange between culture and environment, perhaps continuous dialectic interchange, if in adapting the culture transforms its landscape and so must respond anew to changes that it had set in motion. I think the best answer to the received controversy over which is the determinant, culture or environment, should be this: both—the answer lies at both extremes.

The significance of given environmental features, as well as their weight upon a culture, is contingent on that culture. Here is a politically developed Asiatic Society relying upon intensive, double-crop agriculture. Subjected to a shortening of summer seasons by five days, it may be under critical selection. A certain isotherm becomes a threshold beyond which the system as constituted cannot be maintained. Yet the same climatic shift means little or nothing to a fishing tribe; its niche is governed by the conditions that directly concern the fishing. Similarly, coal is a relevant resource of an industrial technology, and its distribution in the ground affects the design, the external relations, even the historic fate of an industrial nation. But to a hunting-and-gathering people, to Australian aborigines, say, coal is completely irrelevant: in the ground or no, it is not part of their environment, it has no selective impact on them, unless

Australian Aborigines Hit It Rich
Special to the *Detroit News*

CANBERRA, April 17 [1963]—One of the world's most primitive people—scientists say they are just passing through their stone age—will get a multimillion dollar rake-off from a big Australian mine project.

They are the aborigines on the Arnhemland Peninsula of northern Austrialia. They are sitting [squatting?] on one of the biggest bauxite lodes, the ore of aluminum, ever found in the country.

Because the effects of natural circumstances are thus conditional, one cannot read, with geographical determinists, from the configuration of an environment to *a* configuration of culture.

On the other hand, the equally simple-minded textbook rebuttal to the effect that different cultures may emerge in similar environments—standard example: Manhattan Island 1962 *vs.* Manhattan Island 1492—does not dispose of environmental influence. The environment-culture relation need not be one-to-one, but environment is never, thereby, a powerless term. Natural resources, when relevant to prevailing production, govern dispositions of technologies and populations; a line of rainfall, no matter that the precise line is determined from within, is, as such, a cultural boundary; topographical features are so many barriers to or routes of communication, sites for settlement, or strategic positions of defense.

The circumstances with which most peoples have to deal, moreover, are of two distinct kinds: relations are developed with two environments. Societies are typically set in fields of *cultural influence* as well as fields of *natural influence.* They are subjected to both. They adapt to both. Indeed, terms of the relation to nature may be set by intercultural relations—as when avenues of trade govern avenues of production—and terms of intercultural relations may be set by relations to nature—as when avenues of production govern avenues of trade. It is all so obvious. But until recently the discipline of cultural ecology has operated myopically as if it were biological ecology, without reference to intercultural adaptation. We have, mistakenly in my view, limited the notion of environment and the concern for selection to the geography and biology of a milieu. Research into relations between cultures has been carried on as a thing apart, mostly under the traditional head of "acculturation," and thus not so much from the perspective of adaptation as from that of assimilation. A widespread recognition that cultures act as selective forces upon one another, and with it the realization that culture contact creates complementarity, not merely similarity in structure, seems imminent. Cultural ecology has an untapped potential to provoke useful thoughts about militarism, nationalism, the orientation of production, trade, and many other specialized developments which, if they are not "acculturation" in the conventional sense, still come out of the interaction of cultures.

The dual quality of "environment" is sometimes brought home by actions of nature and of outside cultures from different directions, setting off change in different sectors of an affected culture. Just for this point, let me use the "architectural" or "layer-cake" model of a culture-system that has been popularized in evolutionist writings. The model holds that economic and material elements—"mode of production" or, in another view, "technology"—are basic, the decisive foundation of the cultural order, and that polity and ideology are "superstructure," resting upon and systematically reflecting material foundations. Now ordinarily the imprint of nature may be traced upwards through the cultural order—but external cultural influences may very well impress themselves from the top down. Natural circumstances directly affect technical deployment, productivity, the cycle of employments, settlement patterns, and so forth; from these points the systematic relations of base to superstructure relay impulses to the higher, political and ideological spheres. The material base adapts to nature and the superstructure to the material base. Grant that—even though it is mechanical and oversimplified. A culture, on the other hand, may come to terms with its social milieu in the first place by ideological and political adjustments—the outside cultural pressure itself is often ideological and political in the main and at first. Such has been the classic course of adaptation in primitive and underdeveloped societies opened to Western dominance. The initial revisions appear in ideology, as in conversion to Christianity, and in social-political sectors, by virtue of incorporation in a colonial realm, with radical economic change setting in derivatively or afterwards. Hence the characteristic crisis of the postcolonial period, the "inverse cultural lag" compounded of advanced political norms harnessed to an underdeveloped economy.

For decades, centuries now, intellectual battle has been given over which sector of culture is the decisive one for change. Many have entered the lists under banners diverse. Curiously, few seem to fall. Leslie White champions technological growth as the sector most responsible for cultural evolution; Julian Huxley, with many others, sees "man's view of destiny" as the deciding force; the mode of production and the class struggle are still very much in contention. Different as they are, these positions agree in one respect, that the impulse to development is generated from within. The system by one means or another is self-sustaining, self-developing. The case for internal causes of development may be bolstered by pointing to a mechanism, such as the Hegelian dialectic, or it may rest more insecurely on an argument from logic, which is usually coupled with indifference to the source of change in the presumed critical sector. In any event, an unreal and vulnerable assumption is always there, that cultures are closed systems. Cultures are abstracted from their influential contexts, detached from fields of forces in which they are embedded. It is precisely on this point that cultural ecology offers a new perspective, a counterpoise to conventional evolutionary arguments. For it shifts attention to the relation between inside and outside; it envisions as the mainspring of the evolutionary movement the interchange between culture and environment. Now which view shall prevail is not to be decided on a sheet of paper; the test as always is long-term utility. But if adaptation wins over inner dynamism, it will be for certain intrinsic and obvious strengths. Adaptation is real, naturalistic, anchored to those historic contexts of cultures that inner dynamism ignores. Perhaps it even helps explain why no agreement has ever been had on which aspect of culture takes the lead in development. The various inner dynamisms, though contradictory, have each and all been supportable because, in fact, different sectors, from the mode of production to the view of destiny, at different times are decisive—depending on the point of impact of the selective field.

The trial of the ecological perspective must, and will, be in the empirical arena. The decision rests on its success in handling the facts of this case and that, and indeed an impressive list of accomplishments, headed by the researches of Julian Steward, can already be proclaimed. And it begins to be possible to reflect upon the empirical encounter, to generalize, tentatively, about the adaptive behavior of cultures. The remainder of my remarks are in this vein.

Adaptation implies maximizing the social life chances. But maximization is almost always a compromise, a vector of the internal structure of culture and the external pressure of environment. Every culture carries the penalty of a past within the frame of which, barring total disorganization, it must work out its future. Things get functionally arranged. The present

American industrial system runs on an agrarian seasonal cycle.
The American educational process, legislative process, a whole
host of critical activities virtually cease in summer, as if there
was pressing work to be done, the harvest to be taken in. And
now that in fact 90 per cent of the population has no such
obligation, the summer becomes a holiday, and industrial output
is accordingly adjusted to demands of a travel and sportsminded
market.

There is more to this adaptive compromise than mere contradic-
tion between received cultural order and new conditions of
existence. We see different selective pressures working at cross
purposes, evoking insoluble contradictions within a culture itself.
We see too that adaptive responses can have disadvantageous side
effects, as the modification of one constellation of custom sets off
untoward consequences elsewhere in the system. To adapt then
is not to do perfectly from some objective standpoint, or even
necessarily to improve performance: it is to do as well as possible under the circumstances, which may not turn out very
well at all. In one of the tropical islands of Fiji, if I may draw
upon personal observations, there is a great demand at present
for houses of timber with galvanized iron roofs, houses that
Fijians are pleased to call "European," an allegation that curiously outvalues the fact that these dwellings retain the heat and
are otherwise unsuited to the native climate and mode of life.
At the same time, the number of punts—the most feasible type
of boat for Fijians at present and also, one might note, "European"—declines steadily in this island, which means the decline
of a rare opportunity for getting some needed protein through
fishing. The rise in tin-roof demand is directly related to the
decline in boats: the materials for both must be purchased
and carpenters rewarded, so it is a question of allocation of
scarce finances. Yet, at an obvious cost in personal comfort, and
possibly in health too, this peculiar pattern of desires does neu-
tralize an adaptive dilemma. On one side, the native kinship
organization with its strong ethics of mutual aid has been very
much kept going in Fiji. It is still effective—no, necessary—in
the subsistence sector of their lives. On the other side, the usual
tendencies of individual acquisitiveness have been touched off
by their involvement in copra production and world trade. Now,

while the traditional norm of share-alike keeps people alive, it also weakens the producer's hand in movable things that he has purchased. Boats may just be taken outright by kinsmen in need, or, being scarce, they are frequently borrowed, and the owners saddled with maintenance costs. A tin-roof house becomes desirable, and I suspect is singularly identified with the dominant European (i.e., British) order, because it is, in the cultural nature of things, inalienable—one can neither take it home or decently throw a relative out of his own house. So the Fijian produces copra, continues to have many relatives, fishes less than he needs to, and swelters. An adaptive perspective, goes the moral, must not presume that whatever is there is good, rational, useful, or advantageous. Lots of things people do are truly stupid, if understandable, and many cultures have gone to the wall.

In fact a culture's downfall is the most probable outcome of its successes. The accomplished, well adapted culture is biased. Its design has been refined in a special direction, its environment narrowly specified, how it shall operate definitively stated. The more adapted a culture, the less therefore it is adaptable. Its specialization subtracts from its potential, from the capacity of alternate response, from tolerance of change in the world. It becomes vulnerable in proportion to its accomplishments. Alterations of the milieu are less than likely to be opportunities, more than likely disturbances. By its commitment to an external *status quo* it assigns the negative (negative selection) to environmental change.

Unfortunately, all this is probably convincing in the same measure as it is abstract. How shall we describe in detail the meaning of a cultural specialization, state precisely the mechanisms of its self-defense, assess accurately its adaptive potential? We are in thrall at the moment to organic notions of culture, like the evolutionist "layer cake" model I used before. A beginning on the critical questions can be made by capitalizing that central idea of the organic outlook: "functional interdependence." It should be possible, for example, to uncover chains of interdependent customs that terminate in components directly joined with the environment: an ancestral cult that sanctifies the patrilineal principle, small scale lineages acting as social proprietors, permanent but limited neolithic agriculture—that kind of thing. Professor Wolf remarks in his essay that properties of the elements within such circuits set restrictions on what may be coupled in, and prevailing relations between elements will bear just so much modification in any one of them. Yet what seems truly striking about a mature culture is not so much the organic logic of it as the idiocies of its functional connections, the irrelevancies of its structure. Things bear upon one another that, in the nature of these things, need not do so.

I am saying that there are two kinds of functional couplings in culture, logical and idiosyncratic, and that specialized cultures may be distinguished by an overburden of the latter. The coexistence of a centralized Asiatic bureaucracy and intensive irrigation agriculture is, for an example, logically consistent, in the nature of imperatives. Bureaucracy and irrigation perform necessary services for each other. Each fits within the complementary requirements of the other. But what are we to make of this fact, so painfully familiar in American television: that the style of drama is constrained by the requirements of selling soap or underarm deodorants? The constraint, incidentally is no less compelling for its idiocy, but it is clearly of a different order than functional relations of the irrigation-bureaucracy sort. Irrelevancy is the penalty of a particular past, the structural anomaly of a specialized culture. It is only understandable, and only tolerable, in the context of its own history and the circumstances that have made history. Outside of that context, any mature culture is a monstrosity.

In the past, before World War II, American anthropologists worked from a different model of culture. It was a model of "mechanical solidarity" rather than "organic solidarity," the idea that customs of a society are more importantly alike than they are complementary. Ruth Benedict, in *Patterns of Culture*, unfolded the idea; since then many intellectual descendants and cousins of it have appeared—cultural style, cultural ethos, cultural configuration, and others. "Culture pattern" means design and Gestalt, but more, it means a common alignment of the diverse pieces of culture. It has to do with the singular and pervasive genius of a people. So among the militarist tribes of the American Plains the Dionysian element appears again and

again in many different areas of culture: in their vision quests
and guardian spirit beliefs, in super-machismo definition of the
male role and a corollary acceptance of transvestism among
those who could not live up to it, in military qualifications of
leadership, suicidal pledges of revenge, in Spartan childhood
training. We are confronting a cultural orientation, and although
Benedict saw it artistically as a people's selection from the great
arc of human-temperamental possibilities, in the harder view it
looks to be selection of a different kind. The internal orientation
of Plains culture was cast from the forge of ecological selection:
the Dionysian pattern was hammered out in intertribal battle
over access to trade posts and trade goods, horses and hunting
grounds. I think that the Benedictian models ought to be
revived, to be reconsidered in the light of new interests. We
know already, as Benedict had observed, that an integrated pattern cuts down the capacity for change—in current usage, the
adaptive potential. Innovations are either given the prevailing
polarity or, if they do not lend themselves to it, are rejected.

However cultural specialization be ultimately perceived, in
configurational, organic, or some other terms, many of the little
devices that insulate peoples against cultural alternatives are
already apparent. Among them are negatively-charged ideas
about conditions and customs in neighboring societies. These
are well known under the head "ethnocentrism," but they
have been more despised as unenlightened attitudes than they
have been studied as ideological defenses. For they are "ideology" in the strict sociological sense of beliefs that prevent people
from knowing what is going on in the world. One species of
ethnocentric idea is specially important for this discussion, the
peculiar notions that societies put out about the environments
of their neighbors. The species could be called "great wall
ideology," for like the Chinese wall these beliefs divide the
terrain in which the received way of life is effective from the
terrain in which it cannot survive, and by fantastic allegations
of an outer darkness they keep people within the wall, and so
committed to the traditional order. Consider, for example, the
warnings solicitously tendered by Pathans of Swat State (Pakistan) to an anthropologist who was contemplating a visit to the
neighboring Kohistani people: "Full of terrible mountains," they

said of Kohistani territory, "covered by many-colored snow and emitting poisonous gases causing head and stomach pains when you cross the high passes, inhabited by robbers and snakes that coil up and leap ten feet into the air; with no villages, only scattered houses on the mountain tops." The noteworthy difference the anthropologist discovered between Kohistani and Pathan territories was seasonal temperatures somewhat lower in the former, a small enough matter in itself but sufficient to keep Pathan political economy from operating effectively beyond its proper border.

Adapted and specialized, mature cultures are conservative, their reactions to the world defensive. They accommodate new environmental conditions to their structures more than their structures to new conditions, absorbing fluctuations of their milieus within the prevailing order of things, so that the more they change the more they remain the same. They compensate rather than revise. And new relations to the world suggested from within remain stillborn. These are manifest tendencies of primitive and modern societies alike, dramatically manifest in successful attempts to preserve the old social regime by letting slip new economic opportunities. It is organizational sabotage. It is the essence of Kwakiutl potlatch extravagances during the fur trade, as it is also of the planned obsolescence that saves industries by wasting their productive capabilities. It is the "creeping socialism" that prevents large sectors of private enterprise from falling to pieces. Anthropologists record the herculean technical efforts of the Yakut, an Inner Asian pastoral people pushed into the Siberian forest, to keep horse nomadism alive out of its element rather than switch over to a more functional economy—the Yakut went so far as to develop irrigation, but mostly to grow more winter fodder. From New Guinea comes word of an inland people moved to the coast under missionary aegis who, for forty years, have refused to learn to fish, swim, or handle canoes.

In the final defensive phases of its history, a specialized culture may reach yet greater heights of dysfunction. As normal technical and political competences fail, supernatural reserves are engaged. This foxhole propensity of man and culture we have known for some time, at least since Malinowski's famous observation that the involvement of ritual in Trobriand island fishing increases with the hazards of the enterprise—just as in America religious ikons have been enshrined on the dashboards of automobiles since the advent of overpowered engines and overcrowded highways. The same escapism comes over cultures as wholes when faced by pressures beyond practical control: preservation becomes a supernatural business and what is threatened becomes holy. Just so with some famous millennial movements, such as the American Indian Ghost Dances of the later eighteen hundred's that looked to a magical restoration of the buffalo, the land, dead customs, and dead Indians. (Perhaps modern, overdeveloped nations are showing symptoms of defensive sanctification. Social critics in America, especially the daily syndicated viewers-with-alarum, despair that our healthy respect for the past is sometimes translated into reverent superstition, our historic legacy into the tyranny of an ancestral cult. However that may be, it has been deemed advisable to insert "this nation *under God*" into the pledge of allegiance to the flag, and a fine contrast this makes to the old saw about pioneer days: "Well parson, maybe I did hew this fine farm out of the wilderness with God's help—but you should have seen it when He had it alone!" God help those who cannot help themselves!)

Yet then the question is posed: if highly specialized peoples are conservative, where do the breakthroughs occur? Our theory seems to predict that evolution should grind to a halt, which it certainly does not do. Speculation turns to the idea of "generalized cultures," those with good adaptive possibilities. We find them sometimes on frontiers, among pioneering fringes that of necessity have simplified a heritage of little use at the present juncture. Or, from the analogy of genetic drift in species, we find them among peoples suddenly reduced to small remnants by large catastrophes, a condition that might favor the rapid spread of innovations. Yet these circumstances are too rare, on the whole too insignificant, to bear the grand movement of evolutionary variation.

We know—we take it as premise sometimes—that competition has a salutary effect on development. Even the seeming tragedy of conquest and defeat may have its phoenix aftermath.

Perhaps there is room in ecological theory for some such concept as the "Hamburg effect," referring to the remarkable service performed for German industry by Allied bombers in the last war whose obliteration of entrenched handicraft business in that city finally put production on an all-out military line. The conflict created by expanding, dominant cultures seems specially critical for the creation of evolutionary potential. Throughout history, advanced cultures have displayed a special gift for generating further advance, but not so much in their developed centers as on their ethnic borders.

For the advanced societies, in displacing backward peoples or harnessing them to their own progress, become agents of a disruption that frees the backward region from the dead hand of its own past. "To make scrambled eggs, one must first crack the eggs." But hinterlands are not merely disorganized by dominant cultures, they become committed to main streams of progress as tributaries of it. Thus they are first, involved in development, and second, set politically against its historic agent. They could become, therefore, revolutionary cultures, prepared at the same time to overthrow the old order and overtop the one presently on their backs. Look closely at the so-called nativistic movements along the Melanesian and African peripheries of modern civilization: ostensibly symptoms of cultural bankruptcy, on examination they reveal themselves as capitalizations of advance. Although at certain early phases a Melanesian cargo cult has its inclinations toward a native restoration, in its jealousy of "way belong white man" and its goal of "coming inside" it turns irreversibly from tradition, and its rebellious organization of heretofore autonomous communities is, in the understanding of the most acute observers, the germ of nationalism.

In other words, advanced and dominant cultures create the circumstances for their own eclipse. On one hand, they themselves become specialized. Their development on a particular line commits them to it: they are mortgaged to structures accumulated along the way, burdened, in Veblen's phrase, with the penalty of taking the lead. On the other hand, they restore adaptability to previously stable and backward peoples within their spheres of influence. These underdeveloped orders, rudely

jolted from historyless equilibrium, may now seize "the privilege
of historic backwardness" and overturn their submission by
taking over the latest developments of advanced cultures and
pushing on from there. How many great civilizations have lived
with, and finally died from, the menace of border barbarians? Of
course, as is made obvious today by the struggles of new nations,
it is not easy for the "barbarians," if only because progress in the
hinterland is rarely to the interest of dominant civilizations. Yet
no matter how often underdeveloped peoples fail to gain evolutionary momentum, history shows that progress is not so much
nourished in the strategic heights as in the fertile valleys of the
cultural terrain.

Cultural progress then is an outcome of adaptation and selection. Progress, moreover, is itself adaptive, or at least the complex cultures have the greatest "all round adaptability" in Julian
Huxley's words. So progress will be selected for from time to
time.

Advanced cultures are distinguished by superior means of
coping with the world. The improvements in productive technology that have occurred through prehistory and history, especially the several revolutions from the development of agriculture to the development of nuclear power, are the best known,
but they are not alone. There have been very important improvements in the technology of mobilization, that is, in means for
delivery of power, goods, persons, and messages. These particularly give advantage in intercultural relations, making it increasingly possible to base an advance on the exploitation of
surrounding societies through trade, conquest, or colonial rule.
The existence of one set of cultures, especially rich ones effectively exploiting their several environments, creates a niche
as it were for the cultural predator that can adapt itself to the
adaptations of others. (Perhaps overly impressed with the consequences of the Western Industrial Revolution, anthropologists
have been wont to locate the basis of progress in breakthroughs
of production, forgetting that the development of Rome, of
Greece, and many other civilizations had no such ground.) Finally, there have occurred improvements in still another realm,
that of protective technology: the advances in shelter, clothing,
or medical techniques, for instance, that defend society against

natural hazards; and those in armament that subdue cultural hazards.

It is often said that highly developed cultures are comparatively free from environmental control. But environmental influences are not really put in abeyance by cultural advance. It is rather that advance cannot be put in abeyance by environmental features. The performance of the highest cultures is least constrained by natural conditions. In a way, culture acts to repeal for humans the famous biological law of the minimum. In recent millennia especially, progressive cultures have shown great capacity to wheel and deal in the face of local natural deficiencies. On top of Mt. Everest, Westerners have lived despite the natural lack of oxygen; they have maintained themselves in outer space despite the absence of gravity. What has happened in the long habitable regions of this earth, however, is more important—for the moment. The advanced peoples have sustained imperialist probes of various kinds far beyond their traditional home base, if necessary by provisioning these outposts by the exploitation of the home base. And they maintain high levels of order and complexity at the home base by drawing in resources over long distances. The advanced cultural type is not as confined as the less advanced. It is distributed over greater ranges of rainfall, topography, soil type, whatnot, and it is engaged too with a greater external cultural diversity. A higher culture has more environment than a lower one.

Thus the rise in the first place of dominant cultures. Deploying power and personnel in a variety of zones, advanced cultures often compete successfully with the indigenous occupants of these zones for resources that have become indispensable to the developed peoples. The higher orders typically displace less developed ones in regions similar to, and available to, centers of progress. Societies more distant, and those exploiting other natural settings, are harnessed to the centers of development and thereby are partly acculturated. This closes a circle: we had seen that dominance can initiate progress; we see now that progress sets off dominance. I suggest that the Hegelian interplay of these main adaptive processes provides the momentum by which culture continuously transcends itself.

Anthropology was conceived in the first place out of the

dominance power of high civilization. In those "new worlds given to the world" by the European expansion were peoples and customs that could not fail to provoke an anthropological curiosity. One hopes that anthropology and its sister human sciences will keep pace now with the accumulating consequences of dominance. To do so, the development of the ecological perspective is a first requisite. The era of world history has begun. The scale of functional dependence between societies expands, drawing together the histories of different parts of the planet. The several cultures of mankind become subcultures, subsystems, differentiated parts of a larger complex of cultural relations. Cultures cannot any longer be understood by contemplation of their navels. None is intelligible in isolation, apart from its adaptation to others in the world-cultural net. As each society's history so becomes the history of every other society, and each society becomes an environment of every other, it becomes for us common sense and necessity to learn how to interpret cultures as much from the outside, from their environmental contexts, as from their inner values.

BIBLIOGRAPHICAL NOTE

The tradition of environmental determinism is discussed at length and in detail by Lucien Febvre (see Febvre and Bataillon 1925). The characterization of environmental determinism and the quote from Montesquieu in the introductory passage of the present essay have been cribbed from Febvre. His work is also a useful introduction to possibilism.

Anthropological interest in the relation between culture and nature—mostly from a possibilist vantage—developed markedly in America in connection with the culture-area approach (see Wissler 1926 and Kroeber 1939). It was Julian Steward, however, who self-consciously initiated the study of cultural ecology and placed the question in an evolutionary framework. *Theory of Culture* (1955) expounds Steward's view of ecology and the conclusions of his concrete ecological research.

Among the many contributors to current ecological thought, Frederik Barth deserves special recognition, not simply for artful brilliance in handling ethnographic data but also for his explicit inclusion of external cultural influence within the concept of environment; for examples, see Barth (1956, 1959, 1961). I have drawn heavily from Barth's work—the citation concerning Pathan views of Kohistani territory is from Barth (1956). Owen Lattimore's *Inner Asian Frontiers of China* (1951) is a classic study of historic interplay between culture and environment. The greatest single contribution to the adaptive or ecological perspective (in my opinion), it raises and speaks directly to all the critical theoretical issues.

At the risk of making invidious distinctions, a few more empirical analyses of note might be listed: Wittfogel (1957); Suttles (1960); Fried (1952); Krader (1955); Secoy (1955); Gluckman (1941); Palerm and Wolf (1957); and Conklin's contribution in *Transactions of the New York Academy of Sciences* (Ser. 2, 17:133-42). June Helm (1962) has recently reviewed the anthropological study of ecology, and her paper ought to be consulted for further bibliography.

The discussion of dominance, progress and evolutionary potential in the latter part of my essay has its basis in Sahlins and Service (1960).

12.

PERSPECTIVES GAINED FROM FIELD WORK

Laura Nader

AS PART OF THEIR training, professionals in every discipline develop a particular way of looking at the world—especially that part of the world which is the subject of their study. This paper will be about how anthropologists look at the world of man.

It is no exaggeration to say that nearly everybody, at one time or another, exhibits an interest in the language, physical type, and customs of other groups, whether they be foreign nationalities or minority groups at home. This was true of the Egyptians and, even more, of the Greeks, who touched on most modern anthropological interests in their philosophical explorations. However, it has been only during the past century that Western scholars have really grappled with the problem of understanding *all* the cultures of the world, from those of the Germans and Chinese to those of the Eskimos and Australian aborigines. This development in scholarship came after Europeans had been traveling to distant corners of the globe for something like four hundred years; ever since the age of Columbus, explorers had been voyaging to all parts of the globe, sometimes entranced and sometimes repelled, but always reacting to the diverse customs of the peoples with whom they visited, traded, and lived.

These early explorers were soon followed by missionaries, traders, and government officials who wrote reports of what they had seen, reports which pointed out to other Europeans that human life was much more varied than anyone had before supposed. The field reporters of that day were first and foremost nineteenth-century Europeans, so it was only natural that the

148

things which impressed them most about non-European cultures were exactly the customs that were unknown to European civilization: things like cannibalism and plurality of wives. It was only natural, too, that societies with such strange and barbarous habits should be thought of as somehow lesser developments in the total history of mankind. When some of the earlier explorers came to the New World they found Indian tribes in which no one seemed able to tell the difference between uncles and cousins; but this was because the Indians used one term for what the Europeans thought of as two distinct categories. In the same way the early explorers believed that primitive people who always spoke in proverbs did not know how to think properly. The problem here was that Europeans saw everything in terms of the values, attitudes, and ideas that they had learned from European civilization. Their thinking was circumscribed by a lack of self-awareness. Regardless of their biases however, it is interesting that these early observers did think it was worth writing down their observations. The information that they made available stimulated the minds of many, and by the nineteenth century anthropologists were reading these detailed collections of facts and trying to find some sort of order in the great potpourri of data.

Following this initial period of anthropology—the study of man primarily based on the accounts of travelers, missionaries, and government men—a new practice developed, that of first-hand, systematic exploration of the variety of human cultures by the anthropologist himself. This foray into the field was the exciting step which was to force a twentieth-century revolution in thinking about the many questions asked by the nineteenth-century anthropologists. The very fact that the anthropologist abandoned his comfortable armchair for the rigors of life in the field was destined to expand the field of factual knowledge upon which theories of human behavior are built. It functioned also to affect radically the anthropologist's image of himself as scientist and humanist.

In the early days of field work, which began in wide-scale form at the turn of the century, a man went to live with a group of aborigines, either accompanied by several other scientists or alone. When he proceeded alone it meant that he was isolated from his family, from his friends, from the whole of his cultural setting. He found himself among a people whose culture was often quite alien to his own, but which need not be truly alien if he learned something about it.

The early fieldworkers—men like Rivers, Boas, Malinowski, and Radcliffe-Brown—began, in a sense, to find new identities by learning about the people they found themselves living among. What they learned they painstakingly recorded. Their notebooks were filled with details of what they saw and heard, and their resultant monographs attempted to render their experiences intelligible in terms, not of Western European culture, but of the native culture itself. A prime problem the field anthropologist has to face was expressed by the famous jurist Cardozo, "No matter how objective we may try to be, we must never forget the fact that we see with our own eyes."

The early fieldworker, somewhat like a man shipwrecked upon a desert island, found it necessary to do a bit of everything. He was alone, and a division of labor was impossible, even were it desirable. And so it was that one man alone recorded the economic, the ritual, the technological, the political, and the kinship aspects of a single society. In fact, he found he could only achieve an understanding of some of the more strange and exotic customs by this sort of overview of the whole culture. The fabric of native life seemed to be so intricately woven that Malinowski, for example, could only perceive the meaning of certain fishing patterns among the Trobianders when he had understood certain magical notions. Or take the Andaman Islanders. It was only after Radcliffe-Brown had analyzed their rituals that he could begin to understand the bonds that hold these men together. These early fieldworkers were trying to understand how all the parts fit together to make a working "whole" society—a society which had adapted to and was adapting a local environment for the purpose of life.

This functionalist approach—the view of culture as an interwoven whole—was not new. Armchair anthropologists of an earlier time, such as Maine and Fustel de Coulanges, had this same view of culture. What was new was the act of going out with this point of view and collecting raw data. The results were not just more data on the variety of cultures in the world, but a different sort of data from that picked up by traders and government officials. It was now more than an interest in exotic minutiae torn out of context; these field studies were explorations in the commonplace and familiar, as well as the strikingly different. Customs which had previously been conceived of as strange or unusual were described as parts of the general design of living.

Since the time of the early fieldworkers, the detailed, and often tedious process of recording the social and cultural life of a people has been replicated by anthropologists in a variety of cultures the world over. The range of societies covered is great—from hunting-and-gathering groups like the American Shoshone and South African Bushmen to large scale civilizations such as Japan and India, from the study of nomadic societies such as the Bedouin, to an industrial American town like Yankee City. And the topics which anthropologists focus upon are equally diverse—child-rearing practices, culture change, language, or law, politics, music, and religion. As a result of this unprecedented ethnographic activity we are now beginning to document in detail the range of variation in human societies. We are now beginning to realize what men have been capable of in social and cultural creations.

The anthropologist lives and works in two worlds. When he is in the field he is recording data by observation and interview. In all his studies he investigates patterns of behavior and this much of his work is descriptive (and, as mentioned by Hymes in his discussion of linguistic anthropology, "an adequate ethnographic description is truly a theoretical task"). Beyond this, however, there is the interpretive part of the science—that part which seeks to relate direct observations to a logical framework of concepts and to a body of general statements about human culture. The anthropologist has to keep both the particular and the general in mind at once. His experience with cultures through time and space stimulates him to work at the complementary tasks of recording unique historical events and generalizing about such events. The special perspective of the anthropologist requires him to be aware of time events—for example, the development and diffusion of certain ideas and material objects, such as tobacco or the alphabet. He also has

to be aware of what we might call timeless events—the fact
that certain cultural phenomena recur in the same way under
special circumstances. For example, in many societies in the
world people practice a custom we refer to as the postpartum sex
taboo. It is taboo for a husband and wife to have intercourse for
a specified period after their child is born. John Whiting *et al.*
(1958) has suggested that in societies where this taboo extends
into many months or even years it is quite likely that we will
find another customary practice, namely that of plural marriage.
Another custom which has world-wide distribution is that of
male initiation rites, and again the anthropologist is curious as
to why some societies have male initiations and what may be
associated with them. Whiting *et al.* (1958) also looked into
this question and came up with the intriguing hypothesis that
in patrilineal, male-dominated societies, where the mother nurses
her son for a very long period, we are likely to find very severe
male initiation rites. It is important in male-dominated societies
to have men that are *men,* and the purpose of male initiation
rites is to emphasize this. These rites are designed to make a
man out of a boy who has, for so many years of his life, had a
much closer identification with his mother than with his father.

In every culture, however simple or complex, we find some
kind of family, some kind of political and economic organization,
religious beliefs, ways of settling grievances and punishing
crimes, aesthetic and recreative expression, material culture, and
so on. I have indicated that we study a wide range of societies
in order to understand the universal features of human societies,
as well as to understand the particular nature of any idea or
institution in a society. At this point I would like to mention
some observations that have been made about culturally patterned aggression and conflict.

Conflict between husbands and wives occurs, in different degrees, in all societies. Sometimes such conflict ends in what we
call "divorce," but again this varies with the culture. In working
with two societies in Africa the English anthropologist Max
Gluckman (1959) noticed that among the Zulu of Natal there
was a very low incidence of "divorce" and that among the Lozi
of Northern Rhodesia there was a high incidence of "divorce"
—and he wondered why it should be that some societies are

characterized by brittle and others by long-enduring marriage partnerships. He puts forth an interesting hypothesis: namely, that "divorce" rates vary with the type of descent system. A high divorce rate would be expected to occur in matrilineal societies, a low divorce rate in patrilineal societies; and bilateral societies such as ours would be expected to fall somewhere between the highest and the lowest rate. Another anthropologist, Lloyd Fallers (1957), worked with an African group which was patrilineal in descent but not characterized by stable marriage as Gluckman would have predicted. This led Fallers to reformulate the original hypothesis as follows (1957:121): "Where a woman either through the complete transfer of her childbearing properties, or by other means, is socially absorbed into her husband's lineage, patriliny tends to stabilize marriage; where a wife is not so absorbed [into her husband's lineage group] and thus remains a member of the lineage into which she was born, patriliny tends to divide marriage by dividing the loyalties of the spouses." While such theories do not take cognizance of the total range of variables relevant to marriage stability, they do center our attention on a very pertinent point—namely that an understanding of the context of marriage is crucial to an analysis of marital stability. There are certain conditions where the prognostication for a lasting marriage is not good. We tend to approach the problem of divorce in Western society by looking at case histories of particular couples in conflict, but we would profit by looking also at the relation between the couple and the larger kin and non-kin groups in society. As Gluckman states this (1959:79), "Social factors and not only personal disharmonies may control divorce rates in Western society." Regardless of whether one is interested in the Zulu or the Lozi, the theories formulated to explain specific aspects of these and other particular societies will be useful as points of comparison for viewing marriage stability in our own society. The study of divorce is a study in the conflicts between a man's or a woman's interests and allegiances—a study which has broad implications for society, above and beyond an interest in the elementary family.

The anthropologist also argues that the functions of conflict are multiple. Traditionally, the study of conflict has been the

study of the disruptive or disintegrative factors in society, but
conflict may produce ties that bind as well as those that divide
people. Using African data, for example, Gluckman examined
the cohesive effects of conflicts of interests. Referring to the
Nuer of East Africa, he describes a situation where an individual
is, on the one hand, linked with a group of people through the
bonds of kinship, and, on the other hand, to another group,
which may be an enemy of the first, through bonds of residence.
He concludes, "If there are sufficient conflicts of loyalties at
work, settlement will be achieved and law and social order maintained" (Gluckman 1959:17). Such a theory does not of course
make a case for the cohesive effects of strife or contentious behavior, but rather suggests that conflicts of interest may bring
people together.

Conflict may also be a way of maintaining order. Let us
take the study of the feud for instance. The feud as an institution has often been described by ethnographers as an important mechanism of social control in societies which lack formal
governmental institutions and officers. A classic case is the
Ifugao of the Philippines. Another would be the Scottish High-
landers where the feud has historically been viewed as a "lawless" institution. But is it a lawless institution? A close analysis
of the feud in context illustrates that in a very real sense the
feud was a "legal" institution, whose function was to punish serious transgressions and act as a brake to prevent aggression.
Among the Nuer of Africa we could say that the feud was a
valuable institution, necessary for maintaining and integrating
social groups in a society where the principle of opposition is
basic to the social structure.

Research on conflict and aggressive behavior bears serious
thought because the implications are so important to modern
man and the dilemma of war. Anthropologists are not pessimistic
about warfare. We know that destructive behavior is not a necessity for human life, for there have been enough cases recorded
of the constructive channeling of human behavior so that warfare was not necessary. Evidence indicates that warfare was unknown during the earlier part of the Neolithic in Europe and
the Orient; organized warfare was unknown in aboriginal
Australia and in certain parts of the New World. What we have

been able to establish is that different types of culture carry
with them varying degrees of propensity for war. Groups like the
Pueblo Indians of the American Southwest for many centuries
rarely engaged in offensive warfare. On the other hand, among
the Tupinamba of Brazil warfare was a major activity. We need
to look into such cases. The suggestion that severe inhibition of
aggression *within* a society such as the Tupinamba "encourages"
outlets for aggression by means of warfare is not to be taken
lightly.

All the examples previously mentioned of marital conflict,
feuds, and societal inhibition of aggression have in the main been
concerned with the impact of such behavior on the society at
large. Other anthropologists have been concerned with the ways
in which a society inculcates in its children certain ideas about
aggression—attitudes about aggression are taught to children in
all societies. Clyde Kluckhohn (1953) and Whiting and Child
(1953) have explored the general question of what happens
when aggression is severely inhibited in early childhood—that is,
when children are taught never to express anger by aggressive
behavior towards their fellow men. Preliminary findings suggest,
for example, that if such feelings can not be expressed between
people there will be a high degree of phantasy projection of such
feelings onto sorcerers and witches. And this hypothesis, when
followed through, leads us into the generally fascinating problem
of why some societies practice witchcraft and others do not.

Thus far, I have talked principally about anthropological experience in preliterate societies. Anthropologists, however, have
not found it difficult to shift their focus from the small, preliterate society to the modern world, and today this is evidenced
by the kinds of research they are doing. We find anthropologists
not only in the university, but also in government, in industry,
and in hospitals, and their research is not so different in general
method and approach from that of their field trips in preliterate
societies. Gregory Bateson and his colleagues (1956) for example
find themselves, as anthropologists, working with schizophrenic
patients. Their research in psychotherapy utilizes some ideas
very basic in anthropology. Mental illness is viewed as both a
cultural and a genetic problem. Several years ago Beaglehole
(1939) noted that there were strong tendencies among certain

Pacific Island groups to particular kinds of mental illness. The Filipinos, for example, tended towards catatonic schizophrenia; among the Hawaiians there was a predominance of paranoia; and manic and depressive states were common among Japanese patients. All these patterns suggest the influence of cultural factors, although there is some evidence that this remains to be clarified (Böök 1950). Urban ecologists have found that certain types of mental illness characterize the center of a metropolitan area whereas others are usually found on the periphery, and these findings again suggest the importance of environment. It has also been suggested that mental illness may be communicable, much as other kinds of behavior diffuse from one society to another. Bateson in dealing with schizophrenic patients abandoned the idea that a patient can be treated as an isolate. He and his colleagues (Weakland, 1960) investigated the patterns of parent-child interaction which seem to characterize the families of schizophrenics, and they have developed a theory about the kind of interaction which is conducive to the development of schizophrenia. The mental patient is treated simultaneously with his family. Owing in great part to the studies of anthropologists, the patient is no longer viewed as a single thread; if he is to be understood he must be examined in the fabric of his whole cultural *and* genetic heritage.

The main point to remember in all these examples is that what we learn about one society can tell us something about another. Margaret Mead (1928) gained insight into American problems of adolescence by investigating the lives of young Samoans. Political movements such as Zionism can best be understood if compared with a variety of similar nativistic movements that have been recorded through time. Similarly the deterrent effects of capital punishment can be evaluated by the study of societies where capital punishment is not used. What we discover in the study of an institution such as the family in any one society makes more intelligible the nature of the family in our own culture, while the comparative view enables us to see mankind as a whole.

The phrase "viewing culture as a whole" is an oft-repeated one in anthropology, and it is often repeated because it has led to some valuable insights as to what makes men tick. Statements such as "people drink too much," may be relatively meaningless unless they are supported by a detailed description of drinking in a particular context. In my own work among the Zapotec Indians of Mexico I recorded the various settings in which drinking took place. In each context drinking meant something in particular: it was considered bad for a man to drink alone, good to drink in company, courteous to drink in the courts of law, improper to drink in the presence of ritual kinsmen unless invited, and so on.

Many years ago Donald Horton (1943) demonstrated that the higher the level of anxiety in a society the greater the frequency of alcoholism, and now the interesting question becomes—in what settings does alcoholism increase and with what kinds of anxieties? When I left the Zapotec there was a generally worried atmosphere about what would happen to them now that the rapidly expanding Mexican system of roadways had put them in closer contact with modern Mexican national culture. They were worried as to how this contact with the non-Zapotec world would affect their mores and customs. Merchants would now be able to come in from the state capitol; there was already an increase in the production of cash crops, and many of them realized that their economy would no longer depend solely upon the fluctuations of climatic conditions, but would also be affected by price conditions of the nation and the world. These people are facing new crises, new anxieties, and alcoholism is on the increase. Will they increase their consumption of alcohol by drinking in groups, or will there be an increase in solitary drinking—drinking which is not traditionally sanctioned—and why?

The anthropologist realizes, and painfully so at times, that few problems involving humans can be defined and solved within the confines of any narrow analysis. Any kind of anthropological research itself is a multilevel investigation. We are aware that cultures which appear to be quite similar in many basic features of form may nevertheless show striking behavioral dissimilarities, and it is necessary for the anthropologist to investigate simultaneously form, content, and the various levels of culture, such as what people do, what they think they do, and what they feel they ought to do. It has been pointed out by anthropologists working in industry, for example, that you can not always find out what will motivate efficient work production simply by asking people—and the reason you often can not is because so much of culture is out of the range of the conscious. This is why an anthropologist doing research in a factory does not only sit in an office and interview workers, but also spends hours working and observing in the production room (Warner and Low 1947).

The emphasis that anthropologists have placed upon participant observation cannot be overstressed, especially for those interested in the development of the so-called underdeveloped countries of the world. One of the problems faced by those who plan economic development is that of social distance—those patterns of behavior which separate men. Certainly in many contexts social-distance mechanisms are useful and indeed necessary for maintaining order, role identity, and predictability, but they may also serve as barriers to communication. In many underdeveloped countries today we observe the development of an elite educated class—a class that is striving to utilize modern technical knowledge for the improvement of their peoples' lives. This goal implies change, but the social distance between the educated and the masses of the people often stands in the way of communication and thus in the way of diffusion of ideas and material culture. Participant observation by this educated elite may be useful in breaking down the barriers to communication.

Several themes have been underlined in this description of anthropological exploration: how anthropologists view culture as a whole, how their description of particular societies permits them to generalize for mankind, how anthropological techniques have been applied to modern societies, and how perspectives gained in other societies enable viewing our own with some measure of detachment. Participant observations and more recent techniques developed as part of the ethnoscientific enquiry equip anthropologists to discover both unconscious and conscious levels of culture not easily reported by informants or observed by the anthropologist. Much has been accomplished in less than a half-century of field work, but we have yet only a glimmer of the possibilities for anthropology.

BIBLIOGRAPHICAL NOTE

For a brief introduction to the early beginnings of social anthropology see Evans-Pritchard (1954: 21-03) and Hallowell (1960). A cross-cultural study of male initiation rites may be found in Whiting (1958); a critical and complementary analysis of this paper was recently published by Norbeck, Walker and Cohen (1962). For a discussion of marriage stability see Gluckman (1950, and 1959: 54-80), Fallers (1957), and Cohen (1961). An interesting statement about conflict and feuds may be found in Gluckman (1959: 1-26). For further literature on conflict and aggressive behavior see Kluckhohn (1944), Whiting and Child (1953), Levine (1961) and Whiting (1963). Review discussions of anthropology in modern life will be found in the papers by Caudill and Chapple in Kroeber (1953); also pertinent is Mead (1928). My own comments on mental health have been abstracted from Bateson, Jackson and Weakland (1956) and Weakland (1960). An earlier study of drinking by Horton (1943) is still a good starting point for students interested in the subject. And finally, Kluckhohn (1954) provides an excellent picture of the variety of subjects which interest the anthropological fieldworker.

13.

SOCIAL ORGANIZATION

James L. Gibbs, Jr.

EPIGRAMMATISTS MAKE MUCH of the fact that man is the only animal who knows that ultimately he must die, and of the impact that this has on man's actions. Man is also the only animal who studies himself and his way of life. Clyde Kluckhohn has called anthropology a "mirror for man" in which he can see himself in his infinite variety. Since the early workers in our discipline first silvered that mirror, we anthropologists, along with laymen, have been interested in describing the variations in the form of the human family and in human social groups and relationships. Why do some peoples inherit position and property through the mother while others inherit through the father? Was a matrilineal form of the family its earliest form? Is father-right or patriliny identical in all societies in which it exists?

We anthropologists have always asked ourselves questions like these, but the answers we have given have varied between one of two extremes. On the one hand, we have explained man's family forms and kinship behavior in terms of some factor external to family and kinship—a factor in another segment of culture or even apart from culture itself, yet something which is part of the matrix or setting in which the family and kinship rests. Such an explanation accounts for matrilineal residence —where a man goes to live with his wife and her family after marriage—in terms of economic patterns. For example, where women are the owners of fields, and agriculture is largely in their hands, men will live with their wives' families. Such a theory we

160

can call a "matrix-centered theory" because it explains family forms in terms of an element in the wider matrix in which they are found.

At the other extreme we have explanations that are narrower, which explain the family and kinship in terms of themselves, in terms of some inner dynamic. Such theories are tight and well ordered because they relate significant features of the family to other features of kinship or to very closely related institutions. Such an explanation uses the residence pattern to explain another feature of kinship, unilineal descent, which is the transmission of important social rights more through one parent than the other. For example: where men live in their wives' households, children will come to acquire the most important social rights through their mothers rather than their fathers. Such a theory we may call a "kinship-centered theory" because it explains one aspect of kinship in terms of another.

Which kind of explanation is right? Actually, the two types of theories are not mutually exclusive, but at different periods in the history of social anthropology one or the other type of explanation has been predominant. In recent years kinship-centered theories have been very dominant, but there is a current move in the other direction which is gathering momentum.

The matrix-centered theories which are re-emerging in American social anthropology represent a trend established by our early colleagues, the social evolutionists of the last century. These men, strongly influenced by Darwin's theory of organic evolution, were dominated by two concerns: to explain the variations in forms of marriage and the family in human society and to explain the development or evolution of human culture through time.

A view firmly held by most of the evolutionists was that matriliny, where descent is traced through the mother, is a very primitive form of family organization. It was found, they suggested, in societies in which the biological role of the father was unknown or where mating was so promiscuous that paternity would necessarily be in doubt. Moreover, many of them held, matriliny would lead to matriarchy or the concentration of economic, political and ritual power in the hands of women.

That would be a natural reflection of the fact that matriliny was stronger in gardening societies where women performed most of the labor. In their unilineal view of human history, matriliny would, everywhere, ultimately be succeeded by patriliny, supposedly a higher form of family organization in which women hold a less exalted position.

The evolutionists were imaginative in framing matrix-centered theories to explain the presence of matriliny. We have seen that in turning to factors outside of kinship they noted beliefs about conception and the mode of subsistence. They placed a lesser stress on narrow kinship-centered explanations.

However, later advances in our knowledge proved the evolutionists to be wrong in some major ways. It was proven that matriliny is not associated with the simplest forms of subsistence and technology, nor with promiscuity, nor with the concentration of power in the hands of women. Finally the conclusion that matriliny preceded patriliny in the history of human society was also overthrown.

When evolutionism died out in the 1890's social anthropology in America veered off in a new direction. The evolutionists who had used broad, matrix-centered interpretations were wrong. Consequently, many anthropologists seemed to conclude not that those particular theories were faulty, but that *all* wide-scale systematic theories would probably prove to be incorrect unless they were based on more adequate knowledge of nonliterate societies.

Under the strong leadership of Franz Boas, American anthropologists energetically turned to the firsthand study of nonliterate societies, especially those of the vanishing North American Indians. These men did not deny the importance of seeking theoretical explanations of human behavior, as some have claimed; they simply felt that this task was so important that it should be postponed until they had gathered adequate descriptions of nonliterate societies from which *sound* deductions could be made.

While many evolutionists had been especially interested in the family and kinship, Boas and his followers were interested in man in each of his aspects. As field workers they concerned themselves with physical anthropology, archaeology and linguistics. With such breadth of interest, the problem of understanding family and kinship was no more important to them than many other problems such as the role of folklore or the historical spread of American Indian cultures in the New World. Thus, studies of family and kinship were usually made only as a part of wider studies.

Both in their empiricism and in their moderate, cautious theorizing, the anthropologists of the Boasian period were reacting against the evolutionists. They avoided matrix-centered theories and turned to less speculative kinship-centered theories. Why, in some societies does a person call his mother's sister by the same kinship term that he uses for his mother? The evolutionists would have explained this first in terms of residence, saying that where my mother and mother's sister live in the same household they both care for me. Thus, I think of them as being alike and call them by the same term. Moreover, the residence pattern would, as we have seen, be explained in terms of economic matrix-centered notions. Kroeber, re-examining this question during the empiricist reaction, took a much more cautious view which some years later he renounced. He said that the use of kinship terms is really a matter of linguistics, of the way in which a language categorizes the world, and has nothing to do with either household composition or economic patterns.

The empiricists left us full descriptions of kinship practices in many societies, but they provided only incomplete answers to such questions as *why* people who speak widely divergent languages categorize their relatives in identical ways, or *why* in some matrilineal societies a man lives with his wife's people while in others, he takes his wife to live at his mother's brother's house.

In the 1930's American anthropology veered in still another direction. At this time in England Radcliffe-Brown and Malinowski were pioneering figures in a new approach in anthropology which can be called the comparative sociology of nonliterate societies. The impact of this school on America was intensified when both men came to teach in this country: Radcliffe-Brown at the University of Chicago, and Malinowski at Yale.

Social anthropology brought a blending of systematic theory building and systematic empiricism which led to a great refinement in the sophistication of explanations of social organization, especially of the family and kinship. This development of a specialized concern with social organization was given unique impetus and flavor by the fact that many American academic departments of anthropology were and are departments where anthropology and sociology are taught together.

The central concern of social anthropology is social organization, which has two aspects. One aspect is social structure, i.e., the network of social relations. This is the total pattern or repertoire of social position or statuses which a society offers its members and to which it fits them. The other aspect of social organization is the behavior or roles associated with the statuses or positions. Social organization, then, is a network of recognized statuses and the behavior patterns followed by people who occupy those statuses.

It was clear even to the evolutionists that most of the statuses that comprise social structure in nonliterate societies are kinship statuses. Thus, in studying social organization in the simpler societies, social anthropology is concerned largely with kinship, and kinship studies came to the fore again as social anthropology rose as a separate subdiscipline within cultural anthropology. The kinship organization of a society, like its general social organization consists of two parts: (1) a *structure* of kinship roles *and* (2) associated behavior. We have discovered that kinship organization has the attributes of a system. That is to say, the statuses and roles are arranged in an orderly pattern such that changes in one aspect of the system will lead to changes in other aspects. In recent years social anthropologists have discovered and stated rules about such changes—about the conditions that precipitate them and about the directions they will take under given circumstances.

Lewis Morgan, the evolutionist, first noted that the key to the system which underlies any kinship organization is its terminology. The kinship terms which members of society use for each other are themselves ordered in such a way that they reflect other features of the kinship organization such as the types of kinship groups and the kind of descent. It is by analyzing kinship terms as a kind of cryptogram that we social anthropologists have gained many insights into kinship *as a system.*

Such analyses are very detailed and abstract—almost mathematical. Detractors refer to them as "kinship algebra," while others use the more neutral term, "componential analysis." Thus, explanations of kinship organization in the 1950's were in terms of highly refined kinship-centered theories, not matrix-centered ones.

An influential classic study which demonstrated that kinship organizations are systems which therefore change in predictable ways was George P. Murdock's research on kinship in a sample of 250 societies. Professor Murdock demonstrated that kinship organization as a system is arranged in such a way that when the residence pattern changes, the form of kinship groups changes and this in turn leads to a change in descent which finally leads to a change in the kinship terms which people use for each other. For example, if in a matrilineal society most couples begin to reside after marriage with the husband's family rather than with the wife's, this leads to a change in the composition of households, later to a change to bilateral descent and perhaps later still, a change to patrilineal descent. Finally, there will be a change in the kinship terms with which people refer to each other.

The systematic quality of other aspects of kinship organization was studied by other writers. For example, the interest in matrilineal kinship organization which first aroused the evolutionists continued in the fifties. In 1954 the Social Science Research Council sponsored a summer research institute on matrilineal kinship systems and the papers which were prepared for that institute have recently been published in a lengthy monograph. Part one of the monograph is by David Schneider and it describes the features which characterize matrilineal kinship systems in general and explains, in kinship-centered terms, why these features occur together. For example, matrilineal societies everywhere are characterized by a very close tie between brother and sister, and a weak tie between husband and wife. In a matrilineal society a man's children do not belong to his kinship group, but to his wife's, because they trace their descent through their mother—his wife. They inherit major property from their mother's family, not from his family. As a result, he has limited authority over them. In some ways he has stronger ties to his sister's children who do belong to his kin group because their mother does. As an adult male of their kin group he has authority over them. Moreover, as their mother's brother he will leave his property to them. These characteristic allegiances and cleavages are also reflected in kinship terminology.

From Schneider's analysis, we note that in matrilineal societies it is men, not women, who make the major decisions with regard to property and other matters, although the men are related through women. When we understand the reasons for the weak link between husbands and wives in matrilineal societies, we can better understand why such societies generally have higher divorce rates than patrilineal societies.

We have here a kinship-oriented explanation for the nature of sibling ties and marital ties. They are explained in terms of other connected kinship features, namely the type and locus of authority over women and children, and descent group membership.

Marital ties, in fact marriage in general, is an element in kinship organization which has always interested anthropologists. It remained a significant focus of analysis in the fifties. Some of the most sophisticated attempts to gain new insight into the role of marriage in kinship organization have started with an examination of kinship terminology which as we have already noted is a key to the way in which kinship organization is a *system*. As the evolutionists, the empiricists, and contemporary social anthropologists have all noted, there are a limited number of patterns of kinship terminology which recur again and again in human societies. We classify the patterns of kinship terminology in terms of the way in which they categorize cousins. Other research has shown that these basic patterns of kinship terminology are partly influenced by marriage customs.

A deduction from this principle led to an important insight into the function of a preferred form of marriage among the Algonkian-speaking hunters of the northern regions of North America. These North American hunters have a kinship terminology in which cross-cousins, the children of one's father's sister or mother's brother are called by a special term. All the other cousins are called by the same term as a brother or sister. In these societies, one cannot marry a cousin who is called brother or sister, just as one cannot marry one's real brother or sister. Similarly, one *can* marry a cross-cousin whom one does not call brother or sister. This suggested to some anthropologists that the Algonkian hunters practiced cross-cousin marriage, a type of marriage in which a man marries a woman who is his cross-cousin. An examination of kinship terminology for in-laws gave further evidence for this.

One might ask: what difference does it make what form of marriage is preferred by the Algonkians? Anthropologists had been puzzled as to what held together the small hunting bands of the Algonkians. There was no inherited political office and even no unilineal descent groups to assume important duties, and a constant shifting of families from one band to another. Fred Eggan has suggested that these bands were given unity and strength by the presence of cross-cousin marriage which enables them to remain small and isolated and thus able to successfully exploit their traditional hunting territories. This is because cross-cousin marriage is a way of linking related families over and over again in matrimony. Other studies such as that of Kimball Romney and P. J. Epling of the Kariera in Australia have also indicated the way in which marriage patterns can be strongly integrative in social organization.

Such an interpretation would not have been possible without componential analysis and the slow accumulation of precise principles concerning the interrelationship of terminology and other aspects of kinship.

However, the amount of range in kinship organizations is inherently restricted by the limited variation in the elements which are part of kinship organization. Because of this, we have reached the point of diminishing returns in making involuted studies of kinship organizations as relatively self-contained systems. In graduate seminars, at professional meetings, and in prophetic articles in professional journals critics of the work of the fifties have suggested that kinship processes and behavior have been neglected in favor of a narrow concern with structure. This restlessness is reflected in a current trend to studies which attempt to understand kinship not in terms of itself, but in terms of matrix-centered elements such as other aspects of culture or even environment.

Francis Hsu has recently reminded us that kinship organizations with identical *structures* may, nevertheless, be different in actual operation and feeling. This is because kinship organizations are partially shaped by the values or basic premises which pervade and direct each culture. Thus, individuals who live in societies with identical patrilineal kinship structures may behave quite differently even though they occupy parallel positions in those kinship structures.

To document this view, Professor Hsu uses a more intuitive and literary approach than that characteristic of most kinship studies in the fifties. He compares China and India and notes that while their kinship organizations are almost identical in structure they are very different in content, content which is molded by each society's basic values. The pervading value in Chinese culture is continuity of traditional ways from generation to generation. In the patrilineal kinship organization this results in a stress on the ties which link father and son in a chain of father-son bonds stretching far into the past. It results in a mutual dependence between father and son which inculcates submission to authority within the individual. It also leads to a very subordinate role for women whose primary duty is not to their husbands or even to their brothers, but to their husband's parents and their sons.

In India, on the other hand, with a virtually identical patrilineal kinship structure, the behavior patterns of kinship organization are quite different. There, one major value is diffuse spirituality or supernatural dependence. In the proper Hindu household there is segregation of the sexes which means that the young Indian boy spends his early years primarily with his mother or other women who answer all his needs. In the kinship system, this leads to a stress on the mother-son tie. Moreover, Hsu argues, the implication is that the dependence on the supernatural is first learned as this dependence on one's mother in the household. A related outcome is the lack of strong father-son tie in a society which is apparently heavily male centered. Although there is a male-centered descent group, it is one which is oriented about a pantheon of deities, many of whom are female. Thus, we see a strong contrast to the Chinese descent group centered on the ancestor cult.

I have simplified Dr. Hsu's argument which is very subtle and most provocative. We are left with the intriguing chicken-and-egg aspects of his problem. Is kinship behavior strongly shaped by a society's general values or are the values in the family generalized out to other social institutions? In any case, it is clear that values influence the patterning of kinship behavior.

Robert Levine in a study of political behavior in East African societies makes a similar point, that values are similar both within the kinship organization and outside of it. He points out that in relatively homogeneous nonliterate societies, this makes it possible for early socialization and training in the family to serve equally well as training for political behavior out side the family. Thus, a stress on deference to elders is a strong value in many patrilineal East African societies. One learns this in the family with regard to one's older brothers, father, uncles, and granduncles. Later the same principle serves one in good stead as one becomes a member of the age-grades or a chief's council. We see again that values influence behavior both within the kinship sphere and outside of it, although we are still left with the question of whether kinship values or other values come first.

Values, then, form one aspect of the matrix in which kinship operates. Other recent studies by Service, de Gonzales, Foster and Barnouw have suggested further elements in this matrix which may also affect kinship—elements such as the total level of technological complexity, and the degree of stress in the form of acculturation. Gough and Aberle in the concluding parts of the recent monograph on matrilineal kinship mentioned earlier similarly related structures to outside factors such as mode of subsistence and ecology. In turning to these as explana-tory factors, anthropology of the sixties returns to broader, matrix-centered theories in favor of the narrower kinship-oriented ones which have carried us to this threshold.

This trend indicates eclecticism, which has always been charac-teristic of American anthropology. It also indicates a self-conscious concern with theory, just as the choice of societies in which to gather data shows both a continuing concern with the American Indian and a parallel international focus as indicated by the wave of field studies in Africa, Asia, Latin America, the Middle East, and Oceania.

BIBLIOGRAPHICAL NOTE

A stimulating and clear presentation of the concepts and substance of social anthropology which provides insightful comments on the "meaning" of social organizational studies is in Bohannan (1963). Tax (1955) includes a concise historical treatment of most aspects of the treatment of social organization. A longer treatment of the work and lives of some of the earlier theorists appears in Lowie (1937). Useful, concise and astute overviews of kinship and social anthropology appear in two articles included in the Encyclopedia Britannica (1963 edition): "Social Anthropology" by Raymond Firth (20:862-70), and "Kinship," by J. A. Barnes, (13:403-407). Two works which are basic to the work of most contemporary American anthropologists who deal with social organization—especially kinship—are both oriented to the matrix-centered approach to kinship; they are Murdock (1949) and Radcliffe-Brown (1950).

Noteworthy examples of newer studies in social organization which reflect some of the recent trends noted in the present article include Eggan (1955), and Schneider and Gough (1961). Shorter contributions such as journal articles reflect new trends in research more quickly than monographs, and they contain some of the most substantive and provocative contributions to the professional literature. Such briefer social organizational studies are abstracted and commented upon in Harry Basehart's excellent review paper (1959).

14.
THE ORGANIZATION OF ECONOMIC LIFE

Manning Nash

THE ECONOMIC LIFE OF man shows a great variety over time and space. In the New Hebrides islands, the main economic concern is the accumulation of pigs. Men raise pigs, exchange pigs, lend out pigs at interest, and finally in a large ceremonial feast destroy the pig holdings of a life time. Among the Bushmen of the Kalahari desert there is no private property in productive goods, and whatever the hunting band manages to kill is shared out among the members of the group. In the Melanesian islands every gardener brings some of the yams from his plot to the chief's house. There the pile of yams grows and grows, and eventually rots, to the greater glory of the tribe. The Indians of Guatemala and Mexico live in communities each with its own economic specialty. One group produces pottery, another blankets, another lumber and wood, and the next exports its surplus maize. These communities are tied together in a complex system of markets and exchange.

How are these economic activities to be interpreted and explained? What body of ideas can make sense of the gift-giving of the Plain Indians, the personalized markets of Haiti, the elaborate ceremonial of exchange in the Solomon islands? (Malinowski 1922) Less than half a century ago the differences among economic systems were explained by the hypothesis of social evolution. Different economic systems were assigned to levels or stages of the evolution of human society and culture. It was assumed that there had been an evolution from simple hunting bands, with communal property rules, to villages with settled

171

agriculture and clan or family property, and that was followed by a stage of political units with advanced technology and private or state property. This view of economic evolution has not fared well in the face of modern field research. Two chief things have made this mode of explanation lose its force. First, the rising tide of field investigation of economic systems revealed a whole host of economic arrangements which this crude classification by stages could not contain. And second, the idea of stages of evolution shed very little light on the actual processes of economic change. A new model of the variables to explain economic systems and their changes over time is now being fashioned. This model rests on about four decades of accumulated information, and on methods and theories developed in the act of gathering and interpreting that data.

Method in studying economic systems is basically the same as in the rest of social and cultural anthropology. Method is a device to study social regularities, and to give meaning to those regularities. In the study of nonmonetary, or partially monetized economies, getting the basic facts is often a test of the observer's ingenuity. Many new ways of getting measurable or nearly measured data have been invented, and recent research is marked by an emphasis on quantities or relative magnitudes of economic activities.

The distinguishing features of peasant and primitive economic systems fall along four axes. The first is *technological complexity and the division of labor*. These are relatively simple societies, technologically. A simple technology means that the number of different tasks involved in any productive act are few. Usually it is the skill of a single or a few producers which carries production from beginning to end. Many primitive and peasant technologies are ingenious, marvelously fitted to a particular environment, requiring high levels of skill and performance, but still very simple. The Bemba of Rhodesia (Gluckman 1945) wrest a living from poor soil with uncertain water supply by an intricate method of cultivation. With good rains and luck they harvest their crop of finger millet. The system is one of balance in a precarious ecological niche, but the task structure is simple, and the tools involved require only human energy to operate. The specialized operations involved are not the

kind which make an interrelated web of occupations. Men do
most of the agricultural work among the Bemba, and one man
is virtually as good as another in his agricultural skills. The
division of labor follows the natural axes of sex and age. An
occupational list in a peasant or primitive society is not a long
one. Persons tend to learn their productive skills in the ordinary
business of growing up, and within age and sex categories there
is high interchangeability among productive workers. Work and
tasks are apportioned to the appropriate persons, without much
regard to differences in skill or productivity. The technology
also sets the limits of the size of combined working parties. Except at peak periods—planting or harvesting in agricultural communities, an organized hunt at the height of the animal running
season—large working parties are not found. Effort and work
are closely tied to a pattern fitted to the annual and ceremonial
cycle, not to the continuous demands of a highly organized
economy with a wide social division of labor.

The second feature of peasant and primitive economy is the
structure and membership of productive units. The unit of
production, the social organization carrying out the making of
goods, is dependent on, and derived from, other forms of social
life. Peasant and primitive societies do not have organizations
whose only tasks are those of production, and there are no
durable social units based solely on productive activities. The
bonds of kinship which structure families, clans, and kindreds
are often the bonds which organize economic activities. Territorial bonds may serve to create local producing organizations.
And the political structure, especially in societies with hereditary
nobilities, is often used as a mechanism for forming productive
units. This dependence of economic units on prior kinds of social
relations has a typical series of consequences. Productive units
tend to be multipurposed. Their economic activities are only
one aspect of the things they do. The economic aspect of a
family, a local group, or a compound composed of patrons and
clients, is just one area where the maintenance needs of
the group are being met. Therefore, in these societies there
tend to be many productive units, similarly structured, all doing
the same sort of work. These productive units are limited in
sorts of personnel they are able to recruit, the capital they

174

are able to command, and the ways in which they may distribute
their product. There does not exist a labor market, nor a capital
market, nor a system of distribution to factors of production. A
striking example of productive units based on relations derived
from the organization of social groups only partially oriented to
economic activity is the Indian pottery-making community in
southeastern Mexico. This community is composed of 278 households. Each household is engaged in the production of pottery
for sale, with virtually the same technology (Nash 1961). Every
household looks like every other in its productive organization.
Or again, from Mexico, among the people of Tepoztlan (Lewis
1951) many make their living by the sale of services at a wage.
Yet people must be sought out for employment, and hiring a
fellow member of the community is a delicate social job. The
transaction cannot appear as a strictly economic one.

The third distinguishing feature of peasant and primitive
economies is *the systems and media of exchange.* In an economy
with a simple technology, productive units which are multipurposed and derived from other forms of social organization,
and with a division of labor based chiefly on sex and age, a
close calculation of the costs of doing one thing or another is
often impossible, or merely irrelevant. The advantages of a
change in the use of time, resources, and personnel are arrived
at through the logic of social structure, through a calculus
of relative values, not in terms of the increase of a single mag-
nitude such as productivity. This inability to estimate closely
the costs and benefits of economic activity is aggravated by the
absence of money as *the* medium of exchange. Most of the
world now has some familiarity with the use of money. In fact,
some societies developed full, all purpose money prior to contact
with the industrial and commercial West (Davenport 1961).
And many societies have standards of exchange like the Polynesian shell currencies, or the tusked pigs of Melanesia, the salt
currency of the horn of Africa, or the cocoa beans of the Aztecs.
But this is quasi-money, or special purpose money; it is merely
the standard with the widest sphere of exchange. Special purpose
money is confined to a particular circuit of exchange, and the
circuits of exchange in the economy are only partially tied
together. Among the Siane of New Guinea (Salisbury 1962)

there are different kinds of exchange of goods, and each kind of goods is limited to its particular circuit. Some goods can be exchanged only for subsistence items, others only for luxury items, and others only for items which confer status and prestige. The Tiv of Nigeria (Bohannan 1955) have similar multi-centered exchange system with media appropriate to each sphere of exchange. Food is exchanged for food, and can be exchanged for brass rods; brass rods exchange for the highest valued goods, women and slaves. And a reverse or downward movement of exchange items was severely resisted and considered illogical and unfortunate among the Tiv.

The media of exchange and the circuits of exchange are set into various kinds of systems of exchange. The most common systems of exchange are markets, redistributive system, reciprocal exchange, and mobilization exchange. The market system is widespread among peasants, and in Meso-America tends to be free, open, and self-regulating (Tax 1952). In Haiti (Mintz 1961) the market is competitive, free, and open, but special bonds of personal attachment grow up between some buyers and some sellers which cut down some of the risk and uncertainty involved in small peasant trading. Rotating market centers, with a central market and several subsidiary markets, are a fairly common feature in Burma among the Shans, in several parts of Africa, north and south of the Sahara, and in many places in the Near and Far East. These market systems usually operate without the presence of firms, and lack investment in expensive facilities of exchange, including the spread of information. The single complex of markets, firms, capital investments, entrepreneurs, deliberate technical investment, and property rules to facilitate accumulation and exchange is apparently a historical precipitate peculiar to the West. In the ethnographic record it does not appear as a necessary bundle or sequence of events.

Reciprocity of exchanges is exemplified by the practices of gift-giving (Mauss 1925) or kula exchange of the Solomon Islands and tends to lack much bargaining between, to rest on fixed sets of trading partners, and to occur between equivalent units of the social structure. Thus clans exchange with clans; barrios or wards with wards; households with households; tribes with tribes; or communities with communities. The reciprocal exchange is for near equivalences in goods and services. The rates of exchange tend to be fixed. Redistributive trade takes place in societies with some systems of social stratification, but not organized for market exchange. An African paramount chief may collect tribute in the form of goods and redistribute it down the social hierarchy through his clients and kinsmen. Or administered trade at fixed prices, with a political center exchanging with its peripheries is another common example (Polanyi 1957). Redistributive exchange keeps a political and status system operating without great gaps in wealth between the different classes of status groups. A system of mobilization for exchange (Smelser 1959) collects goods and services into the hands of an elite for the broad political aims of the society. The irrigation empires of the early civilizations apparently had these sorts of exchange systems, and some of the new nations of Asia and Africa have systems like this in conjunction with some aspects of market, redistribution, and reciprocal exchange.

The fourth dimension of variation in economic systems is in *the control of wealth and capital*. Generally, investment takes the form of using resources and services to buttress or expand existing sets of social relations. The chief capital goods in peasant and primitive societies are land and men. Tools, machines, terraces, livestock, and other improvements in productive resources are controlled in a manner derived from the conventions of control and allocation of land and human beings. Land tenure is an expression of the social structure of a peasant and primitive society, and the allocation of land results from the operation of the system of kinship, inheritance, and marriage, rather than through contracts or transactions between economic units. Even in those societies where corporate kin groups like clans do not exist as landholding bodies, special devices like the establishment of titles, or kindred-based landholding corporations may be invented as on Truk (Goodenough 1951). Manpower, like land, is also organized to flow in terms of given social forms, not to abstract best uses.

For peasants and primitives to maintain their societies, capital, or property rules, or economic chance may not be permitted to work in ways disruptive of the values and norms of the society.

A fairly common device for insuring that accumulated resources are used for social ends is the leveling mechanism. The leveling mochanism is a means of forcing the expenditure of accumulated resources or capital in ways that are not necessarily economic or productive. Leveling mechanisms may take the form of forced loans to relatives or coresidents; a large feast following economic success; a rivalry of expenditure like the potlatch of the Northwest Coast Indians in which large amounts of valuable goods were destroyed; or the ritual levies consequent on office holding in civil and religious hierarchies as in Meso-America; or the give-aways of horses and goods of the Plains Indian. At any rate most peasant and primitive societies have a way of scrambling wealth to inhibit reinvestment in technical advance, and this prevents crystallization of class lines on an economic base.

This schematic presentation of the major features of peasant and primitive economies serves to place them in a comparative series of economic organizations and to extend the range of social contexts for economic analysis. But charting the range and diversity of economic systems is only a part of the task of anthropology. How economic systems relate to the total social system is a question of major theoretical importance. Economic action is only a part of the system of social action. It is tied to the whole social system in three ways: First by normative integration, second by functional interdependence, and third by causal interaction. The ends sought in the economic sphere must be consonant, or complementary, with goals in other spheres. Economic activity derives its meaning from the general values of the society, and people engage in economic activity for rewards often extrinsic to the economy itself. From this point of view, there are no economic motives, but only motives appropriate to the economic sphere. In peasant and primitive societies the norms and values used to define a resource, a commodity, control over goods and services, the distributive process, and standards of economic behavior, are the norms governing most social interaction. The economy is not so different from the rest of society so that one set of values holds there, and other values hold in other contexts. The economic system does not exhibit an ethic counterposed to the regnant value system.

The functional interdependence of economy and society (Parsons and Smelser 1957) stems from the fact that the same persons are actors in the economic, the kinship, the political, and the religious spheres. The role of father must fit in some way with the role of farmer, and these must fit with the role of believer in the ancestor cult, and these must fit with authority position in the lineage, to take an example from the Tallensi (Fortes 1949). The interdependence of parts of a society means that there are limits to the sorts of economies and societies that may coexist in one time and space continuum. These limits only now are being charted. But it is plain that a system of reciprocal exchange rests on social units that are nearly equivalent in status, power, and size. The marriage and descent system of the Nayar (where husbands were warriors who lived away from wives and where descent was matrilineal) is an instance of the functional compatibility of an occupational and status system with a marriage and descent system.

The causal interaction of economy and society turns on the pivot of the provision of facilities. For given forms of social structure a given variety and volume of goods and services are required, and if there are shifts in facilities available, there will be shifts in the rest of society. Conversely, shifts in the social structure will change the volume and variety of goods and services a society produces. The empirical way of finding these causal interactions is to study peasant and primitive societies undergoing change. The facts of change are the only sure guides to generalizing on the sequences, forms, and processes of economic and social interaction. Much of the change in the economic life of peasants and primitives comes from the expansion and spread of the Western forms of economic activity.

The expansion of the economic frontier can be seen in places like Orissa, the hilly tribal region of India (Bailey 1957). Here economic opportunity in the wake of the spread of the money economy has allowed some castes to move quickly up the status ladder and forced some traditional high status castes downward. The economic frontier in the form of money and new opportunities tends to change the role of corporate kin groups and place more emphasis on smaller familial units (Worsley 1956), to introduce a re-evaluation of the goods of a society (Bohannan 1959), and to put pressures on traditional authority systems.

The chief way that peasants and primitives get involved in the world economy is through entering a wage-labor force, or by producing something that can sell in international trade. The effects of entering a wage-labor force (Watson 1958) often start conflicts between generations, raise problems about the control of income, and sometimes depopulate the society so that its social structure collapses. A rural proletariat may replace a tribal society. Income from entrepreneurial activity by peasants poses larger problems for the social system (Firth 1954). It may result in greater wealth differences, in modifications of the use of capital, in loosening the integration of the society, and in changing the authority patterns. The boom involved in peasant agriculture (Belshaw 1955) often involves a change in religious and ethnical concepts, and an increase in the importance of economic activity relative to other forms of social activity.

The introduction of factories to peasant primitive societies (Nash 1958) provides, in theory, the widest possibilities for transformation. The change induced by a factory may be akin to that from the increased use of money from wage labor, or the expansion of the economic frontier, but it tends to tie the community more closely to a national and international economic network, to provide a new context for political change, to give a base for new voluntary groupings, and to exert great pressures on extended familial networks, and above all to demand a sort of flexibility and mobility of persons and institutions usually not found in traditional societies (Moore and Feldman 1960).

What the studies of economic change have taught is that modifications in economic activity set up a series of pressures and tensions in the society and culture and that there are limited possibilities for their resolution. There is no generally agreed upon sequence of change, and hardly more consensus on final forms, but the evidence seems to indicate that economic systems are among the most dynamic parts of a society, and that economic activity, in the sense of the provision of facilities for the organization of the rest of society, is one of the most pervasive and determinative aspects of social life. It sets the limits within which social structures and cultural patterns may fall.

The field of economic anthropology has mainly, thus far, worked on the description and interpretation of small-scale societies, but by principle and method it is not limited to them (Berliner 1962). It is moving into problems of economic and social change, and illuminating the relations of economy and society, and the causal interaction of economic variables and other parts of society and culture. Its greatest challenge and potential is the fashioning of a theory encompassing both economic and noneconomic variables in a single explanatory system. It may then provide a framework for a truly comparative study of the form, function, and dynamics of economic systems (Dalton 1961).

BIBLIOGRAPHICAL NOTE

Modern studies in economic anthropology stem from Malinowski's *Argonauts of the Western Pacific* (1922). Raymond Firth's *Primitive Polynesian Economy* (1929) is a landmark in field studies. Melville Herskovits' *Economic Anthropology* (1952) is a good catalog of the empirical work to date. Sol Tax's *Penny Capitalism* (1953) is probably the most complete and detailed description of a small scale non-Western economy. Specialized studies like Bohannan and Dalton (1962) and a growing interest in economic and social change (Salisbury 1962 and Epstein 1962) now dominate research and theory.

15.

ANTHROPOLOGY AND THE STUDY OF POLITICS

Morton H. Fried

THE MEANING OF THE WORD "politics" or of the phrase "political organization" is often uncertain because of wide and varying usage. Yet to take the problem of definition seriously would be to exhaust the space at my disposal. Even doing this, it is likely that the result would be indefinite and of marginal utility. Still, some initial point of definition is needed, even if to merely and arbitrarily establish a basis for the ensuing discussion.

Harold Lasswell, well known political scientist, offers an aphorism, telling us that politics is "who gets what, when and how." Superficial and apparently cynical, this definition has merit for drawing immediate attention to at least two crucial aspects of political phenomena. The first has to do with power, the other with the relation of politics to other phenomena.

Power, the ability to forcefully compel the behavior of others, exists in all societies. Also a universal characteristic of cultural societies is authority, the socially approved ability to orient the behavior of others. Authority, it may be quickly said, is usefully distinguished from power on two grounds: authority is not necessarily associated with force nor with compulsion; conversely, there can be considerable power without approval, hence without authority in this sense. Further discussion of this admittedly difficult matter cannot be undertaken during this brief presentation.

Returning to power, we note that it is so universal that one social anthropologist, Edmund Leach, has stated flatly that it is "necessary and justifiable to assume that a conscious or unconscious wish to gain power is a very general motive in human affairs." Yet, as Leach quickly adds, the social conceptions of status, with which power is inextricably entwined, differ greatly from culture to culture. This means that we are misled if we seek any universal political pattern; yet this is precisely what is done when, for example, the power relations within family groups are taken as the model of the nascent state. In the usual conception, for example, the frequently cited opinion of Aristotle, the power organization of the family is seen to revolve about the role of the father, and to some extent urban middle class families in my own country are so structured as to have the paternal role the focus of authority. Yet we know of many cultures in which the organization of the family differs markedly from this, and power in those structures tends to flow and concentrate in other statuses. Furthermore, there are many societies in which leadership, the organized application of power to concrete situations, is so diffuse as to approach nonexistence. The Kung Bushmen of the Kalahari Desert exemplify this. Even hunting parties, the most crucial form of organization among the Kung, frequently lack formal leadership. As Lorna Marshall says, "Often an informal leadership develops out of skill and judgment and the men fall in with the plans and suggestions of the best hunter or reach agreement among themselves somehow." In such a situation the forceful compulsion implicit in power is lacking; in its stead is consensus based on authority in the sense of favorable reputation.

When we say that politics relates to how someone (or some group) gets something and then holds on to it, we obviously implicate power. We also immediately bring in the whole social system. While evidently referring to persons in a society, we are talking—on another level of abstraction but in an equally real sense—not about people as such, but as holders of formal positions in a social system. In other words, we are concerned with statuses. These may be *kinship* statuses, as in the situation, "*Father* will not permit me to smoke cigarettes;" or they may be *non-kin* statuses of the widest variety of types, as in the situation, "*My neighbor* will not allow me to walk on his land," or "*The policeman* allowed me to pick a flower in the park."

Whatever else "the political" may be, it is a subsystem of a larger social system.

Furthermore, if we turn to what it is that one gets or holds through politics, we discover that political action frequently has as its context some other aspect or aspects of culture. Thus an economic or an ideological concomitant often appears simultaneously. For example, a man might desire the high priest's crown because with it goes great prestige, considerable wealth, access to theological exaltedness, increased control over his fellows, and many other advantages (as well as certain limitations and disabilities). Rephrasing, we may note that what we are referring to as "the political" is not only a subsystem of the larger encompassing social system, but a collection of allocations. In a sense, the political aspect of a society comprises the means whereby that society defines its component statuses, equips these statuses with roles, attempts to manage the fulfillment of these roles, and rationalizes all of the implicated interactions in terms of larger groups rather than in terms of individual behavior.

In order to better show the locus of political functions, we may have recourse to two hypothetical limiting cases. In the first limiting case we imagine that power is exerted in order to achieve, validate, legitimize or otherwise obtain or hold on to power (power being used in the previous sense of "means of compelling the behavior of others"). The redundant use of power is by no means universal, for reasons already indicated. To the extent that it exists we may adapt our usage from John Austin, the nineteenth century English jurisprudent, and speak of "politics proper."

In the second limiting case power is exerted in order to obtain, validate, or legitimize access to something other than power. The senior person in a lineage, for example, might discipline a refractory member in order to maintain peaceful relations with another neighboring lineage. Or he might invoke penalties upon a member for attempting to find a wife whose relationship was deemed too close, thereby protecting the larger group from supernatural disaster. Examples might easily be multiplied; in each case they might be called, following Karl Polanyi's treat-

ment of certain types of economic integration, "imbedded
politics."

It should be made clear that while psychological study of the
motivation of political behavior, particularly decision-making, is
of great interest, we are advocating focus on the cultural or
societal dimensions of the phenomenon, rather than upon individual responses. It is well, at this juncture, to remind ourselves that political behavior and institutions are not and cannot
be confined to individual interactions, but have great significance
in terms of the relations among groups. Some of our examples
have already introduced this characteristic, though none have
emphasized it. Thus, the problem of maintaining order in a
lineage is often related to the interaction between lineages: if a
member of lineage "A" kills, or wounds, or rapes, or defrauds,
etc., etc., a member of lineage "B," the problem becomes simultaneously three—what shall be done by each affected lineage,
and what shall they do in concert?

Returning to the limiting cases previously offered, and adding
the concept of interactive groups, we might consider, by way
of illustration, the use of the power of the Chinese Communist
Party to drive out or thoroughly discipline all non-Communist
political parties. That this has been done is a matter of record.
The purpose of this drive could be summed up by saying
that it was to consolidate and extend the power of the Chinese
Communist Party. Indeed, Leninist political theory is most relevant to our present discussion, since it includes a body of
practical directions relating to the seizure, consolidation, and
enhancement of the power of an oligarchical group which is
said to represent the power of a specific class, the proletariat.
Though very far from modern revolutionary struggles, the administration of the court in the traditional society of Buganda
in East Africa is theoretically similar. In the instance of Buganda
the organization and control of a large number of functionaries
and specialists—some involved in ritual, others in military operations, in provisioning, entertainment, etc.—is directed toward
the central goal of demonstrating, maintaining, and extending
the power of the king and the sector of the society which he
represents.

However illustrated, the point of cases such as these is that political activity in these societies is recognizable as such. It seems to me that this separation and identification of the political can only be undertaken in such cultures (societies) as already have achieved a precipitation of their major political institutions into a set form known as the "state." In the absence of a polarized state, political relations will inevitably be imbedded. Permit me, at the risk of pedantry, to underscore this point. I do so because the issues contingent upon this problem have attracted the attention of many great minds. To some degree this is the matter that separates the "historical" school of jurisprudence from the "analytical" school.

The historical school, particularly in the phase associated with Frederick von Savigny, who died a century ago, tends to view custom as law and sees no qualitative difference between the political organization of the most simple hunting-and-gathering society and those based on intensive agriculture and industrialism and urbanism. Whether or not they are intellectually aware of the existence of this school of jurisprudence, many anthropologists have taken similar stands and continue to defend this general point of view. For example, E. Adamson Hoebel, one of the few United States' anthropologists to have made a specialty of the study of legal systems, has written that, "where there is political organization, there is a state. If political organization is universal, so then is the state." It needs but little reflection to realize that this is essentially the position known more broadly as "cultural relativism." While its main benefit, a very great one, has been in freeing our minds from errors of ethnocentric bias, cultural relativism makes exceptionally difficult, perhaps even impossible, the task of scientifically analyzing and comparing cultures.

Analytical jurisprudence, on the other hand, is anti-relativistic. As a consistent body of definitions and theories, the school is the product of English utilitarianism and is closely associated with the name of John Austin, who died in 1859. Very briefly, the analytical approach so defines "law" and the "state" as to restrict the appearance of these phenomena to social systems which have already undergone a high degree of internal differentiation. Extrapolating from the original Austinian position, it may be said that such societies would have already evolved or otherwise acquired socioeconomic classes and a fixed locus of authority and power. Quite evidently, materialistic views of history, cultural evolution, or the cultural process in general are most compatible with the analytic approach.

What are the disadvantages of the historical school's approach which makes law equivalent to social control? Perhaps the major difficulty is the loss of very useful differences. All societies have mechanisms for "compelling the behavior of others." In a sense, some societies are aided by the biological processes of genetics in achieving this end. Social insects, with their problems of differentiated function, worker, reproducer, warrior, etc., come immediately to mind. In cultural societies the problem is equally intense but rather different because there are no genetically determined allocations of role. One of the extreme reactions to this lack of clear-cut innate difference has been the assertion that all human societies are common subscribers to certain cultural universals which include law and the state. The reaction, though emotionally understandable, is destructive of analytical comprehension. There are intermediate categories in the classification. The means by which simple societies regulate social behavior are aspects of "social control," but they are not thereby equivalent to "law."

If we now combine some of the points which have already been made, we may be able to offer some ideas about political organization that will be useful in any future attempt to think constructively about this phenomenon. First, political activity is generally an aspect of some other activity, carried out for some other purpose. Second, political activity, in the final analysis, deals with the compelling of the behavior of other members of the society. Third, societies differ in the degree to which compulsion of the behavior of others is permitted; some societies concentrate their compulsion in their systems of enculturation and in a general adherence to "customary" rules based, in final analysis, upon the simple powers of reciprocity. Other societies, though equally reliant in initial stages upon enculturation, and though dependent to some degree upon conformity based upon generalized social pressure and the effects of reciprocity, must, because of complexities introduced through a proliferation of specialized statuses, very large population, or great extent of the area under control, begin to regulate behavior by different principles. The most convenient means of designating these new and different principles is by use of the rubrics "law" and "state."

The state may be regarded as an assortment of institutions which organize and channel the power of a society on a supra-kin basis. It comes into existence because the network of kin relations fails to coincide with the network of personal relations. This has been brought about, in turn, by the steady expansion of a number of factors: population, area, number of distinct statuses, complexity of the means of production and distribution, and others, all cumulative results of trends released by the switch to domestication.

All societies are witnesses to internal conflicts among members. The reasons for conflict are varied; there is competition for persons, things, prestige, etc. Yet, in most simple societies such as those based upon hunting and gathering or many of the less densely populated farming societies, the opportunities for conflict are relatively limited by the structure of society. Why compete for land if it is free to the clearer and there is ample virgin forest or second growth timber? Why compete for sexual favors if marital norms are not monogamous and the culture permits a considerable freedom to youth or to the adults? Why compete for scarce goods to the extent of stealing or committing violence for them when these very goods move easily from hand to hand, being exchanged by relatives in societies where all are kin? I repeat; there is conflict and the need for mechanisms of adjudication in *all* societies, but some have far less conflict and need for these mechanisms than others.

Two important things happen more or less simultaneously and create a new model of society with new requirements for social control. One of these is limitation of access to the resources and scarce goods of the society. The other is the enlarging of the society beyond the bounds where interpersonal relations can be maintained on the basis of existing kinship ties or the fictitious extension of those ties. Actually, the second need not develop from the physical expansion of the society; it can and does develop as a concomitant of the first process which is the formation of incipient socioeconomic classes.

The first and most important task of an emergent state is to maintain general order both within and without. But evolving states generally lack the technical capacity to keep control of an entire range of social institutions; indeed, even the most tightly organized modern states cannot do so. That being the case, the emergent state in particular must maintain social order by defending the keystone of that order—the order of stratification. It is for this reason that the data of comparative primitive state government so often contain examples of the crime of *lèse majesté*, and why, in modern states, the legal system may be seen to run between such ultimate extremes as treason and contempt. These crimes are against the system as such. To walk on the grass, if king, or congress, or court has said no, is to incur a penalty. The penalty may be for an explicit offense but, as in *lèse majesté*, it may be for breaking the rules in general.

If it be asked, what turns a society from generalized "social control" of interpersonal relations to rules of law administered by determinate judges according to formally prescribed procedures, we face a great and fascinating problem. We are asking for the origins of the state.

To begin with, the stage was set for the invention of the state rather late in history. If we assume culture to be a round million years old on this planet, the earliest states appeared only some five- or six thousand years ago. Quite evidently, the preparatory event was the mastery of plant and animal domestication, what V. Gordon Childe called "the Neolithic Revolution." Equally evident is the conclusion that the mastery of domestication was not sufficient cause for the development of the state. We know of many regions of the world where domestication has existed for tens of centuries but where the state has not developed. In my own work I have found it useful to distinguish two kinds of states according to their geneses: the "pristine" state, which developed *sui generis* out of purely local conditions, and the "secondary" state, which is assisted or directed toward this form of organization by interaction with a social system that has already taken state form.

It is not a simple job to identify pristine states. Shall we, for example, place the development of ancient Egypt posterior to and make it dependent upon the formation of state polity in Mesopotamia? Or, in another part of the world, do we deem Shang China a secondary state because of evidence indicating a substantial flow of traits from Southwest Asia? What of relations between Peru, Mexico, and Yucatan in the New World?

Yet, despite certain empirical difficulties, the utility of the distinction lies in its application to the understanding of the genesis of the state. The foremost theorists of the nineteenth century who considered the question of the origins of the state did so largely in terms of Greece and Rome, which I would identify as secondary states. Yet the processes which go on in the development of secondary states may differ very greatly from the processes which produced pristine states. Secondary states may see the rise of socioeconomic classes as the result of conquest, or the extension of a web of trade relations frequently of an exploitative kind, or of the introduction of wage-labor or multipurpose money, etc. In a pristine state the mechanisms of control would arise out of indigenous changes in the subsistence economy, means of distribution, and the pressure of population on the land. The new society, growing out of the old, would have to grapple in a different way with the alteration of the ideology of kinship and coresidence. In brief, the reconstruction of the original development of stateship cannot be read with accuracy from the acculturation situations which, in fact, are the beginnings of each secondary state.

In a brief interval we have covered a range of topics relating to the anthropological approach to the understanding of political systems. The presentation offered here has stressed certain definitional problems and the question of origins. Various other approaches are favored by other students, such as the functionalist attempt to understand the relations between particular polities and particular economies, or religions or social systems in general. Some anthropologists also specialize in the study of a particular kind of secondary state, that which has recently been generated as the result of the advance and retreat of imperialism and colonialism.

Anthropological interest in the study of political systems is not limited to simple societies, to the evolution of ancient states, or to modern problems of political enculturation. We may look

forward to increasing interaction between scholars specializing
in the realm of politics and those who take wider behavioral or
cultural frames as their systems of reference.

BIBLIOGRAPHICAL NOTE

A good beginning overview of the evolution of law and political systems is available in a strongly partisan work by a lawyer,
William Seagle (1941). A somewhat broader view, of considerable interest because it incorporates a large number of selections from the works of some of the most important students of
the problem in the late nineteenth and early twentieth centuries, is in Simpson and Stone (1948: esp. pp. 1-312).

On the evolution of the state, Friedrich Engels' *Origin of the
Family, Private Property and the State* (1902) is still worthy of
attention. It is especially rewarding in conjunction with Lewis
Henry Morgan's *Ancient Society* (1878), Sir Henry Maine's
Ancient Law (1917), and Robert Lowie's *Origin of the State*
(1927). Also interesting is Franz Oppenheimer's *The State*
(1914).

For more recent political science approaches see Lasswell and
Kaplan (1950), Easton (1953), and a very interesting survey
of the newer approaches in Eulau (1963). More conventional anthropological approaches may be found in Hoebel (1954),
Schapera (1956), the now classic *African Political Systems* edited
by Fortes and Evans-Pritchard (1940), and the recent paperback by Mair (1962).

My own views are being prepared for book-length presentation (Fried, in press). A summary statement is available in my
article (Fried 1960).

16.

ANTHROPOLOGY AND THE LAW

Paul J. Bohannan

THE GOLA PEOPLE, OF the hinterland of Liberia, have a proverb that "the law is like a chameleon—it changes form in each place and can be controlled only by those who know its ways." That proverb can be matched with an aphorism by one of the foremost twentieth-century Western jurists, who tells us that the law has no subject matter of its own, but is as broad as life itself.

If the law is as changing as a chameleon, and as broad as life itself, its entirety is obviously beyond the competence of any one man, or even of any one profession. There must be many specialists to study it, understand it, and apply it. These specialists fall into two broad groups; there are those who are concerned with the law in its relation to behavior, and there are those who are concerned with the law in its intellectual and philosophical aspects. The first are the lawyers, judges, policemen, and legislators. The second sort of people are the students of jurisprudence, of the history and art of government, and those anthropologists who have concentrated on the ways in which different peoples throughout the world settle their disputes, and maintain at least a modicum of political order.

Lawyers are the specialists who are brought into situations in which people dispute about their rights or even about the correct path of conduct. Lawyers and judges settle cases of trouble in accordance with the written or customary law, and with the deeper basic values to which the society subscribes. These are men who, with many others, provide a means for minimizing the upset which trouble and disputes cause. They are also

191

the people who are the guardians of the most basic and valued moral and ethical precepts of the culture. And like all specialists who deal in morally charged matters, they are sometimes considered suspect.

Jurisprudence, in its way, and legal anthropology, in its way —and the two ways are quite different—deal with the same subject matter as do lawyers and judges. But they do not aim at practical ends, with programs of behavior for maintaining the society or ordering its change and growth. They want rather to understand the ways in which a society's law works to uphold its basic values, and also to change them. They might be called the moral preceptors of the judges and legislators, just as the judges are the preceptors of the people. Jurists also want to compare the basic values from one society with those of the next, and to understand and analyze the institutions by means of which different societies provide for their citizens a set of norms within which it is possible both to find rewards and to predict the behavior of others seeking their rewards.

Therefore, the student of legal anthropology has to take into consideration two initial matters. He must discover first of all what a people say that they should do. He has at the same time to discover what it is that they actually do. In the process, he will find that some people in the world are very strict about making individuals live up to the social ideals. Others are lax. Some people have high standards and high demands; others with the same standards do not make nearly the same demands.

Jurists and anthropologists, thus, are interested not so much in whether in a specific case a person broke the law. That is to be determined by the lawyers and the judges. The jurist and the legal anthropologist rather are concerned with the ways that the law maintains the institutions of society, in the way in which breaches of law are defined in relation to the rest of the ideals of the culture—ideals so deep that they often, in fact usually, cannot be stated in words by the people who hold them.

Thus we can see that it is the lawyer's law to which the Gola proverb refers. Lawyer's law does indeed change color and quality from one culture to the next. It is a real chameleon. It is on the other hand to the jurist's and the anthropologist's

law, that the statement about the breadth of the law refers, for
although any single system of law may have only a fraction of
the ethical, moral and other required behavior encapsulated
within it, it can draw from the entire range of the culture.

Thus, the jurist and the anthropologist approach the chameleon of law not in terms of its color, or of its capacity for blending into the background and ultimately to camouflage itself
into the totality of its surroundings. Rather, jurists must study
the structure of the chameleon: its skeleton, its circulatory system, and the very device which allows it to change color, and
to seek camouflage among its surrounding moralities.

However, jurists have not always been successful in studying
the legal systems of peoples other than those in the direct line
of legal tradition of the West. Jurists of the Western world
are experts in the common law and in the Roman law, and in
the present-day manifestations of those legal systems. They
know and deal in the *Code Civile* of France, the Roman-Dutch
tradition in South Africa, and in the Common Law of Britain
and the American and Australian versions of it.

Yet, too often these very jurists have taken the categories and
ideas found in Roman law and in the Common Law to be
universals. They have tended to overlook the fact that the subject matter and even the legal processes involved in these
laws were tightly associated with the cultures of which they
were a part. There has been, therefore, some tendency to
create false analyses of African, Oceanian and American Indian
law by the mere device of raising the legal peculiarities of the
West to the place of a universal analytical device.

In order to avoid this kind of trap, which anthropologists
call ethnocentrism, it is well to look at the legal situation
stripped of any particular cultural context. Instead merely of
defining law, which is a sticky business at best, as a glance into
any good English dictionary will show, it becomes advisable to
examine the kind of social acts by means of which individuals
or groups within a society make the members live up to agreed
expectations.

For a legal situation to exist, there must be a social act which
people regard as a wrong way to behave, so wrong that
unless something is done the most valued institutions of the

society may be undermined. Laws obviously are not social acts. They are precepts in terms of which people are supposed to act. Now there are many kinds of precepts which govern behavior. The social scientist can afford to beg the question of whether a precept is a "law" or some other sort of demand. Indeed, he cannot afford not to beg it. He begins rather by examining the acts which follow upon a breach of the standard of behavior which the society has set for itself, whatever that may be. Following the commission of an act which is in violation of the recognized standards of conduct, there may or may not be a reaction on the part of society, or some institution of it. As we have seen, every culture allows its people a certain range of deviation from its own standards—that is, the law does not expect that all of us always live up to all of the ideal norms. However, once we overstep the accepted permissible range of deviation, if the standard is indeed a law, some sort of social mechanism will swing into action so that the breach of standards can be corrected. In modern nation-states, this counteraction takes the form of specialist lawyers, of complex police systems, and of courts. Either the police of their own volition or on the recognized demand of a citizen, or a private citizen himself, bring wrong doers before the courts.

Counteractions against crimes are much easier to illustrate than are counteractions against breach of contract or agreement. Contract law not only came late in our own society, it is still more precarious than is the criminal law. We shall, here, for the sake of clarity, deal primarily but not entirely with what we would call the criminal law.

There are, besides courts, many kinds of counteracting institutions. One of the most common—it is found in all societies—is "self-help." Within certain defined limits, a wronged person every place has permission from general society to bring about the correction of the situation by which he was wronged. Modern peoples in all legal systems are expected to help themselves against burglars, for example. There are, however, certain lengths beyond which they must not go in applying self-help. These boundaries can be writ very much more precise in the presence of a police system than they can in the absence of such a system. Many societies of the world, for example, not merely allow but demand that a man who has suffered robbery must go out, if there is to be any retribution, and steal back, so to speak, his own property. If a dispute or fight ensues, he will have moral right on his side, and therefore the backing of his community. Such institutions of self-help are commonly found throughout the world.

Another widespread type of social counteraction to breach of law is the "game" solution, found in very widespread areas. Indeed, modern courts have been compared to games in which we take the whole of life, and reduce the range of rules to a controllable span. Disputes which cannot be settled in the wide arena of life can be examined in the narrower arena of the courts, and settlements made which can then be sent back to the wider stage. More to the point, however, are the gladiatorial contests and ordeals which were and are commonly used to solve disputes.

Still another form of counteraction is the town meeting. In many parts of the world a whole community meets to discuss the problems of some of its members and ultimately to provide the solution for them. The town meeting sort of arrangement is very different from a court. The court is a specialist body appointed in a stable political system—a specialist body which has the task of settling disputes. The town meeting is not a specialist body; it is a gathering of all the citizens of the community.

When a counteraction of one of these sorts occurs, we can be sure that a law of the society has been broken. The counteraction, as we have called it, and under which we have classified courts and police systems, gladiatorial contests and ordeals, town meetings, and self-help, is the way that we can begin to define a situation as legal. Like the original breach of norm, the counteraction is a series of social acts. The social acts can be observed, and they can be discussed at length with the people who participate in them.

If the counteraction is successful, it is followed by another series of acts that we can call the correction. This English word "correction" has a neat ambiguity in it, which it is wise for us to utilize. There are really two ways in which a deviant act can be corrected. First of all, the person who committed the original wrong may be required subsequently to carry out the action in terms of the norm which he violated. Thereupon, the community can pretend that no breach of the standard ever occurred at all. The other way in which correction can come about implies some sort of penalty. It is this use of the word correction which we underline when we speak of a prison as a house of correction. Thus the word correction within itself means both that restitution is made or, if that is impossible, that some sort of retribution must be made.

It is these three social acts, one following upon another, that creates the legal behavior in any society: first, the breach of standard, next, the counteraction, and finally, the correction. Lawyers, jurists and anthropologists all study this same series of acts, but they do so for different purposes, and in somewhat different ways.

Legal anthropologists take the standards as well as the acts which are violations of them, as their data. They then investigate the ethical axioms that lie behind the standards, at the same time that they focus on the institutions of counteraction rather than upon the law, or standard, itself.

Here we will take a series of disputes from several societies to show different ways in which the institutions of counteraction work to apply the law and maintain the moralities that underlie the law. One of the most famous cases in anthropological jurisprudence is the case of Qijuk, an Eskimo who, after his wife died, stole the wife of a neighbor in another community. Being without a wife in Eskimo society is an extremely serious situation because getting a living is so demanding that there *must* be two persons, a man and a woman, to divide the labor in order to do it at all. Qijuk, accompanied by two of his brothers, stole the woman while her husband was out hunting. Qijuk had obviously broken the law, and it is obvious not just because the Eskimo say that a husband has certain rights in his wife, but more specifically because of the fact that certain recognized customs of counteraction came immediately into play. This one was simple. The wronged husband, with the help of friends from his own community, in this case, killed Qijuk; they also killed one of Qijuk's brothers, although the other brother escaped.

Now in this particular case, the matter ended there. Qijuk had broken the law, and he got his comeuppance. The counter-action was self-help, carried out with the consent of the community. For had Qijuk not been in the wrong when he was killed, the Eskimo society would ultimately have formed a re-solve, probably taken informally and over a period of time, to execute his killer. The ritual head of the community would have gone to the killer's closest kinsmen and charged them on behalf of the community with carrying out the execution. Ultimately, it would have been up to the brothers of the killer to perform the execution in the name of the community. They may, or may not have done it, but there are several instances in the records of Eskimo cases in which kinsmen have carried out such a charge—in one case, it was even carried out by the mother. Obviously, the reason that it is the next-of-kin who must carry out the execution is that only so can it be assured that feuds will be avoided.

There is another kind of concerted counteraction that an Eskimo community can take. Either the principals to a dispute or the community itself can decide that the dispute must be settled in terms of a song or "buffeting" contest. Sometimes, they even combine the two, and the two disputants sing insults at one another, at the same time that they bump foreheads till one cries a halt.

At the other end of the world, in central Nigeria, I have myself seen singing contests used as a legal device. In this instance, which happened among the Tiv people of central Nigeria, a dispute arose between Torgindi and Mtswen. Mtswen's ward had been married to a son of Torgindi. When the marriage proved to be unsuccessful, there was some difficulty about the return of the bride-wealth that had been paid. The two men were neighbors, and rather than disgrace himself by calling a close neighbor before the courts, Torgindi hired a song-maker and brewed a great supply of beer. When the beer was ready, and the song-maker had had time to perform his task, Torgindi threw a big party. The song-maker taught his songs to all of the guests. They were scurrilous attacks on the behavior of Mtswen. They were sung loud, long, and lustily into the night. Everyone in the countryside for as much as a mile or so about could hear, and Mtswen was among the listeners. Mtswen did the only thing that an honorable man could do under the circumstances. He too hired a song-writer and began to brew beer and to give parties in direct competition with Torgindi. This situation continued for about three weeks. Thereupon, the most influential elder of the community invited, indeed demanded, that Torgindi and Mtswen come, each with his song-writer and his guests and partisans, and submit both the songs and the original dispute about the bride-wealth to decision by the elders. It is interesting that the elders of the community decided the dispute about bride-wealth in favor of Torgindi, but agreed that Mtswen had the most entertaining and best songs.

Africa is however one of the homes of advanced legal institutions. Perhaps the most famous of these institutions is the court found among the Bantu in the southern third of the African continent. Here the head of the community, be he chief or king, was one of a number of judges on a large and inclusive bench. The bench included men who represented all of the important pressure groups and segments of the community. There was a pronounced and well-known hierarchy. The headman sat in the middle, and at his immediate right was the second most senior person. To his left, the third most senior, and so on, right and left, until the whole court was deployed more or less in an arc. Then, after the principal disputants had each told his side of the dispute, and after witnesses had been heard, the most junior member of the bench, down at the far end, pronounced a decision. His decision probably included a moral lecture, statements about the proper kind of behavior that should have been carried out in the situation, and he may have cited precedent. His judgment was then followed by that of the man at the other end of the line, the next junior, who might disagree, and who added new views and new opinions. The third most junior man followed, and so on until they arrived at the middle where the headman pronounced the final decision and sentence. He had heard everything that the representatives of the community had to say. He had a chance to weigh the evidence, the judgments, and the opinions of his junior judges. His word on the decision became law.

The law is indeed a chameleon. It changes to fit in with its surroundings, but like the chameleon there is underneath it all a recognizable animal. Its very changeability is one of its most important and strengthening capacities. The law, whatever it may be in any particular society, is, for the student of anthropological jurisprudence, always to be studied by first discovering the way people handle disputes and cases of trouble; that is, the ways in which they organize the institutions of the society to cope with deviations which, if they were allowed to go unchecked, would destroy the very fabric of the society. At the same time, the law must look out in the other direction to avoid any opportunity for tyranny. In this sense, every community we have ever discovered has a pronounced system of legal institutions. There are always institutionalized counteractions to repeated breaches of standards of behavior. Ultimately they swing behavior back into recognized and accepted channels so that social life can persevere. Law is society's way of healing and maintaining itself.

BIBLIOGRAPHICAL NOTE

The literature in legal anthropology is small and almost all good—neither claim can be made for very many other branches of the subject. Background classics are Henry Maine's *Ancient Law* (1917); Paul Vinogradoff's *Commonsense in Law* (1959); and Roscoe Pound's *An Introduction to the Philosophy of Law* (1954). For comparative purposes, I find the following particularly helpful: Joseph Schacht, *The Origins of Muhammadan Jurisprudence* (1950); Anthony Allott, *Essays in African Law* (1960); Hubert S. Box, *The Principles of Canon Law* (1949).

Of anthropological writings, the best general book is E. A. Hoebel, *The Law of Primitive Man* (1954). Bronislaw Malinowski's *Crime and Custom in Savage Society* (1932—a short book about the Trobriand Islands) has been influential among both anthropologists and lawyers, not always for the better. Some noteworthy ethnographic reports are Max Gluckman, *The Judicial Process among the Barotse* (1955—Nothern Rhodesia); Paul Bohannan, *Justice and Judgment among the Tiv* (1957—Nigeria); R. F. Barton, *Ifugao Law* (1919—Philippines); Leonard Pospisil, *Kapauka Papuans and their Law* (1958—New Guinea); Karl Llewellyn and E. A. Hoebel, *The Cheyenne Way* (1941—North America).

17.

EVOLUTION AND THE ILLS OF MANKIND

Steven Polgar 4/26/86 aloud

MAN DID NOT EVOLVE alone. He evolved in the company of a goodly number of microorganisms. We should remember that many of these small creatures are necessary and beneficial to man in many ways: they help to digest the food in his intestines, to leaven his bread, to dispose of his wastes, to ferment his cheese—not to mention their help in brewing his beer. But our present concern will be with the diseases they cause.

Before turning to my main topic, I should perhaps explain how a social anthropologist can become interested in the evolution of human disease. Most social scientists in our great universities keep themselves busy, like other scientists, in trying to put facts together into meaningful combinations. Their habits of scholarly detachment are often carried over into aloofness to the miseries and dangers engulfing the peoples of the world. Our professional standards, too, reward those who remain in their ivory towers, contributing to the pages of periodicals and training successors to themselves.

Anthropologists have been noted, nevertheless, for the sympathetic way in which they regard the people from whom they collect their data. They have, on occasion, spoken out against injustice and stupidity. Some have written reports relevant to a question vexing an administrator, regarding their task completed when they handed over a piece of paper. It is but in the last decade or two that a few anthropologists have recognized that seeking a solution to the difficulties experienced by the groups we study—and the frustrations of those who wanted

200

to help these people—could simultaneously add to the body of
scientific knowledge (Gearing, Netting and Peattie 1060).

One of the groups of practitioners who have become frustrated
in their attempts to help are medical workers, particularly in
public health. They have encountered two kinds of difficulties in
which the collaboration of anthropologists can be important:
first, understanding the causes of certain diseases; and second,
persuading people to do what they—the medical people—
think will prevent or ameliorate disease. Let us look at the
latter question first. Anthropologists and other social scientists, it
was hoped, could provide some of the answers as to why people
are reluctant to take pills brought by doctors to rid them
of worms, why they are slow to build latrines and prefer
using the fields for defecation, and—to quote an example about
supposedly advanced people living in cities in the United States
—why they will not vote in favor of adding fluorides to their
water supply in order to cut down on tooth decay. We do not
have ready answers for the hygiene workers about how they
can change people in a short time to be more coöperative, but
we have made progress in identifying some of the relevant
variables (Foster 1962; Polgar 1963). Sometimes it is even
important to point out to our medical colleagues that not all of
their recommendations have a strict scientific basis, but may
well include some preferences based on their own way of life.
Thus, in order to understand the factors influencing the success
of a public health program, the social scientist has to study
not only the culture of the people receiving attention, but also
the culture of the professional workers who would provide the
help. These kinds of studies make up a large part of applied
social science in health, but I will not deal with them any further
on this occasion.

The other problem I mentioned, where cross-disciplinary collaboration is useful, relates to the causes of disease and its
distribution. In this field the great bulk of the joint work done
until now relates to diseases of the nervous system. There is increasing interest, however, in looking at the social, cultural and
psychological factors involved in such disturbances as heart disease, traffic accidents, or even the common cold. When an anthropologist, reared in the tradition of anthropology which unites the

study of social man and physical man, comes to learn about the complex ecological relationships involved in human diseases, it is logical that he should begin asking questions about the changes that might have occurred during human evolution. It is by working on the answers to questions such as this that the applied anthropologist, too, brings back to his own discipline the fruits of his collaboration with medical workers.

So, let us move on to the main topic of our discussion. There are essentially two ways in which we can make guesses about the antiquity of human diseases: by examining the prehistoric and historic record and by looking at the present-day ecology of a disease among other species of animals and among different human populations.

Written history only takes us back about five thousand years and then only in a few places; in other parts of the world this type of evidence is not available until the most recent centuries or even decades. For everything before that time the record is limited to whatever we can dig out of the ground. Paleopathologists rely mainly on the examination of bones to see if any malformations are present. From such investigations, they have concluded that diseases like arthritis, spondylitis, dental caries, and pyorrhea predate even the appearance of primates (Ackerknecht 1953). Other archeological evidence from sculptures or paintings can occasionally be useful too.

The second type of evidence is entirely inferential. We do not know what the ancestors of our present parasites were like, most of them being too soft and too small to get into the fossil record. But some human parasites are known to infect many kinds of animals; others may be quite uniquely adapted to man. The bacterium of tularemia for example is known to infect insects, birds, rodents and mammals. Man is quite susceptible, and the disease is fatal in about 5 per cent of the cases (Maxcy 1956:413). Several species of birds and rodents, as well as a number of domestic animals are only slightly susceptible to tularemia, while other species of a similarly wide range of animals that carry the infection without severe disease; this makes it likely that humans have been affected a long time also. The inference that a disease is old when different species or populations show great variation in resistance is based on studies

showing that successive epidemics of a disease in a single population cause less and less mortality or inconvenience (Burnet 1953).
Although new disease strains can arise through mutations which
once again produce a more serious form of the disease, it is
to the parasite's advantage in the long run to kill as few of its
hosts as possible—to do otherwise would be to "bite the hand
that feeds you" as the saying goes (Zinsser 1960).

I will now turn to the discussion of the ills that beset mankind throughout its evolutionary history. I will divide this history
into five stages: hunting and gathering; settled villages and food
production; preindustrial cities; industrial cities; and the present. It is important to note that once cities came into existence,
for example, all peoples exposed to their influence entered a new
era. Today, the influence of the metropolitan city extends into
every part of the world, and even the Australian aborigine
who still obtains his food through hunting and gathering is
part of the present era and can both receive the benefits and be
exposed to many of the ills that characterize our period. It would
be erroneous therefore to argue that all the diseases that plague
him today were the same diseases that afflicted mankind before
the invention of agriculture. Studying the patterns of illness
among present-day populations, however, makes it possible to
make inferences about diseases of the past which could have
flourished under similar cultural and environmental conditions.

Studies on contemporary monkeys and apes (Washburn and
DeVore 1961b), as well as evidence from other organisms,
make it seem likely that predatory animals were important only
in killing off individuals who became separated from their social
group. Periodic hunger might well have been a problem to early
man after he spread into the temperate zone and came to rely
upon the hunting of larger game whose availability fluctuated
seasonally (Schultz 1961). Evidence of pyorrhea, the disease of
the gums, is reported in Neanderthals (Ackerknecht 1953), but
since we still do not know much about its causation today,
we cannot assess the significance of this finding. Accidents have
surely played an important part in man's early history; and
somewhere along the way he invented murder and war as well
—phenomena unparalleled within other species (Bates 1959).

The most important points with respect to infectious diseases in the hunting-and-gathering stage are the size of the social group and the intensity of contact between groups. Several biologists have already made the point that in preagricultural times no epidemic-inducing parasites could have maintained themselves with man as their exclusive host (Bates 1955; Haldane 1956; Livingstone 1958; Cockburn 1959). There would just not be a large enough number of new susceptible people available for the parasite to infect once the disease ran its course within a small band.

The parasites that did affect early man were of two types: those which were already adapted to the prehominids and those which were only accidentally transmitted to man, with other species acting as the main hosts. The first group of long-standing parasites might include the head and body louse *Pediculus humanus*, pinworm, yaws and malaria (Cameron 1958; Schultz 1961). This kind of louse and the pinworm are found only among primates. Yaws, a tropical skin disease which is being rapidly reduced at present, has also been found among apes. Many animals have parasites resembling those causing human malaria, but they become increasingly similar to the human types as we go from non primates to monkeys and to apes— indicating that this disease may well have evolved along with the primates, becoming differentiated as their hosts broke up into separate species (Cockburn 1959). Diseases which are accidentally transmitted to man today through insect bites, wounds, or the consumption of the meat of infected animals, such as scrub typhus, sleeping sickness, tick-borne relapsing fever, tetanus, tularemia, leptospirosis, liver fluke and trichinosis could well have infected early hunters and gatherers also.

The second major stage of human evolution began during the terminal phase of the last glaciation; men began settling down into more permanent encampments and eventually came to rely largely on domesticated plants and animals for their food. One of the immediate problems of a more settled existence involved the disposal of human excreta and other garbage. While dogs can perform some sanitary tasks and the cultural habits of personal modesty can demand that stools be deposited at some distance from habitation, neither of these are sufficient to prevent the proliferation of diseases which follow the route from the

bowel to the mouth. Pigs, sheep, cattle, fowl and other domestic
animals are, significantly enough, carriers of many of the
human types of salmonella—the group of bacteria which includes
the agent of typhoid fever—as well as of ascaris worms. They
also harbor related species of hookworms and many other
parasites spread through fecal matter which occasionally infect
man. The shigellae, causing bacillary dysentery, are more
closely associated with man although several domestic and wild
animals are also susceptible.

Nomadic or seminomadic hunters and gatherers changed the
environment very little. When man settled down into permanent villages he began to alter the landscape around him in many
important ways. These alterations created opportunities for some
animals and plants to establish new niches for themselves closely
associated with human habitations (Bates 1956). Certain species
of insects and rodents domiciled this way have an important role
in the transmission of many diseases. A type of mosquito, breeding in small bodies of water collected in man-made receptacles,
is mainly responsible for the transmission of the viruses of
yellow fever and dengue. The clearings created in the West
African tropical forest by the introduction of agriculture were
probably a causal factor in making malaria an endemic disease
thereby allowing the proliferation of another kind of mosquito
which does not breed in the dark shade of tall trees (Livingstone
1958). Murine typhus is mostly a disease of wild rodents, but
domestic rats can become infected and man can get the disease
if bitten by the rat flea. Deforestation by man also leads to the
establishment of new breeding places for field rodents and their
mites which are implicated in many parts of Asia in the transmission of scrub typhus—when farmers begin to cultivate land
once allowed to run to waste, they become exposed to the bites
of these insects and thus catch the disease (Audy 1961). The
housefly is often involved in the spread of diseases associated
with fecal matter. The milk of domestic animals as well as
their skin, hair, tissues, or even the dust in the places where
they are kept are also vehicles for passing on to man a number
of diseases like anthrax, Q fever, brucellosis and tuberculosis.

On the whole, the domestication of animals and plants provides a more secure supply of food than hunting and gathering.

The larger units of population this makes possible are also at greater risk of famine if the harvest is poor or the flocks become decimated. No sudden changes in the composition of the diet took place either from the prehuman to the hunting-and-gathering stage or from the latter to early agriculture (Schultz 1961), but after the gradual shift to a diet higher in cereals there is some evidence that rickets became more frequent in certain places like Scandinavia (Ackerknecht 1953). This was probably due to changes in climate and clothing as well as diet (Newman 1962). Much of the mortality among infants and children in contemporary villages is caused by a combination of a poor diet with intestinal parasites and malaria. It is quite likely that this pattern is old, but we will see that certain conditions introduced later might have aggravated the dietary situation. Chronic deficiencies in certain nutrients can also result from the more settled way of life—thus, if a population happens to live in an area where there is insufficient iodine available, endemic goiter can develop. We have an interesting bit of evidence about Pre-Columbian goiter in Guatemala from the examination of pottery figurines among which there were two pieces clearly showing enlargement in the thyroid area of the neck (Borhegyi and Scrimshaw 1957).

The next stage of evolution, that of preindustrial cities, is the first one for which some written historical evidence is available to supplement archeology and conjectural reconstruction. While many hunting-and-gathering groups, pastoralists and settled agricultural villagers remained separate from the cities and their civilized way of life, others were increasingly influenced by this new type of culture. Toward the end of this period, stretching from the time of the earliest Sumerian cities to the industrial revolution in Europe, all the continents of the world were brought into direct contact with one another. This stage in human history was without doubt the one which saw the greatest suffering from widespread epidemics of infectious disease.

The concentration of large numbers of people into a relatively small area had two important consequences from the point of view of disease. The first of these was a problem of supply: large quantities of food and water had to be distributed and waste materials taken away. The second consequence was that

a critical ratio was arrived at in the frequency of contact between
a large enough number of people, which allowed for the development of diseases spread directly from person to person.
Supplying an urban center with clean water and carrying away
the sewage without these two streams ever becoming mixed
presents major problems even in the wealthiest countries today.
In the era of preindustrial cities the two bodies of water often
did mix and such diseases as cholera could result. In the agricultural village, if food was contaminated, it was by parasites
of the villagers themselves for which the adults had often acquired a tolerance. In the city, food brought in from far away
might have pathogens on it that were new to the city dweller
and consequently more dangerous. A serious shortage in the
amount of food brought in often led to famines of great severity,
famines which were usually followed by epidemics of infectious
disease (Cook 1946). It is possible to relate the prevalence of
disease to the organizational effectiveness of political systems:
Angel (1954 and 1957) estimated the rise and decline of the
mean age at death for adults in Greece from hundreds of
skeletons dated from 3500 B.C. to 1750 A.D. and obtained good
correspondence to the levels of material civilization; Celli
showed that variations in the prevalence of malaria in the Roman
Campagna of Italy also correlated with the ups and downs of
prosperity—he went a little too far, perhaps, in attributing to
the disease a causal power on history (Rosen 1957).

The second group of diseases which became important during
this time, those spread by direct person-to-person contact, contains a number of viruses. Measles, mumps and chickenpox
are mild diseases today, but were more lethal in previous times
(Dubos 1961). Smallpox, on the other hand, remains a disease
much to be feared. In addition to these viruses which cannot
usually live outside of human cells, some other parasites became
adapted also to spread by close contact between people. The
plague bacillus can be passed from lung to lung, although
between human epidemics it is maintained among rodents and
their fleas. Typhus fever epidemics are transmitted by lice crawl-
ing from one person to another under conditions of extreme
crowding. The venereal diseases probably became important during this period also; syphilis was first recorded in Europe during

the sixteenth century, first causing serious epidemics and then
changing into a stubborn endemic disease. Gonorrhea is much
older, being mentioned in the Bible, but we have no reason to
believe that it was important in the settled village stage.

The period of the preindustrial city is also the time when
warfare assumed major proportions. The conditions engendered
by these intercity, interstate and imperial wars had much to
do with the spread of the diseases I have been describing.
Medical historians have also written about the ways in which
epidemics have decided battles, and in this connection I would
heartily recommend a scholarly and witty book by Hans Zinsser
called *Rats, Lice and History* (1960) which contains a chapter
entitled "On the influence of epidemic diseases on political and
military history, and on the relative unimportance of generals."
Yet another type of epidemic disease arose during this time,
namely the dancing manias and similar cults of religious or
secular fanaticism. Sometimes, as in the so-called holy wars, these
epidemics of mental illness are translated into wholesale mas-
sacres. In other instances they manifest themselves in the tor-
ture of witches or similar representatives of illusory danger
(Rosen 1960).

The transition from preindustrial to industrial city cultures was
marked by the intensification of many factors already in existence. We have a fairly good chronology, for example, on the
epidemics of the various "fevers" which swept through Europe
in the late eighteenth- and nineteenth centuries. These included
typhus, typhoid fever, smallpox, diphtheria, measles, malaria,
yellow fever and others already familiar from the previous era
(Rosen 1958). Occupational diseases of miners and tanners had
also been described prior to this period, but they do not become
numerically important until the advent of full industrialization.
With the crowding of many more people into the city slum, the
long hours of work and the utilization of many new materials,
tuberculosis became the most characteristic disease of this
period. The rise in other diseases of the respiratory tract like
pneumonia, bronchitis, streptococcal sore throat and the non-
infectious toxic irritations of the lung is caused by the same
conditions.

Infant and child mortality had always been high, but child

labor and malnutrition put a new strain on young people.
Parental and juvenile delinquency, alcoholism and organized
crime became prevalent too; these conditions, together with
tuberculosis and veneral disease, came to be called the "social
diseases" as if all the other ills of mankind did not also have
their roots in the type of society where they prevail.

Despite the sustained high infant mortality rate, the nineteenth
century also saw the beginnings of the population explosion. The
industrialization of some countries changed world trade from
one where mainly luxuries were transported to the exchange
of manufactured goods for raw materials and staple foods. This
also meant that the industrialized countries sought to assure for
themselves trade areas in the rest of the world over which they
had firm control. The political ills of colonialism were also
accompanied by the conversion of many new areas to a money
economy including a change from subsistence crops to crops
for sale—which often resulted in detrimental changes in the
diet (Mead 1955:194). Colonialism also brought about the
transmission of the epidemic diseases of urban societies to prac
tically every remaining agricultural and hunting-gathering group
in the world. Measles, smallpox, and tuberculosis in particular,
were responsible for the extinction of many cultures in the
Americas and the Pacific and for the decimation of many more
(Roberts 1927; Stearn and Stearn 1945; Cook 1946). The struggle for colonies brought with it also a new type of war, one
which now embraced practically the whole world. Armies were
no longer made up of nobles, volunteers, or mercenaries, but
were conscripted from the general population.

I have pointed out how the arrival of rodents and insects as
permanent guests had been an unintended by-product of settled
village life, how in the preindustrial city the coming together of
people in sufficient numbers allows certain microorganisms to become entirely dependent on man, and how colonialism was accompanied by the export of these same diseases to all corners of the
globe. It is the ills of our present era, however, which are the most
glaring examples of unplanned disaster following the deliberate
actions of man. We are keeping tuberculosis in check fairly well,
but we are probably ruining our lungs with smog instead,
produced by factories and millions of cars! These same cars

are now responsible for thousands of accidental deaths every year! We use antibiotics in our hospitals at such a high rate that we have epidemics of resistant staphylococcal disease! We buy so many vitamin pills that some of our children develop hypercalcemia! We eat a diet so abundant in calories and saturated fatty acids that we expose ourselves to heart disease! We can keep people alive who suffer from genetically based diseases like phenylketonuria, but we add to our load of harmful mutations by the overuse of x-ray equipment and by the atmospheric testing of atomic bombs! We fight wars to end all war only to arm again with weapons that could exterminate mankind in an hour! And perhaps most cruel irony of all: in exporting public health without exporting adequate means for family limitation to countries with high fertility rates we slow down their ability for economic development by widening the excess of births over deaths!

But our present development of science and technology is advanced enough to prevent and remedy these ills to some extent. To the degree that we become aware of what the consequences of our actions will be, we can also take steps to alter these consequences (Polgar 1961). It is important to realize, however, that we are not the only living inhabitants of this planet and that we could not survive without the presence of other animals and plants. And this includes microbes and insects, fungi and rodents too. René Dubos has argued in his book *Mirage of Health* (1961) that the hope for a disease-free future is not very realistic. Nevertheless, the ability of scientific medicine to forestall and alleviate conventional diseases is phenomenal. When it comes to the anthropogenic diseases of our present era, biological knowledge alone is insufficient. Social scientists know far less about societies and people than human biologists know about tissues and cells. Unlike the controlled situation in the medical laboratory when sociocultural experiments are performed, it is the subjects of the experiment who decide what to do—while the anthropologist tries to discern and write down what happens. In action anthropology we go beyond this and tell the people what we have found out, what we think it means, and to the extent of our ability try to help in carrying out mutually agreed upon solutions to difficulties.

I hope that this discussion has contributed toward the recognition of our responsibility in facing the ills that plague mankind today.

BIBLIOGRAPHICAL NOTE

The main considerations in bringing anthropology to bear on practical problems are set out in *Some Uses of Anthropology: Theoretical and Applied* (Anthropological Society of Washington 1956) and in Tumin et al. (1958). Applications in the field of health have been recently surveyed in Polgar (1962) and Straus and Clausen (1963).

No single source is available for a more extensive treatment of changes in disease accompanying human evolution. The books by Burnet (1953), Dubos (1961) and Zinsser (1960), referred to in this article, are nontechnical but authoritative descriptions of communicable diseases in relation to man. The article by Bates (1956) and, in fact, much of the symposium on "Man's Role in Changing the Face of the Earth" (Thomas 1956) wherein it appears, bear on the questions of human ecology, of which disease is only a limited aspect. Rosen's book (1958) can be profitably consulted for additional data on the industrial period, while E. H. Sigerist (1961) is an excellent source on pre-industrial city societies in the West. Present patterns of disease and what is done about it are admirably summarized in F. Brockington (1958).

18.

THE STUDY OF RELIGION

Edward Norbeck

MAN'S EXAMINATION OF his own behavior in a systematic and objective way is one of the newest facets of science, which has turned its eyes to a growing number of phenomena as fruitful subjects for investigation. Religion is among the latest additions to the roster and the progress of its investigation has been less rapid than that in other fields. The basic philosophy of Western religions had not been seriously challenged until about a century ago. To be sure, conflicting religious interpretations had long existed, but all were variants of a common underlying theme, a common interpretation of the universe that met with general acceptance. Western religions were regarded as divinely revealed, a circumstance that did not provide the groundwork for even formulating the questions related to religion that concern modern scholars.

As scientific interpretations of the nature and genesis of man and natural phenomena were advanced during the past several centuries, skepticism was inevitably directed toward conventional theological counterparts. The reaction is well known to us, but it is doubtful that the warfare between science and theology that we know in the history of the Western world is an inevitable concomitant of the growth of science. The emotional defense of dogma when it seemed to be threatened by science is doubtless in part a reflection of the history of Christianity itself. Arising among people seeing troubled times, Christianity emerged in an atmosphere of opposition from adherents to fundamentally similar faiths. Its later history saw much struggle with competitors from within its own ranks. The threat seemingly imposed by science, although different in nature from previous challenges, was thus not an entirely new experience.

In view of this history of struggle, the strength and emotional depth of Christian opposition to scientific interpretations are not surprising. Similarly, it is not surprising that the scientific study of religion has had relatively little development. Yet many of the basic data required for the objective, comparative study of the religions of the world are available to us, placed on record by early travelers, missionaries, and, during the past century, by scholars in the social sciences. The modest beginnings of a comparative study of religion were made long ago, and recent years have seen a resurgence of scholarly interest in the subject. Old problems for investigation have been recast, and new problems have been formulated. We may note that publication of the first scholarly journal devoted solely to the scientific study of religion began in 1961 in the United States.

One of the newer problems that should be stated in the outset concerns the definition of religion itself. Until recent years, the prevailing scholarly conception of religion centered on supernaturalism as against the naturalism of scientific or mundane conceptions. Religion was seen as ideas and behavior associated with beliefs in forces and entities—unexplainable in conventional, naturalistic terms—which control the universe and the affairs of man. A new conception of religion held by a growing number of scholars and members of the general citizenry sees it as ideals or values, often ethical in nature, that are highly cherished and surrounded by intense emotional feelings. We may note that this conception of religion omits supernaturalism. Thus it imputes religion to all men whether or not they regard themselves as members of a church or followers of any recognized religious faith. This definition reflects modern times, and it is a subject to which we shall return. Our discussion here will center principally upon supernaturalistic beliefs and acts as the principal identifying feature of religion.

From its beginning, the scientific study of religion has attempted to account for similarities and differences in religious ideas and acts. Following the expansion of Europeans into Asia and the Americas, information that became available on exotic religions provided many examples of apparent diversity. But examination also revealed that much was held in common in the religious as well as other spheres of life. Objective observation soon led to the conclusion that all living races and peoples are sufficiently similar in biologically inherited traits so that recourse to racial differences cannot explain cultural differences. Similarities in man's religions are, of course, in part reflections of the essential uniformity of human nature. However, understanding of variations in religion was seen to depend chiefly upon consideration of factors external to the human organism; that is, upon similar and different circumstances of man's life that influence his religious beliefs and practices. Although scholarly conceptions of problems of religion worthy of investigation have changed greatly in the past century, these fundamental ideas have remained.

Scholars of religion of the nineteenth century were strongly concerned with questions of the origin and evolution of religion. Viewing religion as a form of interpretation of and adjustment to the universe, they tried to imagine circumstances that might have led to the noteworthy similarities in religion among all known societies. None was seen to lack supernaturalistic ideas and acts. None lacked beliefs in souls and spiritual beings or conceptions of an afterlife. Repeatedly, religious conceptions included beliefs in malevolent or benign supernatural beings, acts of magic, and rites held at critical times in people's lives to propitiate or coerce supernatural beings.

Several theories were presented of the origin of religion and its subsequent evolution culminating in monotheism. Of these the best known is the theory of animism, or the belief in spiritual beings, as the least common denominator of religion. According to this idea, man arrived at the concept of a spirit or soul separable from the body to explain the events that he saw in dreams, hallucinations, and while unconscious. Spirits or souls left the body to do the things that one seemed to observe at these times. The presence or absence of the soul also accounted for the observable differences between the living and the dead. Once man had hit upon the idea of souls, so the reasoning went, he extended it to other animals and the inanimate world. Gradually, as hierarchies emerged and grew in human societies, so did they among the spirits, leading to gods with variable power and finally to monotheism.

The French sociologist Emile Durkheim thought totemism, the belief in mystic affinity between man and certain animals or plants, was the original form of religion because it stood out prominently in the religion of Australian aborigines, whose crude culture he regarded as representing the way of life of primeval man. The totem was then both the symbol and a divinization of society itself. By periodic group rituals centering upon the totemic figure, the members of society affirmed their common sentiments and thus maintained social unity.

These and other early theories of religious genesis and evolution into monotheism were discarded in the twentieth century, and the question of religious origins ceased to be a matter of interest. The prevailing view has long been that no theory of genesis can be more than reasonable speculation because the data required for its verification are beyond reach.

Although their theories regarding religious origins have been discarded, these early studies have borne other fruit. Characteristically, they saw religion as a form of interpretation of and adjustment to the universe, a view that scholars continue to hold. They regarded religion as a means of promoting social solidarity and continuity through joint beliefs and acts and through the support it often gives to moral codes and other values of society. They also pointed to the role of religion in providing psychological support for the individual. These are all lines of thought which have received their greatest elaboration among scholars of the modern era.

Contemporary scholars in the social sciences characteristically interpret supernaturalistic beliefs as creations of man, expressions of his hopes and fears. Cast into these forms, hopes and anxieties become more readily intelligible, and ways of dealing with them are suggested. Supernatural beings and whole theologies are then conceptual expressions of things in man's universe that importantly affect his life. As expressions of social experience, theologies are conditioned by habitat, techniques of gaining a livelihood, the manner of ordering society, and the whole of culture.

According to this scholarly view, it is no mere coincidence that

Christians worship God the Father and that the aboriginal Fox
Indian of the United States had a private tutelary spirit which
he addressed as "my nephew." The social relationships implied
by these terms are important in the lives of the peoples involved. It is no coincidence that maritime peoples worship gods
of the sea while agriculturists pay homage to gods of vegetation
and conduct fertility rites. Like birth, physical maturity, marriage, parenthood, and death, which are characteristically surrounded by ritual observances, these gods and acts represent
things of importance to the individuals and social groups
concerned.

Holding these views of religion, contemporary scholars have
not concerned themselves with the question of the validity in
a scientific sense of religious beliefs. Mental constructs need
not of course exist in the "real" world in order to have important effects. Their principal goal has been to gain an understanding of the role of religion in human life, its relationship
to other elements of culture, and the manner in which it grows
and changes. To reach this goal they have gone beyond the
study of theology to give attention to the observable acts of
religion—the identity and social relationships of participants,
what they do, and when the acts are performed. In particular,
scholars have tried to deduce unintended effects of religious
acts, effects not ordinarily perceived by the participants. From
the view of the participants, the goal of ritual may, for example,
be merely to worship a god for the reason that he is thought
to have power over men and to require propitiation. Unperceived
effects may include the binding of society through common acts
and beliefs; the encouragement of harmonious social life through
adherence to moral precepts interpreted as commands of the
god; and the psychological assurance given to the individual
by the belief that divine aid is available.

Much of the foregoing may be restated in somewhat more
technical terms. Contemporary scholars of religion customarily
take a view of culture, all of the man-made part of the universe,
as comprising a system composed of interrelated parts. As is
customary in physics, chemistry, astronomy, population genetics,
and other sciences that employ the concept of systems, social
scientists implicitly or explicitly use the idea of equilibrium. Like

any other system, the parts of culture—technology, economy, social structure, social institutions, and religion—are conceptually seen as enmeshing in order for the system to operate. Change in any important element of the system then results in change in other aspects, leading to a new enmeshing or state of equilibrium, or otherwise to breakdown. The term "equilibrium" does not, however, necessarily imply perfect harmony of the parts. Many societies may be seen to limp along in poor states of articulation. Nevertheless, a fair measure of congruence is seen as essential for continued maintenance in any given form of a society or culture.

Equilibrium implies functional relationships between parts of the whole, and it is this subject which has been the principal interest of modern scholars of religion. Some have presented an interpretation of function as the part played by any element of culture in maintaining the social system. Psychologically oriented scholars have concerned themselves with the role of religion in maintaining the psychological well-being or integration of the individual. For the most part, scholars have seen positive or supportive effects, although negative or disruptive effects of religion have not been entirely neglected. Here scholars have often been faced with the problem of judgments of the relative value of positive and negative effects. How, for instance, may one make final judgment of the supportive versus disruptive roles of a religion that sanctions a code of ethics vital to the maintenance of smooth human relations but at the same time instills severe anxiety by the nature of its rewards and punishments? No objective techniques have been devised for settling questions of this nature, and modern trends of scholarly interpretation tend increasingly to look for functional relationships between religion and other aspects of human culture without attempting to deduce societal or individual "needs" that they might serve. That is, functional relationships or covariations are sought between and among religion, social and political organization, technology, and other aspects of human culture which scholars have chosen for attention.

The successful pursuit of studies of religion has depended strongly upon progress along other lines of investigation. We may take as an example one of the "rites of passage," ceremonies that mark the passage of individuals from one social state to another. In their attempts to account for similarities and differences, scholars have been struck with the fact that, although the social custom of marriage exists in all historically known societies, rites marking marriage vary greatly. Among societies of equal cultural elaboration marriage ceremonies vary from the extremely simple to the exceedingly elaborate. In some societies marriage is a religious event. In others, it is not.

Considerable light has been shed on this subject by recent research into the nature of societies based upon different principles of organization. We shall take for comparison only two of these, found among the simpler societies of the world, where the principal basis of organizing society into groups for living, production, and defense is kinship. Some of these societies trace their kinship and take their important social affiliation through male lines only; others through female lines only. The first of our examples is called patrilineal reckoning of kinship and the second, matrilineal. The great nations of the modern world trace descent through both male and female forebears, but we shall limit our discussion here to the first two examples.

The coöperating social groups of our examples are either matrilineal or patrilineal relatives. Matrilineal and patrilineal societies have distinctive patterns of interpersonal relations and distinctive sets of problems arising from these relationships. In matrilineal societies, where the important social group consists of related women, their brothers, and the offspring of the women, husbands must come from outside the immediate matrilineal kin group. To perpetuate the matrilineal kin group, it is necessary to maintain strong ties with children, and these ties may be created and maintained at the expense of bonds between husband and wife.

We shall take as a concrete example the Zuni Indians of the southwestern United States. The scant attention given to wedding ritual among the Zuni is consistent with their social organization. The Zuni are matrilineal and thus the important social affiliation of the children is with the mother, her brothers, and other matrilineal relatives, who form an important social group. Upon marriage, a man resides with the kin group of his bride, but retains important ties to his own matrilineal kin group, in which he holds a secure status. The minimal role of the husband in a society such as this is as procreator. If divorce should come, the vital matrilineal kin group suffers no severe blow. Matrilineal descent, residence after marriage with the kin of the wife, and the unity of brothers and sisters assure a suitable home and economic support as well as approved social identification for the children. At the same time, continuance of Zuni social groups is also assured, despite divorce, since the social groups are based upon matrilineal descent and residence. Special sanction of marriage is not a vital issue.

It is not surprising that the incidence of divorce is higher in matrilineal than in patrilineal societies, for among patrilineal societies the maintenance of strong ties of marriage are of paramount importance. Although the patrilineal social group is perpetuated through male lines, this can be accomplished only through wives, coming from other social groups. The patrilineal kin group suffers not at all in giving up its female members in marriage so long as they are replaced by wives coming from other kin groups. Wives are necessary not only for giving birth to the children but also for nursing and caring for them. In congruence with these circumstances, rituals of marriage among patrilineal societies are commonly well developed, with supernatural sanction for the union. Secular binders, such as the transfer of valuable property that must be returned if the marriage falls asunder, are also common.

As our discussion of marriage rites suggests, much modern study of religion relates to sources of tension or conflict in social relations brought about by the ordering of society. The scholar looks for sources of stress in customs governing such things as the composition of social groups, spatial arrangements in living, interpersonal privileges and obligations, the division of labor according to sex, age, and other considerations, and the basis of social prestige. Beliefs and practices of witchcraft, for example, are seen as both channels for the expression of hostile feelings when other avenues of expression are closed or excessively costly and as indicators of stressful human relationships. Both practices and accusations of witchcraft may be seen to follow patterns. Witches and those bewitched are persons who fail to conform with standards of behavior or appear to threaten their fellows in some other way. Both witches and bewitched stand in stressful relation to each other.

Institutionalized rites that symbolically or actually violate important rules of behavior have received a similar interpretation. These are rites, existing in many of the simpler societies, in which rulers and other figures of authority are impugned and reviled, men and women deride the opposite sex, obscenity is officially sanctioned, sexual license is permitted, and other normally cherished customs are violated with full social approval. Hypotheses advanced concerning rites of this sort interpret them as both indices of tension in the social system and socially-regulated means for its harmless release.

The emergence of new religious movements has similarly been linked with social disturbances and has for many years been a subject of interest to scholars of religion. Religious movements have risen repeatedly among simpler societies of the world during the past two centuries as these societies have come into sustained and demoralizing contact with European cultures. Movements continue to wax and wane among primitive societies, and they are also a common occurrence among the lower social strata of great industrialized nations. As attempts at self-aid to meet crises, they are also markers of stress.

Although religious movements of this kind long ago struck the attention of scholars, early accounts of them were primarily descriptive. Far better understanding of these movements— why they are accepted by one people and rejected by another, explanations of their relative intensity and their peculiar local forms—has come as a result of increased knowledge of human society and culture. Similarly, a better understanding of witchcraft and rites violating social rules has come from examining the social order and other aspects of the cultures of the societies in question.

Psychiatric studies of religion have dealt with human tensions in another way, examining religious dogma and ritual for its therapeutic aspects. It is clear from these studies that psychotherapy is very old. The techniques of modern psychotherapy have long been followed by primitive curers, who were both religious specialists and physicians. Even Freudian theory concerning dreams and repressions seems ancient. Among the Iroquois Indians of the eastern United States similar ideas served as the basis for rites to cure the mentally ill that allowed the controlled fulfillment of desires expressed in dreams. It is interesting to note that a modern Japanese technique of psychotherapy was consciously derived in part from Zen Buddhism.

The bearing of religion upon human motivation toward achievement is another subject which has continued for many decades to interest scholars. The ideas embodied in the "Protestant ethic," an expression which came to us several decades ago from the German sociologist Max Weber, remain alive among modern scholars of religion. Weber used this name for a set of values—thrift, unremitting industry, the eschewing of luxury, and the valuing of work for its own sake—which he thought characterized Protestants and arose from Protestantism. He describes this ethic as an important motivating force in the industrial revolution. Subsequent interpretations have seen these values as arising from changed technological and economic conditions of the early years of the industrial revolution and shaping Protestantism, which in turn reinforced these attitudes by sanctioning them. A similar interpretation concerning religious motivations toward economic development and allied growth in other spheres of culture has been attempted for Japan, and the subject will doubtless continue to hold scholarly attention.

If we review these and other trends of research on religion of the past three decades, we find certain characteristic ideas and methodological approaches. One of the guiding concepts, which we have already mentioned, is the systemic nature of society and culture. Religion is examined in its relationship to the whole of culture, not as a discrete element that may be excised from its cultural matrix and observed in isolation. In sharp contrast with theologians, who have concentrated on religious dogma, scholars in social sciences have seen religion as a system of social interaction with important influence in human affairs. Accordingly, much attention has been directed toward observation of the acts of religion. This procedure has been one of choice, on the reasoning that much of the importance of religion may be inferred only from observation of such things as the identity and interrelationships of social groups and individuals involved in ceremonial observances, the values expressed in rites, and the occasions on which ritual is performed. Consideration of these things has rendered intelligible many things, including witchcraft, rites of passage, rites connected with agriculture and other economic enterprises, and rituals that express conflicts of interest.

The groundwork is laid for the comparative study of many features of religion, and, from all indications, the next decade will see much progress in that direction. Of special interest among the newer trends is a revived interest in the nature of religious change. If, as scholars assume, religious beliefs and practices arise out of other circumstances of life, we might reasonably expect that the great cultural changes the world has experienced during the recent past should exert great influence on religion. As one might infer from our earlier reference to changing scholarly conceptions of religion, profound change has already taken place in the religions of the Western world. We may recall that the emerging conception of religion appears to be one that allows no place for supernaturalism. It seems reasonable to state that we may expect in the near future the scholarly formulation of new theories of the evolution of religion. Before this may be done, however, much remains to be accomplished in the formulation of points of reference. We must first formulate typologies of religion, philosophy, society, technology, and economic structure suitable for deducing and intelligibly expressing the relationships between and among these categories.

BIBLIOGRAPHICAL NOTE

For the earliest detailed anthropological study of religion, evolutionist in interpretation, see E. B. Tylor, *Primitive Culture,* Vol. 2 (first published 1871; many subsequent editions). The appendix to Goode (1951) provides a review of nineteenth-century theories of the origins of religion. Important works in the formulation of modern functionalist interpretation of religion are Durkheim, *The Elementary Forms of the Religious Life* (1954); A. R. Radcliffe-Brown, *The Andaman Islanders* (first published in 1922); and Bronislaw Malinowski, *Magic, Science and Religion and Other Essays* (1948). A recent functionalist interpretation of a single ceremony is provided in Richards (1956). The outstanding interpretative study of witchcraft by an anthropologist is Kluckhohn, *Navaho Witchcraft* (first published 1944; various later editions). For the most recent survey and appraisal of anthropological studies of religion and for additional references, see Norbeck (1961).

19.

THE ARTS AND ANTHROPOLOGY

Alan P. Merriam

THE RELATIONSHIP BETWEEN the arts and anthropology is a problem which has been discussed from time to time, but unfortunately usually without much result. While anthropologists have long been interested in the arts, particularly among nonliterate peoples, it is only recently that significant studies have begun to appear. Herta Haselberger (1961:342) tells us that "specimens of ethnological art had been included in European collections as early as the fifteenth century," and references to African music extend well back into the seventeenth century (Dapper 1676). In dance, the study of European forms received impetus from the research of Cecil Sharp in England early in the twentieth century, but a survey of studies made in the Soviet Union shows materials dating back to 1848 (cf., Kurath 1960). Concentrated studies of oral literature were begun in Germany by the Grimm brothers early in the nineteenth century, and the word "folklore" was coined by William John Thoms in 1846 (Emrich 1946). The earliest publications in ethnomusicology as such, date from 1882 with Theodore Baker's doctoral dissertation at the University of Leipzig, *On the Music of the North American Savages*; and the study of the visual arts among peoples other than ourselves began to receive significant impetus in the decades surrounding the advent of the twentieth century.

We can thus look back on the study of the arts in cultures other than our own and see a slow development over a rather extended period of time: at least four hundred years ago we find interest being shown, though it is not until the turn of this
224

centuiy that extensive and serious studies begin to appear. And it is not until very recent times that a major attempt has been made to deal with anthropology and the arts in more than descriptive terms.

Interest in specific arts as aspects of anthropology has also varied enormously. The study of drama, for example, has hardly been touched upon in anthropology, though a very few studies such as Γ. E. Williams' *Drama of Orokolo* (1940), and Melville J. Herskovits' "Dramatic Expression Among Primitive Peoples" (1944) are to be found. Similarly, architectural studies have played a very small part in anthropology, although descriptions of house types are found in almost every ethnography; and even dance has not received the attention it deserves. On the other hand, the anthropological literature is full of references to the graphic and plastic, or visual arts, to music, and to oral literature; and so it is that the study of the arts remains unbalanced, with much emphasis on some forms and very little upon others. It seems reasonable to say that, with the possible exception of oral literature, the study of the arts in anthropology generally has been seriously neglected and undervalued when viewed in broad perspective. The average text in anthropology, for example, devotes a single chapter or a portion of a single chapter to all of the arts taken together, and the contrast between this allotment and the space given to problems of social structure or political organization is indeed striking.

This relative neglect of the humanistic aspects of culture derives in part at least from two major misunderstandings about the arts and how they should be handled in the investigation of the patterns of human behavior. The first of these stems from the failure to understand the essential nature of the content of the social sciences, on the one hand, and the humanities, on the other, and the basic relationship between them. I have argued this point at some length elsewhere (Merriam 1962), but essentially the content of the social sciences—that is, the subject matter which is of concern to them—derives from the institutionalizing behavior of man through which he solves the problems which arise from his own biosocial existence. That is, man must regulate his economic, social, political, and encultura-

tive behavior with his fellow men, and these are problems which
arise, on the one hand, from the needs of the biological organism,
and on the other, from the group life to which man is so irretriev-
ably committed. The essential nature of the content of the
humanities, however, seems to arise from man's need to supply
himself with what A. I. Hallowell (1947: 550-51) has referred
to as ". . . mediative factors in man's cultural mode of adaptation
. . . whereby a world of common meanings has been created
in human societies." In other words:

> Through the humanistic elements of his culture, man seems
> to be making pointed commentary on how he lives; he seems in
> the humanities to sum up what he thinks of life. In short, man
> lives as a social animal, but he does not live as a social animal
> alone. For his social life in itself seems to bring about conditions
> under which he is unable to restrain himself from commenting
> upon himself and enunciating and interpreting his actions, his
> aspirations, and his values. (Merriam 1962:14)

The social sciences, then, deal with man as a social animal
and the ways in which he solves his social and biological
problems in daily living, while the humanities take man beyond
his biosocial living into his own distillations of his life experiences which he uses, in turn, as an expression of his basic
sanctions and values.

It may conceivably be argued that the social sciences are
necessarily prior to the humanities because they deal with
absolute fundamentals of existence. I think this is a proper conclusion only in the sense that man as a social animal *is* basic; that
is, men do live together. But at the same time, both the social and
the humanistic aspects of man's life are universals in his culture
and experience, and thus the question is not at all one of
priority, but rather one of unity. If man cannot live, as apparently he cannot, without either his social institutions or his
humanistic responses, then the two become merely two sides of
the same coin and neither can be examined without involving
the other (cf., Merriam 1962).

The second major misunderstanding about the arts and their
anthropological context derives from the nature of the arts
themselves, and from the ways in which they have previously
been studied. The arts are perhaps peculiar among man's cul-

tural creations simply because the behavior involved in their creation produces a product which, as an object of study, can be treated quite divorced from cultural context. The same, of course, is true of tools and house types, for example, but there is some argument as to whether these may not most logically be treated as arts as well. Herein, of course, lies the difficulty in the treatment by anthropologists of what are commonly known as the "arts and crafts," or simply as "crafts." In reality, these seem to me to be of such a nature as to be classed with the fine arts, and it is but a convention of our own culture that prevents us from doing so, and leads us, instead, to set them apart. In any case, what is important here is that the art product is conceptually, and in certain ways practically separable from its cultural context. Thus musicians, no matter in what culture they are found, produce a product, musical sound, which can be recorded, transcribed to paper, and analyzed as a structural entity. Dance is objectified by a system of graphic shorthand; oral literature is reduced to writing; the visual arts cannot exist without a tangible product; architecture results in buildings; and drama, reduced to writing after observation, shows structural characteristics of sequence in time, plot, climax, and the like.

This peculiar characteristic of the arts seems to set them apart from those organizations of society which we call its institutions, for in the case of institutions what is important is the organization itself which is directed toward shaping the behavior of the individuals concerned. With the arts, on the other hand, the importance lies in the product, and artistic behavior is directed toward it; without musical sound, music does not exist, but society is behaving.

At the same time, what draws the two broad fields of inquiry together is not only the fact that they are inseparable, but also the fact that both must inevitably deal with human behavior. That is, the artist produces a product, and this is his ultimate and direct aim, but in doing so he behaves in certain ways.

This distinction between the product, on the one hand, and the behavior which produces it, on the other, is one which has not often been made in studies of the arts. On the contrary, most investigations have tended to concentrate exclusively or almost exclusively upon the product which is visualized as a structure or system, the parts of which interact with each other to form a cohesive whole. Our studies of the visual arts are primarily concerned with the painting or sculpture itself, not with the artist; our studies of oral literature concentrate upon the tale or proverb or myth, not with the teller; our investigations into music deal almost exclusively with the musical sound and not with the musician.

Behavior, then, is separable from the product conceptually; in fact, of course, it is inseparable because no product can exist without the behavior of some individual or individuals. And this behavior is exemplified in two major ways: first, because the producer of music, for example, conceptualizes his product in certain ways; and second, because the producer of music is a musician and thus shapes his behavior to accord with what the society at large conceive to be musicianly behavior. Thus, the behavior of any artist is underlain by his conceptualization of the product he wishes to produce as well as his concept of himself as an artist.

Finally, the product as such has a feedback effect upon the artist's conceptualization. If the musical sound produced is pleasing to the performer and to his audience, then the particular concept is reinforced; if it is not pleasing, the artist is forced to change his concept, which in turn means a change in behavior, resulting finally in a changed product.

There is, then, a fourfold organizational pattern involved in the arts: concept, leading to behavior, resulting in product, which in turn feeds back upon the concept. Of these four aspects of the art process, only the product has been studied in anything approaching detail; concept, behavior, and feedback upon concept, have been almost totally neglected. In these terms, it is perhaps not surprising that the study of the arts has not been of central concern to anthropology, for studies of product are essentially descriptive in nature. And any descriptive study must develop a technical terminology which quickly surpasses the competence of individuals who are not primarily concerned with the object of the study at hand. Thus in dealing with the music product, ethnomusicologists speak of "melodic level," "modal analyses," or "triadic split fifths," and use a large number of further terms incomprehensible to those not directly involved in this sort of analysis. Artists have their own technical vocabulary to describe visual products; students of dance deal in special ways with dance forms, and so forth. The study of artistic product is a highly technical field of inquiry, and it is also a restricted one.

But if we look at art as behavior in the kinds of terms I have just suggested, then it becomes apparent that the product is but one part of art, and that our frame of reference falls very sharply into the kinds of inquiry which are of primary interest to anthropology. Anthropology seeks descriptive facts, it is true, but of much more importance are the reasons that lie behind those facts. The straight description of a kinship system is not our ultimate aim; what we want to know is how this system works, and particularly, why it works in the ways it does. I submit, then, that in the study of the arts, the major emphasis has been placed upon the product, with the result that such systemic, structural, or synchronic descriptions dominate the literature, leaving little room for behavioral studies which will help us toward an understanding of the how and why of human behavior. If we look past the product as a product, and consider some of the deeper manifestations which it and the behavior which underlies it represent, we arrive at an understanding of the kinds of questions which are beginning to preoccupy more and more students of the arts and human behavior.

Perhaps these various levels of analysis can best be illustrated by one or two examples from the music system of the Basongye people of the Kasai Province in the Republic of the Congo (formerly the Belgian Congo), with whom I spent a year in 1959-60.

> The Basongye conceptualize music as a uniquely human phenomenon through distinctions made between noise on the one hand and music on the other. These distinctions are summarized in a series of aphorismic statements made by individuals as they discuss the problem:
> When you are content you sing; when you are angry, you make noise.
> When one shouts, he is not thinking; when he sings, he is thinking.

A song is tranquil; a noise is not.

When one shouts, his voice is forced; when he sings, it is not.

On bases such as these, the Basongye separate noise from music, or more precisely, non-music from music. Thus non-music includes such sounds as those made by birds or animals, wind blowing through the trees, a single pulse upon a drum or xylophone, whistling, or blowing into cupped hands when these are used for signalling. Music, on the other hand, includes the sound of the drums when played together and over a period of time, the human voice when it is not "shouting" or speaking, whistling when it is co-ordinated and used as accompaniment to the dance, and other like productions. The Basongye "theory" of music, then, seems to involve three essential features in the distinction between music and non-music: first, the fact that music always involves human beings, and that those sounds emanating from non-human sources are not music. Second, the musical sounds that humans produce are organized; thus a single tap on the drum is not music, but the drums playing together in the patterned forms which the drummers use, do make music. And third, there must be continuity in time; even all the drums struck but once simultaneously do not make music; they must continue over time.

This conception of music as distinct from non-music is, of course, an abstraction of principles expressed in a variety of ways by a number of informants; yet the statements of the Basongye point to a conception of music which underlies all musical production. Music is a non-mechanistic, humanly-produced phenomenon, and this conception colors the entire attitude of the Basongye toward their music. (Merriam 1962:27-8)

On a somewhat different level it is clear that the conceptualization of his instrument by the musician clearly affects the music he produces upon it. For example, the Basongye think of every known bass xylophone pattern as having definite starting and ending points, and these points are not those at which the Western-oriented musician would place them. Without a knowledge, then, of the Basongye distinction between music and non-music, of their concept of music and musical instruments, and of a large number of further points, we cannot hope to understand clearly the sound product.

Similarly, concept is translated into behavior, and here our wider approach to the study of the arts leads us, for example, into investigation of the creative person, both as an individual and as a member of his society. Ruth Benedict's remarkable study of Zuni mythology, for example, at one point discusses the individual narrator of myths, and how the personalities of the tellers affect the eventual product. One of her informants was a social deviant, a man of considerable self-reliance, individualism, and ability, and a person with a deep-seated need for achieving personal eminence; the myths he told differed markedly from those given by other informants (1935:xxxviii-xl). And similarly, the artist in society plays certain roles, thinks of himself in certain ways *vis à vis* the society of which he is a member, and is thought of in special ways by persons who are not artists; inevitably this particular social role shapes the product he produces.

If we look at the arts, then, as human behavior, we stretch our concepts considerably, for our studies are no longer only descriptive and thus synchronic, but become instead processual. And this applies to studies of the product as well. For example, most contemporary philosophers are agreed that the arts perform an essentially symbolic function in human society. Thus Ernst Cassirer (1944:168), for example, says flatly: "Art may be defined as a symbolic language"; and speaking of music, Susanne Langer (1953:32) comments: ". . . music is 'significant form,' and its significance is that of a symbol, a highly articulated, sensuous object, which by virtue of its dynamic structure can express the forms of vital experience which language is peculiarly unfit to convey. Feeling, life, motion and emotion constitute its import." While I have no doubt that the arts are symbolic, the problem here is precisely what is meant by the term, for it seems clear that the arts are symbolic in at least four different ways. Let us discuss these briefly.

In the first place, art can be symbolic in its conveyance of direct meanings. Thus, for example, some dance is mimetic, some visual art is representational, and song texts express through the symbolism of language certain attitudes and emotions as well as direct statements of fact. In one sense, perhaps, such behavior is "signing" rather than symboling, for the nature of the product directly represents human action; thus erotic movements in the dance are the same movements used in actual behavior, or a sculptured bust is a direct representation of the person involved.

In any case, this kind of representation is symbolic, though perhaps not technically so, on the most direct level (see White 1949: 22-39; Morris 1955).

On a second level, the arts are symbolic in that they are reflective of emotion and meaning; we can refer to this as "affective" or "cultural" meaning. In this case, the symbolism is distinct and culturally defined. In our own Western music, for example, we assign the emotion of sadness to what we call a minor scale; certain combinations of musical instruments playing together suggest certain physical or emotional phenomena, and selections of particular combinations of notes can and do symbolize particular states of being. Edward Lowinsky (1946:79) has noted that:

> Chromaticism always represents the extraordinary . . . Again and again we find chromatic treatment given to such highly emotional concepts as crying, lamenting, mourning, moaning, inconsolability, shrouding one's head, breaking down, and so forth.
>
> In the Italian madrigal the same concepts find expression through the medium of chromaticism. There they represent man as entangled in his earthly passions, while in the music of the Netherlands they symbolize the devout believer struggling with the burden of sorrow which God has laid upon him to test his faith.

Or again, in oral literature, Lowie (1956:118) reports a number of linguistic usages which function among the Crow Indians as part of story telling but to which are assigned culturally defined meanings: "returning with blackened face" means "triumph," "having one's moccasins made" means "getting ready for a raid," "carrying the pipe" is equivalent to being captain of a party. Similar examples could be quoted at considerable length for all of the arts, but the point is clear; the arts are symbolic in the sense that they indicate affective or cultural meanings through the use of devices that are inherent in their own structures.

A third symbolic level is found in the principle that the arts reflect certain social behavior, political institutions, economic organization, and the like. In the dance, for example, Gertrude Kurath (1960:236-37; Fenton and Kurath 1953:233) has pointed

out how dancing reflects male-female roles and even the clan and
moiety organization of the Iroquois. One of the outstanding
examples of this kind of study is to be found in David P.
McAllester's *Enemy Way Music* (1954:86-88), a study of the
Navaho. Working through the framework of existential and
normative values, McAllester concluded that Navaho music reflects Navaho culture in three major ways. First, a characteristic
of Navaho cultural values is expressed in individualism: in
respect to music, "what one does with one's property, knowledge,
songs, is one's own affair." Second is the fact that the Navaho are
essentially provincial and conservative: in music, "foreign music
is dangerous and not for Navahos." Finally, the Navaho, McAllester says, sustain a formal culture, and in music the same
formalism is expressed in the summatory statement that "there
is a right way to sing every kind of song." In a study somewhat
similar to McAllester's, Alan Lomax (1959:950) has written that
"the basic color of a music symbolizes fundamental social-psycho-
logical patterns, common to a given culture," and suggests that
music sound reflects the sexual code, the position of women,
and the treatment of children in a culture. All these studies,
then, are looking at the arts as reflective of other aspects and
principles of culture; in this sense too, the arts are symbolic.

Finally, the fourth level on which the arts can be regarded
as symbolic is in respect to deeper processes of human thought
and behavior on a world-wide basis and not on the level of any
particular culture. We have very little information concerning
this aspect of artistic symbolism, but Curt Sachs (1937:127-38),
for example, has postulated an elaborate scheme in which three
major types of musical material are correlated with femininity or
masculinity, physical type, size of dance steps, and even such
general cultural traits as "warlike" or "peace-loving" peoples.
Further, in connection with the symbolism of musical instruments, the same writer has made some speculations using a
primarily Freudian conception. He notes, for example:

> Tubular wind instruments, straight and elongated like a man's
> organ, belong to man, and a mixture of symbols arises when a
> flute is globular instead of tubular, or when a trumpet is made
> out of a conch shell which is connected with water. . . .

Sound, also, is a factor as well as form in these connotations. Most of the instruments reserved for men have a harsh, aggressive, indeed ugly tone; most instruments preferred by women have a muffled timbre (Sachs 1940:52).

The quarrel we may have with formulations such as these is not so much with the exploratory nature of the ideas, but rather with the categories of correlation selected; thus the definition of what is to be considered a "warlike" or "peace-loving" people is extremely difficult, if not impossible to reach, and a strictly Freudian interpretation is not convincing to some. However, this approach, which seeks to correlate sound on a human level and a world basis, rather than to specific behavior in specific cultures, is clearly the broadest attack that can be made on the arts as symbolism. What I am trying to stress, however, is that in looking at art as a symbol we are doing more than a description, although the product is our focus. The result of such analysis is an approach to an understanding of the arts as they reflect and as they influence behavior.

In a somewhat different vein it has sometimes been stressed that the function of the arts is their integrative role in society; this point of view has perhaps been best expressed by A. R. Radcliffe-Brown (1948:330-41) in his study of the Andaman Islanders. Radcliffe-Brown cites a legend of the Andamanese which explains the origin of night and correlates the social life of the individual with the alternation of dark and light and with the dependence of the individual on society. Social life, he says, gives a sense of security, and thus when night falls, the individual is less secure because social life ceases. He reports that the particular legend tells of a time when there was no night and thus when social life went on without interruption; this was followed by the disruption of the pattern into day and night in which social life is, of course, interrupted. The tale points up the interpretation that night or darkness is a force hostile to society and thus stresses the individual's participation in and dependence upon the social group. The function of the tale, then, says Radcliffe-Brown, is to emphasize the importance of society, thus contributing to its integration by reinforcing the notion of the individual's dependence upon society.

This is, of course, but one interpretation of the function, in this case, of oral literature, but it stresses meaning and importance both of the product as a product, and of man's behavior in creating and using it.

In the past, then, the arts have been studied in anthropology, primarily as products, that is, on a descriptive level which stresses their own internal structure. What is argued here is that the product must inevitably be produced by human beings who behave in certain ways in so doing. Further, all human behavior arises out of peoples' thought and concepts of what proper behavior should be; and finally, the success or failure of the product itself causes changes in concept which accounts, in part at least, for internal change and stability. The approach argued here is essentially a broadening one which calls for the real combination of techniques of analysis from both the social sciences and humanities. It is the kind of study which is gradually emerging in the investigation of the arts and anthropology.

BIBLIOGRAPHICAL NOTE

Although the amount of published material concerning anthropological views of the arts is enormous, most of it tends to treat the art product rather than viewing the arts in terms of human behavior. Thus in ethnomusicology, Nettl (1956) is one of the few book-length expositions in English, but its subject matter is almost exclusively technical, though it is simply written and understandable to the layman. Merriam (1964) expresses in more detail many of the views presented here, but with more attention given to music *per se*. The standard reference in the field of dance is Sachs (1937), which tends to present its information in rather outdated theoretical terms; it remains, however, a very stimulating and useful work. More recently, Kurath (1960) has summarized the field of ethnic dance with considerable expertise; her article also contains an extensive and very useful bibliography. Haselberger (1961) is for art what Kurath's article is for dance, and Boas (1955) has long been a classic in the field. Surprising as it seems, no really general work exists on folklore. Thompson's *The Folktale* (1946) is the most general work on this particular genre of folklore, while the *Standard Dictionary of Folklore Mythology and Legend*, edited by Maria Leach (1950) includes discussion and summary of a great variety of folklore topics. For drama, Herskovits (1944) remains almost unique in the field.

20.

EQUALITY AND INEQUALITY IN HUMAN SOCIETIES

Lloyd A. Fallers

INEQUALITY APPEARS TO BE AN inescapable feature of the human condition. Thus far, the efforts of utopian reformers to eliminate it have failed, leading most students of the subject to conclude, with Robert Michels, that the life of man in society is bound by a kind of "iron law of oligarchy." And yet, in modern times particularly, the pursuit of equality has persisted, in both the aspirations of individuals and the goals of political movements, especially in the Western world. Most observers, while doubting the possibility of complete equality, would at the same time agree that these modern egalitarian movements and aspirations have met with an important degree of relative success. Today, furthermore, they are spreading to an ever widening circle of the world's people in the new states of Asia and Africa.

In what sense, then, is inequality universal and in what sense is equality possible? How far is the somewhat longer Western experience with the modern urge to equality an accurate guide for contemporary Asian and African peoples with similar aspirations—or for Western observers who wish to understand those aspirations? Anthropologists and other students of human society and culture try to answer these questions through the comparative study of societies of diverse kinds. Their investigations suggest that equality and inequality, like most social and cultural features which engage our attention, are complex phenomena which can best be understood by breaking them down analytically into their constituent elements. In this way we are able to see more

237

clearly the different combinations of elements which produce
the differences in actual social life that interest us.

Clearly one universal source of inequality is the tendency of
every human community to develop, as part of its body of common culture, a system of values in terms of which persons may
judge themselves and each other. These values commonly define
for the community's members an image of the "admirable man"
—the kind of man everyone would like to be. Such an image
holds up both a standard of moral evaluation and a goal for
personal ambition—a definition of what is worth doing and
being, and why. Judged by such standards, persons are always in
some measure unequal, though the qualities admired differ
greatly from society to society.

But of course inequality is a more complex matter than this.
If one primary root of inequality is moral judgment, another is
the division of labor or—to use a broader and more accurate
phrase, since what is divided is not always "labor" in the usual
sense—the differentiation of social roles. Societies are never
completely undifferentiated; they always distinguish behavior
appropriate to people who differ with respect to sex, age and
kinship, and usually with respect to other criteria as well. Moral
evaluation takes account of these differentiations, holding up
somewhat different images of virtue for husband and wife,
elder and youth, farmer and priest. The result is a kind of
two-dimensional moral evaluation among a society's members:
Persons judge each other according to how well they perform
their particular roles; but, because a people's system of values
tends to have a degree of coherence, roles themselves are evaluated with respect to some central conception of excellence and
virtue. We know of no people who do not have views concerning the relative merit, for example, of youth and age, of
masculinity and femininity, and of various occupations.

Of course societies differ greatly in the number of roles they
distinguish and in the number of distinct statuses, or bundles of
roles, which are commonly combined in one social person. The
societies which have been called "simple" or "primitive" are so
called, in part at least, because they distinguish relatively few
roles and, even more important, because these roles are typically
combined into a very few statuses. Societies of hunting-and-

gathering peoples often have quite complex systems of kinship roles, for example, as compared with those of modern Western societies, in the sense that they distinguish, and assign distinct behavior to, many more different kinds of kinsmen. But because the occupational structure is simple because there may be only one adult male occupation, that of hunter and warrior, for example—there are very few distinct statuses. Since there are no occupational alternatives, each male and each female moves through the same complexes of age and kinship roles as his or her life progresses. In such societies there is essentially only one kind of man. The possibilities for inequality, apart from the age, sex, and kinship roles into which a person is born and grows, are for the most part limited to differences in the excellence with which he performs in the one occupational role which the society provides. Aboriginal Australian and most North American Indian societies were relatively egalitarian in this sense.

We usually think of modern societies also as being relatively egalitarian; certainly they have often aspired to be so. But their egalitarianism, insofar as it exists, must clearly be of a very different order from that found in aboriginal North America or Australia. For one of the characteristic features of modern societies is precisely the intricate differentiation of occupational roles which they exhibit—the wide range of occupational choices which they offer to their people. In such societies there are many different kinds of men: physicians and lawyers, farmers, priests and industrial managers, white collar and manual workers of many kinds. With this proliferation of alternative life careers —of relatively distinct statuses—the problem of equality and inequality becomes more complex in at least two important respects: On the one hand, this vast range of occupational roles invites relative evaluation in terms of society's common values, thus greatly increasing the possibilities for inequality. And, on the other hand, it also raises the problem of how all these alternative positions are to be filled—the problem of equality and inequality of opportunity to occupy the more highly valued roles. Modern egalitarian ideologies have sought both to reduce the inequality of evaluation of occupational roles and to increase equality of access to them.

But of course this comparison of very simple societies with very complex ones, while it teaches us something about the different meanings equality and inequality can have in different kinds of societies, nevertheless has a certain lack of relevance because it is so very unhistorical. Modern, highly differentiated societies have generally not developed out of very simple ones of the aboriginal North American type; they have rather grown out of the quite complex, but not yet modern, societies which occupied much of Europe, Asia, and Africa in ancient and medieval times. These have sometimes been called "peasant societies," sometimes "traditional civilizations." They were—and are, for some of them still exist—the most unegalitarian societies known to us—societies in which the different orders of men were sometimes so unequally evaluated as to be regarded almost as different kinds of creatures. Because they have provided the setting out of which, and against which, modern egalitarianism has grown, we may learn something about the modern urge to equality by examining the nature of inequality in these traditional peasant societies.

Characteristically, these societies were much more differentiated than the simple societies of which we spoke earlier, but still a good deal less differentiated than modern societies. More important, the kinds of differentiation which they exhibited served to maximize inequality. If we make use of the common image of the pyramid in thinking about inequality, these societies may be described as sharply "peaked" in form, with very small elites at the top and very large masses of peasants at the base.

Part of the gulf between elite and common folk was cultural. Most of these societies lay within the ambit of one or another of the literary world religions—Christianity, Islam, Hinduism, or Buddhism. Religion lay at the center of these cultures and everyone participated in it, but elite and peasants commonly participated in very different ways and degrees. Literacy, and hence direct access to the literary religious tradition, was limited to the elite and their servants. As a result there commonly developed, as Robert Redfield has reminded us, relatively distinct elite and folk variants of the common tradition—a phenomenon represented in medieval Europe, for example, by the aristocratic Christianity of nobility and knighthood, with its emphasis upon honor, *noblesse oblige* and military prowess, in contrast to the submissive piety of the peasantry, organized about the cycle of the agricultural year. The elite variant—more closely associated, as its bearers were, with the leadership of the church—was regarded as the higher or purer one the one more nearly representative of the common values—and this judgment was in large measure accepted by peasants as well as aristocrats. Similar kinds of cultural stratification are revealed by studies of India and the Islamic world.

In some cases the traditional culture, with its religious foundation, added to this tendency toward cultural stratification a positive ideological defence of hereditary inequality. This was true of medieval Christianity, despite the egalitarian emphasis of the primitive gospel message. Medieval Christian philosophers could view the ranks of society as immutably fixed by God's will, like the parts of the human body, and could advise their people to avoid worldliness by serving faithfully in the statuses into which they had been born. Traditional Hinduism was even more explicit: Membership in the castes, ranked in relation to the proximity of their ritual practice to that of Brahmins, was in theory fixed for life. Closer approximation to the religious ideal, and hence social advancement, could come only through reincarnation.

On the other hand, Islamic ideology was apparently more egalitarian in both theory and practice: In the Koran and in the traditions, Muslims found a body of law—the *sharia*—which they sought to make a full and sufficient rule of life in this world for all believers without distinction. Islamic education was relatively accessible, and elites appear to have been more open to lowly-born persons who managed to acquire it. Something like the same situation seems to have prevailed in traditional China, where the acquisition of Confucian learning might enable a capable peasant lad to enter the ranks of the imperial bureaucracy.

However, though these differences in cultural attitude toward hereditary inequality were not unimportant, their practical effect was lessened by the kinds of economic and occupational structure which prevailed in the peasant societies. Where elites are very small and the common folk very numerous, the chances of any particular peasant boy's rising into the elite may be quite infinitesimal, whatever the culture may say about the rightness of his doing so.

(We may note, parenthetically, that the practical effect of such differences may be much greater at the elite level. Because of the small size of the elite, the recruitment into it of even relatively small numbers of persons of lowly origin may greatly affect its character—a phenomenon familiar in the history of the Islamic world.)

Elites in the peasant societies, then, were small and they were supported economically by the surplus beyond their own subsistence needs produced by numerous peasants. Intermediate groups—the traders and the craftsmen, whose products often exhibited marvelously high levels of specialized skill and aesthetic expression—were few, like the elite. They were, in fact, few essentially because they produced *for* the elite. There were no mass markets for their products. Peasants produced most of what they consumed and consumed much of what they produced —or as much of it as they could retain in the face of elite demands for taxes, dues, and tribute.

There was yet another feature of the occupational structure of the peasant societies which tended to fix a man in the social station into which he had been born. A man's occupation was very largely learned and carried out within his household. Both peasant lad and prince learned their occupational roles at home. The king's household was the government; the peasant's homestead was his enterprise. Traders and craftsmen taught these occupations to their sons and other young kinsmen through apprenticeship. For the most part there was neither an educational system nor a labor market external to the family to channel the young man into an occupation other than his father's. For the vast majority of people, family, school and work-place were one.

Thus, while the traditional peasant societies were quite differentiated occupationally—while they contained many different kinds of men—these kinds of men were very unequal, both in the way they were evaluated with reference to the common culture and in their opportunities to occupy the more highly esteemed positions in society. It was out of sharply stratified societies of this kind, as they began to change into societies of

the sort we recognize as modern, that the contemporary urge
to equality developed.

It happened first in the West, in the lands of medieval
Christendom. The reasons for this have been the subject of much
debate among historians and others, but for present purposes
we need not concern ourselves with this problem except to note
that, because modern societies first developed in the West, and
because the Western experience with modernity is more extensive, we are apt to fall into the habit of thinking of modernity as a peculiarly Western possession. We can easily come
to identify as Western social and cultural features which may
in fact be characteristic of modern societies wherever they develop, and vice versa. Let us, then, try to abstract from concrete
historical experience those features of generic modernity which
seem to be associated particularly with the modern urge to
equality.

First of all, there is a cultural dimension of modernity which
we may perhaps characterize as a commitment to the idea that
human life is subject to unlimited improvement through systematic scientific investigation and its technological application. The roots of this idea clearly lie in classical antiquity, but
its pervasive dominance over men's minds is, equally clearly,
quite modern. Only in modern societies does innovation become routine and only in modern societies is it regularly applied
to society and culture as well as to technological problems. Such
an attitude is only with difficulty, if at all, reconcilable with
the great religious systems which lay at the heart of traditional
cultures. In the West, to the extent that it remains religious, a
kind of deistic modus vivendi appears to have been arrived at,
in terms of which the universe is viewed as the handiwork of a
rational God, so that the attempt to understand its complexities
may be regarded not only as permissible, but even as a religious
duty. It would, however, be rash indeed to assert that the reconciliation between science and faith is complete. Outside the
West, the outcome is perhaps still more problematical. For our
purposes, however, the essential point is that the scientific attitude is incompatible with cultural conceptions in terms of
which men were regarded as irrevocably unequal, irrespective
of their needs and capacities. Instead, it tends to apply both

to social roles themselves and to candidates for them the universalistic test of utility. This does not, of course, mean equality, but it does mean a constant questioning of the bases of inequality.

This attitude of innovative utilitarianism is given particular scope in modern societies by a second great differentiating characteristic—the modern type of occupational organization. It seems to have been Karl Marx who first pointed out the manifold consequences for society of the growth of occupational organizations distinct from the family and the resulting separation of work life from domestic life. Marx was preoccupied with one particular manifestation of this phenomenon—the factory worker and the insecurities which he suffered by virtue of having to sell his labor on an impersonal market, unshielded by the personal ties of mutual responsibility which had pervaded the peasant village. In the light of a further hundred years' experience, it is apparent that his insight, while profound, was incomplete. Modern societies have accepted responsibility for securing the worker's place in the labor market, but meanwhile his occupational situation—his position as a paid employee of an extra-familial organization—has spread to an ever increasing proportion of society's members. His employer, who in Marx' time was the owner of a family firm, has become a salaried manager. Civil servants—the employees of government—have become more numerous as the state has assumed wider responsibilities, and an increasing proportion of the practitioners of the learned professions have become employees of either state or industry. Even those islands of family enterprise, the farm and the small business, are increasingly treated—by the tax laws, for example—as organizations in which the owners employ themselves.

In short, there has come into existence a vast complex of organizations, outside the family, devoted to specialized tasks and employing persons in terms of their contributions to those tasks. At the same time, there have developed separate educational organizations charged with selecting and training persons for such tasks. The upshot is a kind of society in which the old connection between family and social status is broken. Not completely, of course, for so long as the family has any part in the training of children more highly placed persons will be in a position to confer differential advantages upon their offspring. But to a very marked degree in modern societies the allocation of occupational roles, and in turn general social status, depends upon performance in relatively impersonal educational and occupational structures. Again, this does not mean equality. The system is highly competitive and offers markedly differential rewards as inducements to achievement. But the logic of the modern industry or bureaucracy does involve continuous reassessment of both roles and persons in the light of technically-defined tasks. They are thus the institutional embodiment of the scientific-technological attitude of which we spoke earlier.

But the kind of equality to which modern societies aspire, and which their institutions enable them to achieve, is not merely a matter of providing scope for occupational achievement. It also has a political side: the demand, expressed in the ideologies of political movements, for some kind of popular participation in the state. This "politics of equality" has expressed itself in two principal directions. On the one hand, the state has been pressed to assume over-all responsibility for the progress of society in the directions defined by the scientific-technological attitude. Differences in view concerning the best means of fulfilling this responsibility—whether through direct state action or through securing the conditions for free competition, for example—tend to obscure what is basically the common attitude of all modern states: All assume the burden of both overseeing the technical efficiency and progress of the occupational structure and supplying their citizens with such services as education and health as means of participating in the occupational system on the basis of a rough equality of opportunity. The other principal expression of the "politics of equality" is the demand that these and other actions of the state reflect the will of the people. The modern state is populistic; whether or not its citizens actually participate in the formation of public policy, it must find means of securing at least the symbols of popular approval. It is precisely in this respect that modern authoritarianisms differ from traditional ones. The rulers of traditional peasant societies required only that their people obey; modern political leaders, whether democratic or authoritarian, must justify their acts as reflecting the popular will, even when this will must be determined by undemocratic means.

Thus the politics of equality in modern societies does not necessarily involve political democracy. Indeed, as Alexis de Tocqueville and others have shown, there is a sense in which equality may work against democracy. When egalitarianism takes the form of an insistence upon the elimination of all loyalties and groupings within society which differentiate individuals and stand between them and the state, the citizens become a mass of political atoms, more readily manipulable by the leaders of the state. Democracy appears to require a compromise with equality: a tolerance of differences among persons, of loyalties based upon occupation, economic interest, ideology, religion, or locality—loyalties which inevitably add to inequality, but which also diffuse the power of the state and provide the individual with the means to express his will within it.

These appear to be the major dimensions of equality and inequality in modern societies. In the past, students of society and culture have inevitably been greatly influenced in their thinking about such matters by the particular historical experience of the West, where modernity is older. But the contemporary spread of this complex outside the limits of the Western cultural tradition holds out the intellectually very exciting prospect of a natural laboratory in which our ideas concerning the nature of modernity, and the place of equality within it, may be tested. We may learn, for example, that different traditional cultures are differentially hospitable to egalitarian ideas, and that they find different kinds and degrees of difficulty in dealing with the scientific-technological attitude. We may discover that kinds of group loyalties unfamiliar to the West are capable of mediating between individual and state in a manner which nourishes democracy. Thus we may come to understand a bit more clearly, and perhaps be able to inhabit with greater comfort, a world in which modern egalitarianism, its privileges and responsibilities, are no longer the monopoly of people of Western culture.

BIBLIOGRAPHICAL NOTE

Robert Michels sets out his "iron law of oligarchy" in *Political Parties* (1949). The most ambitious attempt to systematize the theory of social stratification is that of Talcott Parsons (1953), in *Class, Status and Power: A Reader in Social Stratification* (Bendix and Lipset 1953). This volume also contains many other important papers on the subject. The "fathers" of the study of social stratification are Karl Marx and Max Weber. The best selections from their writings on the subject are in Bottomore and Rubel (1956) and Gerth and Mills (1947). The best discussion of stratification in simple societies is that of Landtman (1938), while the best on peasant societies is that of Robert Redfield (1960). Alexis de Tocqueville's influential ideas concerning social stratification and modern politics may be found principally in his *Democracy in America* and his *Old Régime and the French Revolution*.

21.

THE USES OF ANTHROPOLOGY

Sol Tax

IN THIS SERIES OF essays, nineteen of our younger anthropologists have described some of the directions of their thought and their research. In so doing they have given us some view of man and his works, past and present. They have also given us a view of the sciences of mankind which together we call anthropology. It will be recalled that in 1859 the leading anthropologist of France, Paul Broca called for just such a "general anthropology" to unite the several disciplines studying man. This has become now a reality, perhaps more in America than in any other land. Each of the nineteen anthropologists has described particular phenomena of biology and of culture; of archeology, linguistics, or ethnography; of politics, society, economics, religion, or the arts. All of us are specialists, but despite the diversity of our interests, we are nevertheless closely united in the science of man.

General anthropology today not only unites scholars of all of the disciplines which converge to study mankind; it also is the most world-wide of sciences, uniting scholars of mankind wherever they are. For over a century, anthropologists more than any other group of scientists have vigorously maintained personal communication, through congresses and correspondence and travel. Now there are three thousand of us. It is not surprising that we are the first to find a way to overcome the formidable political and financial barriers that isolate the pieces of a world otherwise so shrunken in size. Through the journal *Current Anthropology* (sponsored by the Wenner-Gren Foundation of

248

New York) we have developed a "communications coöperative" through which almost all of the anthropologists of the world ("wherever the post office reaches") are in constant contact, aware of who the others are and what they are doing.

The science of man thus marches on with new vigor. More and more scholars are trained; the methods of study improve every year; the exchange of ideas and knowledge increases rapidly; and the results of our labors accumulate at an ever increasing rate. These results—some of the newest of which have been recounted in these essays—and the interesting discoveries just beyond the horizon, are sufficient justification for anthropology. The discovery of man and culture is one of the noblest endeavors of the human spirit. But we also live in a world beset with problems; thus it is a fair question whether anthropology also has something to offer to help to solve them.

Like other scientists, we anthropologists believe that our greatest service to mankind is in pursuit of knowledge. This is why society trains us. If we stop being scientists and scholars, what are we? So for the most part we pursue scientific problems, not practical or political or social problems. Paul Broca over a century ago noted that anthropology in America had suffered a period of eclipse because anthropologists had become embroiled in the politics of the Civil War. From this experience, he warned that ". . . science can never, without danger, depart from its proper sphere." But he recognizes the other side of the problem too, and continues:

> "We find fault, and justly, with the *savants* who, under the convenient pretense of concentrating their efforts on one pursuit, flatter themselves that they can remain indifferent to the great questions which agitate society. The very fact of the superiority of their accomplishments, so far from giving such a right, entails on those gentlemen the duty of taking part in political life, and of exercising a beneficial influence on those who surround them. Let them, then, interest themselves in the affairs of their country. They cannot do better than plunge eagerly, according to their several temperaments, into the philosophical, religious, social, or humanitarian problems which surround them. And when, returning to their laboratory or their study, they apply themselves to scientific inquiries, they ought to lay aside their feelings and their

ambitions, and, closing their ears to external influences, listen only to the calm voice of truth. For science ought to hold allegiance to itself alone, and never bend the knee to party. It is a divine power enthroned above humanity, to direct and not to follow it, and of it alone it may be said, that it is born to command and not to obey" (Broca 1871:32).

Following this advice, it is as citizens—not as research specialists—that we participate in public affairs. What Broca did not appreciate is that our experience as general anthropologists would in time give to us a special niche in the world of public affairs. Each of us participates—as Broca says—according to his temperament. All of us tend to believe equally that what we have learned in anthropology is important for everybody in the world to know, and some of us find it difficult not to shout it from the housetops.

But what is it that we shout or do? In this series of essays there are only occasional references to problems in the world, or indications of any practical significance of the knowledge presented. Yet all of the authors in fact believe that anthropology holds lessons for the modern world on a par with those of any science or philosophy. The question remains, then, as to how anthropology finds its uses.

One answer to this question might be suggested by the phrase "applied anthropology." Engineering and medicine are professions which can be said to apply the knowledge gained by the physical and the biological sciences. After this pattern, some have awaited the development of a profession that would apply the findings of anthropology. Indeed, since 1941 we have had in the United States a Society for Applied Anthropology which has attempted to build such a profession. Although this society has encouraged the use of anthropological knowledge by government and private organizations, a profession of applied anthropologists has not come into being, either in the United States or elsewhere. Anthropological knowledge is used by administrators and managers with the wit to use it. If they wish professional assistance, they must turn to anthropologists. Anthropologists indeed become involved in management and administration, just as in social work, education, and public health. These anthropologists are sometimes distinguished from those who work for museums, research institutions, and universities; but in contrast to analogous medical sciences, they do not form a class of practitioners. Instead, all anthropologists conceive of themselves both as pursuing academic research and as putting their knowledge to social use. If an outsider seeks anthropological counsel, he must search out a genuine anthropologist; the anthropologist who gives him counsel will not dissociate himself from either the name of his discipline or his academic pursuits.

Anthropologists study man. Each anthropologist pursues a particular special study—this is what we mean by research—but all are actively interested in the whole study. We are highly specialized as social anthropologists, or human paleontologists, or linguists, for example, but we are equally general anthropologists. As we learn and we teach our specialties, we also learn from other specialists and we teach in a context which we share with them.

Here then we come to the second answer to the question. It is as teachers of the lessons of the whole of anthropology that we put our science to use; and we teach not only in the classroom, important as that is to most of us, but wherever we work and live. Anthropology has become for us a way of life, a set of values to pass on to whomever we touch: our parents and our children; our colleagues at work or play; our fellow citizens wherever they are. What it is that we teach is implicit in this set of essays. The first attraction of anthropology is the very breadth of our subject matter—the study of mankind as a whole—which brings and holds us together, and gives us the special character which we then pass on. Man as an animal, as a population, as a species; man's behavior and his culture, and the behavior of his culture; the origin, characteristics, and distribution of the varieties of man, his language, social forms, ideas; man's genetics, prehistory and history, and the laws of history, which explain all of these in all time over the whole earth; comparative anatomy, personality, religion and ethics, law, sociology, and science; national characteristics, acculturation, socialization—all of these and whatever else may become relevant are parts of the grand problem which anthropologists have chosen to study.

The original anthropologists were anatomists, philologists, geographers, and antiquarians who met together in Paris, in

London, in Moscow, or in New York to listen each to the others. It was their interest in the all-inclusive problem that drew them together and that made all-inclusivenesss a virtue to be felt and extolled. The anatomists might come to read papers on craniometry to philologists and to students of customs, and to listen in turn to papers on chipped-stone industries, on grammar or on folklore. Those first anthropologists surely contributed not only breadth, but a great tolerance for variety in subject matter and in techniques of study. They established these as values for which anthropology ever since has tended to select.

It is not surprising that anthropology should characteristically form a society of scholars open to new techniques, tools, ideas, and men. The tools brought in range from the "law of uniformity" from geology to a Freudian model, or a Carbon-fourteen dating from chemistry. We have freely adopted, reinterpreted, and made our own whatever has appeared useful to our varied problems. People of other fields are drawn in because they are wanted and needed. But if men are not so drawn in, their ideas still are. Sometimes whole new fields of study are added, like culture and personality, but of course all that are added are new answers to the heterogeneous problems already there. Anthropology always has been as broad in conception as it is possible to be; in wandering correspondingly widely for its data and tools, it absorbs into the tradition of the discipline those new men with special ideas who accept the breadth of anthropology.

The breadth, eclecticism, and openness of boundaries of our subject matter are associated not only with an unusual tolerance for a variety of subjects and tools, but also for surprising ambiguity. It is not possible to be (as we say) "wholistic," to take into account all at once all aspects of a problem if we also require a clear structure. Given a choice between fully understanding one piece of a whole, but not in context, or only half understanding a larger whole, we generally prefer the second. This choice is related to our predilection for dealing with the real world. Unlike economists and others who deal with abstractions comfortably, we reflect our origins in natural history by feeling more comfortable the closer we are to nature, and to substantive rather than to theoretical or methodological problems.

The original interest of anthropologists in "other people" is also related to our concern with the reality of man through all time and space. Knowing mankind is to know all varieties of mankind; knowing people means seeing them as people. This is one source of our "liberal" view of other peoples and cultures. When it is recalled that the original Ethnological Society of Paris was formed by members of the Aborigines Protection Association, it is not surprising that anthropologists have generally taken the side of the oppressed. But it is not only tradition, and the circumstance of our founding, that lends us our character. Our tradition takes us out to study different peoples and cultures; though we see them in the broadest context, it is living people whom we come to know. It is because we live with them and come to know them that we learn from them. We keep our liberal tradition because we are the pupils of other peoples. Even if the "other peoples" are only archeological remains (or even not "peoples" at all, but baboons or gorillas!) our point of reference is still other living peoples and cultures, whose accomplishments give us humility and perspective and make us, too, "other" people.

It is precisely our tradition of general anthropology that makes it possible not only to use specialized knowledge, but also to recognize the relevance of new specialties. The question is not whether any piece of specialized knowledge is directly useful, but how the insights of general anthropology can be put to the service of society. Hence that second answer to the question posed: we serve by passing on to others the point of view and the understandings that we have ourselves gained. We have learned and we teach that the peoples of our species are equally human, thus equally able to achieve what is great and what is base. We have learned and we teach that the different peoples have from the very beginning of time developed particular ways and particular values; it is part of being commonly human to differ not simply as individuals, but systematically as communities of individuals. We teach our concept of culture and our tolerance of cultures. We have learned and we teach that a people values its identity, and resists changes which threaten it; that nobody but a people itself can judge what is important in its values, and what is threatening. Thus we teach the wisdom of discovering rather than assuming what other people want and fear, an undertaking the more difficult and the more important as the cultural difference is greater. These lessons we can teach in the classroom, on the lecture platform, in books, and hope that they will become part of a liberal education to be internalized by the many.

What else? When we are asked, we can go farther specifically to influence programs which deal with other peoples. Now it becomes important to distinguish among the kinds of people in a nation or in a community. We have learned that at an operating level we deal not with a culture at all but with many cultures; not even with the many cultures but rather with groups of people who are influenced not only by their cultures but by their position and by their interests as they perceive them. The programs in which we become involved concern what are now called "new nations." A new nation characteristically has an elite culturally perhaps less separated than we are from its tribes and its villagers, but with interests often opposed to theirs. Anthropologists generally see the problem from the village point of view, the administrators of programs, from that of the governing elite with whom they deal. The problem is now not one simply of teaching what we have learned; to be helpful means to become political, and at this point most scientists properly leave the task to others.

Suppose, however, that we stay with the problem: even now—at a time when there are differences of interest and perspectives to which education is not an effective answer—how can knowledge derived from the study of man be deliberately put to the service of man?

"The service of man" is a large phrase. If it could be limited to, say, the service of one's own country, the problem would be more manageable. The country—any nation—is governed by people—in specific Departments, Bureaus, Committees, and as administrators; the scientist simply places his knowledge at the service of one of these, and his problems are resolved. He becomes a technician, an instrument. Indeed the capitals of nations are crowded with social scientists who do just this. This is not to say that they are weak, immoral, dishonorable. Often they will have personal points of view to press: recently I met a young economist working with the Alliance for Progress, in

Washington, who described how the younger men in the agency were fighting to change a philosophy inherited from an older agency. They obviously were passionately working from the inside and probably effecting policy more than if they operated on the outside as independent critics. Similarly with the case of the present Commissioner of Indian Affairs in Washington, the anthropologist Philleo Nash, who clearly presses changes in philosophy and in policy both upon Congress and higher administration officials and also upon the great number of officials who are under his legal jurisdiction, but only by persuasion under his influence. The anthropologist who puts his knowledge to the service of his country need not therefore lose his integrity or his freedom of action, although he may well lose his patience. The difference between serving one's conscience and one's boss; one's boss and one's country; one's country and mankind—the difference in each case is neither clear nor absolute. It is easy to rationalize one's own behavior— whatever it may be—or to blame the next anthropologist.

It is characteristic of the anthropologist that if he does continue his work of education into what is close to the political realm, he acts as an independent agent, taking upon himself the ultimate responsibility for satisfying his conscience in terms of the obligations he feels toward his colleagues and toward his fellow men. It may be because anthropologists cannot comfortably have clients or work for others that a class of applied anthropologists does not develop. The scientist has, as Broca said, but one master, the truth as he learns it, and to teach it requires also the freedom of the academic profession.

Let us accept the independence of the anthropologist. Supposing him to be a research scientist serving only the one master and responsible only to his conscience and to his colleagues, let us give him this problem: What are the circumstances in which a community of people achieves its own goals, or is on the contrary frustrated? Assuming that there is basic agreement on what is wanted, communities of people still fall short of their goals. This happens whether the community one has in mind is a modern city unable to keep itself clean and orderly; or a nation unable to control the growth of a strangling bureaucracy; or even the faculty of a University unable to protect its academic freedom. The problem is one for the tools as well of political science, economics, and sociology; but it is the sort of general problem which anthropologists characteristically tackle, borrowing what tools we need. We would think of beginning the anthropological research in a small community of a culture different from our own, since this is our special method of objectifying the problem; but we would hope to end up with some general understanding of the processes involved. Should we succeed in learning how any community of people can better achieve its own goals, we would have put anthropology to important use.

The method of research that is suited to this problem, however, appears to violate the canon that the anthropologist should not become involved in public affairs. In the three or four cases where the problem has been successfully pursued, the anthropologists found that they had to interfere quite deliberately in social processes. To study such a problem requires helping the people of the community to discover their goals; but since there are competing goals and wants and forces in the society, this cannot be a simple educational process. (If it were so simple, there would be no problem to begin with.) So the anthropologist takes a special position in the community and becomes an actor as well as an observer. He helps people to try various ways of discovering their goals and the ways of achieving them which suit their own cultural norms and their own self-perceived interests. One well-known example of this sort of research is Allen Holmberg's work at Vicos in Peru, where the researchers from Cornell University had to lease a plantation and become the *patrón* of the serf-like Indian community in order to bring the community into a position where it could act freely for itself. The community responded remarkably; and Holmberg's experiment proved an important point not only for anthropology but also for the people of Vicos and Peru, for all others in similar circumstances, and for the policy-making powers in the world. Similarly the University of Chicago's experiment in helping a small community of North American Indians to resolve its problems has led to understandings not only about American Indian problems in general, but about those of other population enclaves like the Maori of New Zealand or tribal peoples in India or Africa. The general lesson that they will adjust to the modern world when their identity and their own cultural values are not threatened is important because such threats may not really be necessary. The understandings gained by this method of research by the anthropologists of Cornell and Chicago could probably not have come in any other way. The results are proving themselves in an understanding of the problems of new nations, of North American cities, even of the organization of universities. Indeed, the unique community of anthropologists of the world that I mentioned as being now in existence was helped into being directly by what was learned from American Indians. The same understanding may some day help the peoples of the world to achieve the common goal of peace.

This new method of research, which Paul Broca could not have predicted, is often called "action anthropology." It does not fit the distinction frequently made between pure and applied research. It requires the intellectual and the political independence that one associates with a pure researcher; it depends upon university and foundation connections and support rather than those of a client or government. But it also requires that the anthropologist leave his ivory tower and that without losing his objectivity he enter into some world of affairs which becomes for the time being his laboratory. But since we are ethical men, and our laboratory is a community of people who are not to be sacrificed for our purposes or for science or even for some larger humanity, the anthropologist who undertakes such research is selected from those who are willing and able to take on unusual burdens and risks. Like a physician with his patients, he accepts the problems of a whole community as his own problems. Since he can never be wholly successful, he must be prepared for disappointments and frustrations, without even the satisfaction of blaming others besides himself. It is no wonder that this method of research has not become common, or indeed fully accepted as legitimate. The stakes are high and the game dangerous; but action anthropology is nevertheless quite in the tradition and spirit of general anthropology, and promises to provide the best demonstration of its meaning and its use.

BIBLIOGRAPHICAL NOTE

The literature relative to the ways in which anthropological knowledge is made useful is found primarily under the rubric "Applied Anthropology." Case studies in applied anthropology, wherein the anthropologist's role has been chiefly one of advising and trouble-shooting, are found in the journal *Human Organization* (formerly called *Applied Anthropology*) published by the Society for Applied Anthropology, and in the following volumes: Spicer (1952), Mead (1953), and Paul (1955). George Foster has written a text for courses in applied anthropology (Foster 1961) which outlines the processes of culture change and the limits within which social science can facilitate such change. The problems encountered by anthropologists in attempting scientifically to implement administrative goals are the focus of H. G. Barnett's *Anthropology in Administration* (1956) and Sol Tax' article, "Anthropology and Administration" (1945).

Theoretical issues concerning the responsibility of anthropologists to apply their knowledge and the possibilities of developing a science of applied anthropology are discussed in Lucy Mair's *Studies in Applied Anthropology* (1957, chapter 1) and are a central focus of Laura Thompson's *Toward a Science of Mankind* (1961). These issues receive attention as well in *The Documentary History of the Fox Project* (Gearing, Netting, and Peattie 1960). For a discussion of the tenets of "Action Anthropology" which emerged from the Fox project, see especially articles in the latter volume by Tax (pp. 167-171), Diesing (pp. 182-197), and Peattie (pp. 300-304).

BIBLIOGRAPHY

ACKERNECHT, ERWIN H.
1953 "Paleopathology." In KROEBER (ed.) 1953, pp. 120-26.
ALLISON, A. C.
1955 "Aspects of Polymorphism in Man." In CSPSQB 1955, pp. 239-55.
ALLOTT, ANTONY
1960 Essays in African Law. London: Butterworth & Co. Ltd.
ANGEL, LAWRENCE J.
1954 and 1957 "Human Biology, Health and History in Greece." In Yearbook of the American Philosophical Society, 1954, pp. 168-72; 1957, pp. 266-70.
ANTHROPOLOGICAL SOCIETY OF WASHINGTON
1956 Some Uses of Anthropology. Edited by JOSEPH CASAGRANDE and THOMAS GLADWIN. Washington: Anthropological Society.
1957 Studies in Human Ecology. ("Social Science Monograph," No. 3.) Washington: Pan American Union.
1959 Evolution and Anthropology. Edited by BETTY MEGGERS. Washington: Anthropological Society.
1962 Anthropology and Human Behavior. Edited by THOMAS GLADWIN and WILLIAM STURTEVANT. Washington: Anthropological Society.
ARMILLAS, PEDRO
1961 "Land Use in Pre-Columbian America." In STAMP (ed.) 1961, pp. 255-76.
AUDY, J. RALPH
1961 "The Ecology of Scrub Typhus." In MAY (ed.) 1961, pp. 389-432.
BAILEY, F. C.
1957 Caste and the Economic Frontier. Manchester: Manchester University Press.

BARNES, J. A.
   1963   "Kinship." In *Encyclopedia Britannica*, 1963 ed., vol. 13, pp. 403-407.
BARNETT, HOMER G.
   1956   *Anthropology in Administration*. Evanston, Ill.: Row, Peterson & Co.
BARTH, FREDERIK
   1956   "Ecological Relationships of Ethnic Groups in Swat, North Pakistan," *Amer. Anthrop.* 58:1079-89.
   1959   "The Land Use Pattern of Migratory Tribes of South Persia," *Norsk Geog. Tidskr.* 8:1-11.
   1961   *Nomads of South Persia*. Oslo: Oslo University Press.
BARTON, R. F.
   1919   *Ifugao Law*. Berkeley: University of California Press.
BASEHART, HARRY
   1959   "Social organization." In SIEGEL (ed.) 1959, pp. 107-54.
BATES, MARSTON
   1955   *The Prevalence of People*. New York: Charles Scribner's Sons.
   1956   "Man as an Agent in the Spread of Organisms." In THOMAS (ed.) 1956, pp. 788-804.
   1959   "The Ecology of Health." In GALDSTON (ed.) 1959, pp. 175-76.
BATESON, G. D., J. JACKSON, J. HALEY, and J. WEAKLAND
   1956   "Toward a Theory of Schizophrenia," *Behav. Science* 1: 251-64.
BEAGLEHOLE, ERNEST
   1939   "Culture and Psychosis in New Zealand," *J. Polynes. Soc.* 48:144-55.
BELL, P. R. (ed.)
   1959   *Darwin's Biological Work*. Cambridge: Cambridge University Press.
BELLAH, ROBERT N.
   1957   *Tokugawa Religion*. Glencoe, Ill: The Free Press.
BELSHAW, C. S.
   1955   *In Search of Wealth*. ("Memoir of the American Anthropological Association," No. 80.) Washington: American Anthropological Association.
BENDIX, R., and S. M. LIPSET (eds.)
   1953   *Class, Status and Power*. Glencoe, Ill.: The Free Press.
BENEDICT, RUTH
   1934   *Patterns of Culture*. Boston: Houghton Mifflin Co.

1935 *Zuni Mythology*. ("Columbia University Contributions to Anthropology," No. 21.) New York.

BERLINER, J. S.
1962 "The Feet of the Natives Are Large: an Essay on Anthropology by an Economist," *Current Anthrop*. 3:47-61.

BIRDSELL, J. B.
1957 "Some Population Problems Involving Pleistocene Man." In CSPSQB 1957, pp. 47-70.

BOAS, FRANZ
1911 "Introduction." In *Handbook of American Indian Languages*. ("Bulletin of the Bureau of American Ethnology," No. 40, Part I.) Washington: The Smithsonian Institution.
1955 *Primitive Art*. New York: Dover Publications, Inc.

BOHANNAN, PAUL J.
1957 *Justice and Judgment Among the Tiv*. London: Oxford University Press.
1959 "Some Principles of Exchange and Investment Among the Tiv," *Amer. Anthrop*. 57:60-70.
1963 *Introduction to Social and Cultural Anthropology*. New York: Holt, Rinehart and Winston, Inc.

BOHANNAN, PAUL J., and GEORGE DALTON (eds.)
1962 *Markets in Africa*. Evanston, Ill.: Northwestern University Press.

BÖÖK, J. A.
1950 "Clinical and Genetical Entities in Human Populations." In CSPSQB 1950, pp. 123-28.

BORHEGYI, STEPHAN, and NEVIN S. SCRIMSHAW
1957 "Evidence for Pre-Columbian Goiter in Guatemala," *Amer. Antiquity* 23.174-76.

BOTTOMORE, T. B., and M. RUBEL (eds.)
1956 *Karl Marx: Selected Writings in Sociology and Social Philosophy*. London: C. A. Watts, Ltd.

BOX, HUBERT S.
1949 *The Principles of Canon Law*. London: Oxford University Press.

BRAIDWOOD, ROBERT J.
1961 *Prehistoric Man*. Chicago: Chicago Natural History Museum.

BRAIDWOOD, ROBERT J., and BRUCE HOWE
1960 *Prehistoric Investigations in Iraqi Kurdistan*. (Oriental Institute Studies in Ancient Oriental Civilization," No. 31.) Chicago: University of Chicago Press.

262   *Bibliography*

BRAIDWOOD, ROBERT J., and GORDON R. WILLEY (eds.)
    1962   *Courses Toward Urban Life*. ("Viking Fund Publications in Anthropology," No. 32.) Chicago: Aldine Publishing Co.

BRIGHT, WILLIAM
    In press (Proceedings of the Conference on Sociolinguistics held at the University of California at Los Angeles, May, 1964.)

BROCA, M. PAUL
    1871   "The Progress of Anthropology in Europe and America," *J. Anthrop. Inst. N. Y.* 1:24-40.

BROCKINGTON, F.
    1958   *World Health*. Harmondsworth: Penguin Books, Ltd.

BROSNAHAN, L.
    1960   "Language and Evolution," *Lingua* 9:225-36.

BROWN, R. W.
    1958   *Words and Things*. Glencoe, Ill.: The Free Press.

BUETTNER-JANUSCH, J.
    1962   "The Relatives of Man," *Annals N. Y. Acad. Sci.* 102: 191-514.

BURNET, SIR MACFARLANE
    1953   *Natural History of Infectious Disease*. Cambridge: Cambridge University Press.

CAMERON, T. W. M.
    1958   "Parasites of Animals and Human Disease," *Annals N. Y. Acad. Sci.* 70:564-73.

CARPENTER, C. R.
    1934   "A Field Study of the Behavior and Social Relations of Howling Monkeys (*Allouatta palliata*)," *Comp. Psych. Monos.* 10, No. 48.

CASSIRER, ERNST
    1944   *An Essay on Man*. New Haven: Yale University Press.

CAUDILL, WILLIAM
    1953   "Applied Anthropology in Medicine." In KROEBER (ed.) 1953, pp. 771-806.

CHAPPLE, ELLIOT D.
    1953   "Applied Anthropology in Industry." In KROEBER (ed.) 1953, pp. 819-31.

CHILDE, GORDON
    1951   *Man Makes Himself*. New York: New American Library.
    1954   *What Happened in History*. Rev. ed. Harmondsworth: Penguin Books, Ltd.

CLARK, E. T.
    1949   *The Small Sects in America*. Nashville: Abingdon Press.

CLARK, J. G. D.
    1952   *Prehistoric Europe*. London: Methuen & Co., Ltd.

1959   *The Prehistory of Southern Africa.* Harmondsworth: Penguin Books, Ltd.

COCKBURN, THOMAS A.
1959   "The Evolution of Infectious Diseases," *Int. Record of Med.* 172:493-508.

COHEN, RONALD
1961   "Marriage Instability Among the Kanuri of Northern Nigeria," *Amer. Anthrop.* 63:231-49.

COLD SPRING HARBOR SYMPOSIA IN QUANTITATIVE BIOLOGY (CSPSQB)
1950   *Cold Spring Harbor Symposia in Quantitative Biology, No. 15.* Cold Spring Harbor, N. Y.
1955   *Cold Spring Harbor Symposia in Quantitative Biology, No. 20.* Cold Spring Harbor, N. Y.
1957   *Cold Spring Harbor Symposia in Quantitative Biology, No. 22.* Cold Spring Harbor, N. Y.

COLE, SONIA
1959   *The Neolithic Revolution.* London: British Museum (Natural History).

COLLOQUES INTERNATIONAUX: SCIENCES HUMAINES
1958   *Les Processus de l'hominisation.* Paris: Centre National de la Recherche Scientifique.

CONKLIN, HAROLD C.
1955   "Hanunóo Color Categories," *Southw. J. Anthrop.* 11: 339-44.
1962   "Lexicographical Treatment of Folk Taxonomies." In HOUSEHOLDER and SAPORTA (eds.) 1962, pp. 119-42.
1964   "Ethnogenealogical Method." In GOODENOUGH (ed.) 1964, pp. 25-55.

COOK, SHERBURNE F.
1946   "The Incidence and Significance of Disease among the Aztecs and Related Tribes," *Hispanic-Amer. Rev.* 26:320-35.

DALTON, GEORGE
1961   "Economic Theory and Primitive Society," *Amer. Anthrop.* 63:1-25.

DAPPER, OLFERT
1676   *Naukeurige Beschrijuinge der Afrikanische Gewesten.* Amsterdam: Meurs.

DAVENPORT, WILLIAM H.
1961   "Primitive and Civilized Money in the Santa Cruz Islands." In GARFIELD (ed.) 1961, pp. 64-68.

DE VORE, IRVEN (ed.)
in pr. *Primate Behavior.* New York: Holt, Rinehart and Winston.

DIAMOND, STANLEY A. (ed.)
1960   *Culture in History.* New York: Columbia University Press.

DIEBOLD, A. RICHARD, JR.
1961 "Incipient Bilingualism," *Language* 37:97-112.
DOBZHANSKY, T.
1962 *Mankind Evolving.* New Haven: Yale University Press.
DUBOS, RENÉ
1961 *The Mirage of Health.* Garden City, N. Y. Anchor Books.
DURKHEIM, EMILE
1954 *The Elementary Forms of the Religious Life.* Glencoe, Ill.:
The Free Press.
EASTON, DAVID
1953 *The Political System.* New York: Alfred A. Knopf, Inc.
EGGAN, FRED
1950 *Social Organization of the Western Pueblos.* Chicago:
University of Chicago Press.
EGGAN, FRED (ed.)
1955 *Social Anthropology of the North American Tribes.* 2d ed.
Chicago: University of Chicago Press.
EMRICH, DUNCAN
1946 " 'Folklore': William John Thoms," *Calif. Folklore Quart.*
5:355-72.
ENGELS, FRIEDRICH
1902 *Origin of the Family, Private Property and the State.*
Reprinted. New York: International Publishers Co.
EPSTEIN, T. S.
1962 *Economic Development and Social Change in South
India.* Manchester: Manchester University Press.
ERASMUS, C. J.
1955 "Changing Folk Beliefs and the Relativity of Empirical
Knowledge," *Southw. J. Anthrop.* 8:411-28.
EULAU, HEINZ
1963 *The Behavioral Persuasion in Politics.* New York: Random
House, Inc.
EVANS-PRITCHARD, E. E.
1937 *Witchcraft, Oracles and Magic Among the Azande.*
Oxford: Oxford University Press.
1954 *Social Anthropology.* London: Cohen & West, Ltd.
FALLERS, LLOYD A.
1957 "Some Determinants of Marriage Stability in Busoya,"
Africa 27:106-27.
FEBVRE, LUCIEN, and LIONEL BATAILLON
1925 *A Geographical Introduction to History.* New York: Al-
fred A. Knopf, Inc.
FENTON, WILLIAM N., and GERTRUDE P. KURATH
1953 *The Iroquois Eagle Dance.* ("Bulletin of the Bureau of

American Ethnology," No. 156.) Washington: The Smithsonian Institution.

FERGUSON, CHARLES A. (ed.)
In press (Papers from the Summer Seminar on Sociolinguistics, Indiana University, 1964.)

FERGUSON, CHARLES A., and JOHN J. GUMPERZ (eds.)
1960 "Linguistic Diversity in South Asia," *Int. J. Amer. Linguistics 26:* No. 3, supp. ("Indiana University Research Center in Anthropology, Folklore, and Linguistics Publications," No. 13.)

FIRTH, RAYMOND
1929 *Primitive Polynesian Economy.* London: Routledge & Kegan Paul, Ltd.
1951 *Elements of Social Organization.* London: C. A. Watts, Ltd.
1954 "Money, Work, and Social Change in Indo-Pacific Systems," *Int. Soc. Sci. Bull.* 4:400-410.
1957 *We, the Tikopia.* 2d ed. London: George Allen & Unwin, Ltd.
1963 "Social Anthropology." *In Encyclopedia Britannica,* 1963 ed., vol. 20, pp. 862-70.

FISHMAN, JOSHUA (ed.)
1965 *Reader in Sociolinguistics* (provisional title). The Hague: Mouton & Co.

FLINT, R.F., and F. BRANDTNER
1961 "Climatic Changes Since the Last Interglacial," *Amer. J. Sci.* 259:321-28.

FORTES, MEYER
1949 *The Web of Kinship Among the Tallensi.* London: Oxford University Press.

FORTES, MEYER, and E. E. EVANS-PRITCHARD (eds.)
1940 *African Political Systems.* London: Oxford University Press.

FOSTER, GEORGE M.
1961 *Traditional Cultures and The Impact of Technological Change.* New York: Harper & Bros.

FRAKE, CHARLES O.
1961 "The Diagnosis of Disease Among the Subanun of Mindanao," *Amer. Anthrop.* 63:113-32.
1962a "Culture, Ecology and Ethnography," *ibid.* 64:53-59.
1962b "The Ethnographic Study of Cognitive Systems." In ANTHROP. SOC. OF WASH. 1962, pp. 72-93.
1964a "Notes on Queries in Ethnography." In ROMNEY and D'ANDRADE (eds.) 1964, pp. 132-45.

1964b "A Structural Description on Subanon 'Religious Behavior.'" In GOODENOUGH (ed.) 1964, pp. 111-29.

FRAZER, SIR JAMES G.
1922 *The Golden Bough.* Abridged ed. New York: The Macmillan Co.

FREEDMAN, LAWRENCE Z., and ANNE ROE
1958 "Evolution and Human Behavior." In ROE and SIMPSON, (eds.) 1958, pp. 455-79.

FREEMAN, H. E., *et al.* (eds.)
1963 *Handbook of Medical Sociology.* Englewood Cliffs, N. J.: Prentice-Hall, Inc.

FREUD, SIGMUND
1922 *Totem and Taboo.* New York: W. W. Norton & Co.
1962 *Civilization and Its Discontents.* 1st Amer. ed. New York: W. W. Norton & Co.

FRIED, MORTON H.
1952 "Land Tenure, Geography and Ecology in the Contact of Cultures," *Amer. J. Econ. and Soc.* 11:391-417.
1960 "On the Evaluation of Social Stratification and the State." In DIAMOND 1960, pp. 713-31.
in pr. *Studies in Anthropology.* New York: Random House, Inc.

FRIED, MORTON H. (ed.)
1959 *Readings in Anthropology.* 2 vols. New York: Thomas Y. Crowell Co.

FRIEDRICH, PAUL
1961 Review of FERGUSON and GUMPERZ (eds.) 1950, *Language* 37:163-68.
1962 "Multilingualism and Socio-Cultural Organization: A Symposium," *Anthropological Linguistics* 4:1.

FROMM, ERICH
1944 "Individual and Social Origins of Neurosis," *Amer. Soc. Rev.* 9:380-434.

GALDSTON, IAGO (ed.)
1959 *Medicine and Health.* New York: International Universities Press.

GARFIELD, VIOLA E. (ed.)
1961 *Patterns of Land Utilization and Other Papers.* ("Proceedings of the 1961 Annual Spring Meeting of the American Ethnological Society.") Seattle: University of Washington Press.

GARN, STANLEY M.
1961 *Human Races.* Springfield, Ill.: Charles C. Thomas.

GARN, STANLEY M. (ed.)
1959 *Readings on Race.* Springfield, Ill.: CHARLES C. THOMAS.

GEARING, FRED, R. M. NETTING, and L. R. PEATTIE (eds.)
 1960 *The Documentary History of the Fox Project*. Chicago:
 Department of Anthropology, University of Chicago.
GEERTZ, CLIFFORD
 1962 "The Growth of Culture and the Evolution of Mind."
 IN SCHER (ed.) 1962, pp. 713-40.
GERTH, HANS, and C. W. MILLS (eds.)
 1947 *From Max Weber*. New York: Oxford University Press.
GLUCKMAN, MAX
 1941 *The Economy of the Central Barotse Plains*. ("Rhodes-
 Livingstone Papers," No. 7.) Livingstone, Northern Rhodesia:
 Rhodes-Livingstone Institute.
 1945 "How the Bemba Make Their Living," *Rhodes-Living-
 stone Inst. J.* 2:55-67.
 1950 "Kinship and Marriage Among the Lozi of Northern
 Rhodesia and the Zulu of Natal." In RADCLIFFE-BROWN and
 FORDE (eds.) 1950, pp. 166-206.
 1954 *Rituals and Rebellion in South-East Africa*. Manchester:
 Manchester University Press.
 1955 *The Judicial Process Among the Barotse*. Manchester:
 Manchester University Press.
 1959 *Custom and Conflict in Africa*. Glencoe, Ill.: The Free
 Press.
GOLDSCHMIDT, WALTER
 1959 *Man's Way*. New York: Henry Holt & Co.
GOODE, WILLIAM J.
 1951 *Religion Among the Primitives*. Glencoe, Ill.: The Free
 Press.
GOODENOUGH, WARD H.
 1951 *Property, Kin and Community on Truk*. New Haven:
 Yale University Press.
 1956a "Componential Analysis and the Study of Meaning,"
 Language 32:195-216.
 1956b "Residence Rules," *Southw. J. Anthrop.* 12:22-37.
GOODENOUGH, WARD H. (ed.)
 1964 *Explorations in Cultural Anthropology*. New York: Mc-
 Graw-Hill Book Co.
GRUBER, FRED C. (ed.)
 1961 *Anthropology and Education*. Philadelphia: University of
 Pennsylvania Press.
GUMPERZ, JOHN J., and DELL HYMES (eds.)
 1964 *The Ethnography of Communication*. (Special Publication of the *American Anthropologist*.) Menasha, Wisc.: American Anthropological Association.

HALDANE, J. B. S.
1956 "Natural Selection in Man," *Acta Genetica et Stat. Med.*
63:321-32.
1959 "Natural Selection." In BELL (ed.) 1959, pp. 101-49.
HALLOWELL, A. IRVING
1947 "Myth, Culture and Personality," *Amer. Anthrop.* 49:
544-56.
1955 *Culture and Experience.* Philadelphia: University of
Pennsylvania Press.
1959 "Behavioral Evolution and the Emergence of the Self."
In ANTHRO. SOC. OF WASH. 1959, pp. 36-60.
1960a "The Beginnings of Anthropology in America." In
LAGUNA (ed.) 1960, pp. 1-59.
1960b "Self, Society and Culture in Phylogenetic Perspective."
In TAX (ed.) 1960, vol. 2, pp. 309-72.
HAMMEL, EUGENE A. (ed.)
1965 *Componential Analysis* (provisional title). (Special Publication of the *American Anthropologist.*) Menasha, Wisc.: American Anthropological Association.
HARLOW, HARRY F.
1959 "Love in Infant Monkeys," *Sci. Amer.* 200:68-74.
HARLOW, HARRY F., and M. K. HARLOW
1962 "Social Deprivation in Monkeys," *Sci. Amer.* 207:136-46.
HARRISON, G. A. (ed.)
1961 *Genetical Variation in Human Populations.* ("Symposia
of the Society for the Study of Human Biology," No. 4.) New
York: Pergamon Press, Inc.
HASELBERGER, HERTA
1961 "Methods of Studying Ethnological Art," *Current Anthrop.*
2:351-84.
HAUGEN, EINAR
1956 *Bilingualism in the Americas.* ("Publications of the
American Dialect Society," No. 26.) Birmingham, Ala.: University
of Alabama Press.
HAYLEY, T. T. S.
1947 *The Anatomy of Lango Religion and Groups.* Cambridge:
Cambridge University Press.
HELM, JUNE
1962 "The Ecological Approach in Anthropology," *Amer. J.
Soc.* 67:630-39.
HERSKOVITS, MELVILLE J.
1944 "Dramatic Experience Among Primitive Peoples," *Yale
Rev.* 33:683-98.
1952 *Economic Anthropology.* New York: Alfred A. Knopf, Inc.
1955 *Cultural Anthropology.* New York: Alfred A. Knopf, Inc.

HOCKETT, C. F.
1960 "The Origin of Speech," *Sci. Amer.* 202:3-10.
HOCKETT, C. F., and ROBERT ASCHER
1964 "The Human Revolution," *Current Anthropology* 5:135-68.
HOEBEL, E. ADAMSON
1954 *The Law of Primitive Man.* Cambridge: Harvard University Press.
HOIJER, HARRY
1962 "Anthropological Linguistics." In MOHMANN *et al.* (eds.) 1962, pp. 110-27.
HOMANS, GEORGE C.
1941 "Anxiety and Ritual," *Amer. Anthrop.* 43:164-72.
HORTON, DONALD
1943 "The Functions of Alcohol in Primitive Societies," *Quart. J. Studies on Alcohol* 4:199-320.
HOULT, T. F.
1958 *The Sociology of Religion.* New York: Dryden Press.
HOUSEHOLDER, FRED W., JR., and SOL SAPORTA (eds.)
1962 "Problems in Lexicography," *Int. J. Amer. Linguistics* 28: No. 2, supp. ("Indiana University Research Center in Anthropology, Folklore, and Linguistics Publications," No. 21.)
HOWELL, F. CLARK, and FRANÇOIS BOURLIÈRE (eds.)
1963 *African Ecology and Human Evolution.* ("Viking Fund Publications in Anthropology," No. 38.) Chicago: Aldine Publishing Co.
HOWELLS, W. W.
1961 *The Emergence of Man.* New York: Random House, Inc.
HSU, FRANCIS L. K.
1959 "Structure, Function and Process," *Amer. Anthrop.* 61: 790-805.
HSU, FRANCIS L. K. (ed.)
1961 *Psychological Anthropology.* Homewood, Ill.: Dorsey Press.
HULSE, FRED
1963 *Physical Anthropology.* New York: Random House, Inc.
HYMES, DELL
1961 "Functions of Speech: An Evolutionary Approach." In GRUBER (ed.) 1961, pp. 55-83.
1962 "The Ethnography of Speaking." In ANTHROP. SOC. OF WASH. 1962, pp. 13-53.
1963 "Notes Toward a History of Linguistic Anthropology," *Anthrop. Linguistics* 5:59-103.
1964a *Language in Culture and Society.* New York: Harper & Row.
1964b "Directions in (Ethno-)Linguistic Theory." In ROMNEY and D'ANDRADE (eds.) 1964, pp. 6-56.

270   *Bibliography*

1964c "Introduction: Toward Ethnographies of Communication." In GUMPERZ and HYMES (eds.) 1964 (pp. in press).

IMANISHI, KINJI
1960 "Social Organization of Subhuman Primates in Their Natural Habitat," *Current Anthrop.* 1:393-407.

ITANI, JUNICHIRO
1954 *The Monkeys of Takasakiyama.* (In Japanese.) Tokyo: Kobunsha.

JACKSON, DON D. (ed.)
1960 *The Etiology of Schizophrenia.* New York: Basic Books, Inc.

KAPLAN, BERT (ed.)
1961 *Studying Personality Cross-Culturally.* Evanston, Ill.: Row, Peterson & Co.

KLUCKHOHN, CLYDE
1949 *A Mirror for Man.* New York: McGraw-Hill Book Co., Inc.
1953 *Navaho Witchcraft.* Boston: Beacon Press.
1954 "Culture and Behavior." In LINDZEY (ed.) 1954, vol. 2, pp. 921-76.

KLUCKHOHN, CLYDE, and HENRY A. MURRAY
1953 "Personality Formation." In KLUCKHOHN *et al.* (eds.) 1953, pp. 53-67.

KLUCKHOHN, CLYDE, HENRY A. MURRAY, and DAVID M. SCHNEIDER (eds.)
1953 *Personality in Nature, Society, and Culture.* New York: Alfred A. Knopf, Inc.

KONDO, AKIHIKO
1953 "Morita Therapy," *Amer. J. Psychoanal.* 13:31-37.

KRADER, LAWRENCE
1955 "Ecology of Central Asian Pastoralism," *Southw. J. Anthrop.* 2:301-26.

KROEBER, ALFRED L.
1909 "Classification Systems of Relationship," *J. Royal Anthrop. Inst.* 39:77-84.
1939 *Cultural and Natural Areas of Native North America.* Berkeley: University of California Press.
1948 *Anthropology.* New York: Harcourt, Brace & Co., Inc.
1952 *The Nature of Culture.* Chicago: University of Chicago Press.

KROEBER, ALFRED L. (ed.)
1953 *Anthropology Today.* Chicago: University of Chicago Press. *Ackerwecht*

KUMMER, H., and F. KURT
1963 "Social Units of a Free-Living Population of Hamadryas Baboons," *Folia Primat.* 1:4-19.

KURATH, GERTRUDE P.
1960 "Panorama of Dance Ethnology," *Current Anthrop.* 1: 233-54.

LA BARRE, WESTON
1938 *The Peyote Cult.* ("Yale University Publications in Anthropology," No. 19.) New Haven: Yale University Press.

LACK, D.
1954 *The Natural Regulation of Animal Numbers.* New York: Oxford University Press.

LAGUNA, FREDERICA DE (ed.)
1960 *Selected Papers from the* American Anthropologist. Evanston, Ill.: Row, Peterson & Co.

LANDTMANN, GUNNAR
1938 *The Origin of the Inequality of the Social Classes.* London: Routledge & Kegan Paul Ltd.

LAMBERT R. D. (ed.)
1960 "Religion in American Society," *Annals Amer. Acad. Polit. Soc. Sci.* 332.

LANG, ANDREW
1898 *The Making of Religion.* London: Longmans, Green & Co., Ltd.

LANGER, SUZANNE K.
1953 *Feeling and Form.* New York: Charles Scribner's Sons, Inc.

LANYON, W. E., and W. N. TAVOLGA (eds.)
1960 *Animal Sounds and Communication.* ("American Institute of Biological Sciences Publications," No. 7.) Washington: American Institute of Biological Sciences.

LASSWELL, HAROLD D., and ABRAHAM KAPLAN
1950 *Power and Society.* New Haven: Yale University Press.

LATTIMORE, OWEN
1951 *Inner Asian Frontiers of China.* ("American Geographical Society Research Series," No. 21.) New York: American Geographical Society.

LEACH, E. R.
1954 *Political Systems of Highland Burma.* Cambridge: Harvard University Press.
1965 "Anthropological Aspects of Language: Animal Categories and Verbal Abuse." In LENNEBERG (ed.) 1965 (pp. in press).

LEACH, MARIA (ed.)
 1950 *Standard Dictionary of Folklore, Mythology and Legend.*
 2 vols. New York: Funk & Wagnalls Co., Inc.
LEAKEY, L. S. B.
 1960 "The Origins of the Genus *Homo.*" In TAX (ed.) 1960,
 vol. 2, pp. 17-32.
LENNEBERG, ERIC H.
 1960 "Language, Evolution, and Purpose Behavior." In DIA-
 MOND (ed.) 1960, pp. 869-93.
LENNEBERG, ERIC H. (ed.)
 1965 *New Directions in the Study of Language.* Cambridge,
 Mass.: M.I.T. Press.
LEVINE, ROBERT
 1960 "The Role of the Family in Authority Systems," *Behav.
 Sci.* 5:291-96.
LEVINE, ROBERT (ed.)
 1961 "Anthropology and the Study of Conflict," *J. Conflict
 Resolution,* symposium issue, Vol. V, No. 1.
LEVI-STRAUSS, CLAUDE
 1949 *Les Structures élémentaires de la parenté.* Paris: Les
 Presses Universitaires.
LEWIS, OSCAR
 1951 *Life in a Mexican Village.* Urbana, Ill.: University of
 Illinois Press.
LINDZEY, GARDNER (ed.)
 1954 *Handbook of Social Psychology.* 2 vols. Cambridge:
 Addison-Wesley Publishing Co., Inc.
LINTON, RALPH
 1954 "Nativistic Movements," *Amer. Anthrop.* 45:230-40.
LIVINGSTONE, FRANK B.
 1958 "Anthropological Implications of Sickle Cell Distribution
 in West Africa," *Amer. Anthrop.* 60:533-62.
LLEWELLYN, KARL, and E. ADAMSON HOEBEL
 1941 *The Cheyenne Way.* Norman, Okla: University of
 Oklahoma Press.
LOMAX, ALAN
 1959 "Folk Song Style," *Amer. Anthrop.* 61:927-54.
LORENZO, J. L.
 1961 *La revolución neolítica en Mesoamerica.* ("Departmento
 de Prehistoria Publicacion," No. 11.) Mexico D. F.: Instituto
 Nacional de Anthropologia e Historia.
LORIMER, FRANK
 1954 *Culture and Human Fertility.* Paris: UNESCO.
LOUNSBURY, FLOYD G.
 1964a "The Structural Analysis of Kinship Semantics." In LUNT
 (ed.) 1964, pp. 1073-90.

1964b "A Formal Account of the Crow and Omaha-Type Kinship Terminologies." In GOODENOUGH (ed.) 1964, pp. 351-93.

LOWIE, ROBERT

1924 *Primitive Religion.* New York: Boni & Liveright.

1927 *Origin of the State.* New York: Harcourt, Brace & Co.

1937 *The History of Ethnological Theory.* New York: Henry Holt & Co., Inc.

1956 *The Crow Indians.* Reprinted. New York: Holt, Rinehart & Winston, Inc.

LOWINSKY, EDWARD E.

1946 *Secret Chromatic Art in the Netherlands Motet.* New York: Columbia University Press.

LUNT, HORACE G. (ed.)

1964 *Proceedings of the Ninth International Congress of Linguists.* The Hague: Mouton & Co.

LURIA, A. R.

1961 *The Role of Speech in the Regulation of Normal and Abnormal Behavior.* New York: Liveright Publishing Corp.

MACNEISH, R. S.

1961— *Annual Reports of the Tehuacan Archeological-Botanical Project.* Andover, Mass.: Robert S. Peabody Foundation for Archeology.

MACCOBY, E. E., THEODORE NEWCOMB, and C. HARTLEY (eds.)

1958 *Readings in Social Psychology.* New York: Henry Holt & Co., Inc.

MAINE, SIR HENRY

1917 *Ancient Law.* Reprinted in Everyman's Library. New York: E. P. Dutton & Co., Inc.

MAIR, LUCY P.

1957 *Studies in Applied Anthropology.* London: University of London.

1962 *Primitive Government. Harmondsworth:* Penguin Books.

MALINOWSKI, BRONISLAW

1922 *Argonauts of the Western Pacific.* London: Routledge & Kegan Paul, Ltd.

1932 *Crime and Custom in Savage Society.* New York: Harcourt Brace & Co.

1948 *Magic, Science and Religion and Other Essays.* Glencoe, Ill.: The Free Press.

MAUSS, MARCEL

1925 "Essai sur le don," *L'Année Soc.* (n.s.) 1:30-186.

MAXCY, KENNETH F.

1956 *Preventive Medicine and Public Health.* New York: Appleton-Century Publishing Co.

MAY, J. M. (ed.)

1961 *Studies in Disease Ecology.* New York: Hafner Publishing Co., Inc.

MAYO, ELTON
   1933   *The Human Problems of an Industrial Civilization.* New
   York: The Macmillan Co.
McALLESTER, DAVID P.
   1954   *Enemy Way Music.* ("Papers of the Peabody Museum of
   American Archeology and Ethnology," Vol. 41, No. 3.) Cambridge: Peabody Museum.
MEAD, GEORGE HERBERT
   1934   *Mind, Self and Society.* Chicago: University of Chicago
   Press.
MEAD, MARGARET
   1928   *Coming of Age in Samoa.* Reprinted. New York: New
   American Library.
   1930   *Growing Up in New Guinea.* Reprinted. New York: New
   American Library.
   1935   *Sex and Temperament in Three Primitive Societies.* Re-
   printed. New York: New American Library.
MEAD, MARGARET (ed.)
   1955   *Cultural Patterns and Technological Change.* New York:
   New American Library.
MEAD, MARGARET, and GREGORY BATESON
   1942   *Balinese Character.* New York: New York Academy of
   Science.
MEDAWAR, P. B.
   1961   *The Future of Man.* New York: New American Library.
MELLAART, J.
   1961   "Roots in the Soil." In PIGGOTT (ed.) 1961, pp. 41-64.
MERRIAM, ALAN P.
   1962   *A Prologue to the Study of the African Arts.* Yellow
   Springs, O.: Antioch Press.
   1964   *The Anthropology of Music.* Evanston, Ill.: Northwestern
   University Press.
MERTON, ROBERT K.
   1949   *Social Theory and Social Structure.* Glencoe, Ill.: The
   Free Press.
MICHELS, ROBERT
   1949   *Political Parties.* Glencoe, Ill.: The Free Press.
MILLER, W. B.
   1955   "Two Concepts of Authority," *Amer. Anthrop.* 57: 271-89.
MINTZ, SIDNEY
   1961   "Pratik." In GARFIELD (ed.) 1961, pp. 54-63.
MOHMANN, C., A. SOMMERFELT, and JOSHUA WHATMOUGH (eds.)
   1962   *Trends in European and American Linguistics, 1932-1962.*
   Antwerp: Spectrum.

MONTAGUE, ASHLEY (ed.)
1962 *Culture and the Evolution of Man.* New York: Oxford University Press.
MOORE, W. E., and A. S. FELDMAN (eds.)
1960 *Labor Commitment and Social Change in Developing Areas.* New York. Social Science Research Council.
MORGAN, LEWIS HENRY
1868 *Systems of Consanguinity and Affinity of the Human Family.* ("Smithsonian Contributions to Knowledge," No. 17.) Washington: The Smithsonian Institution.
1878 *Ancient Society.* New York: Henry Holt & Co.
MORRIS, CHARLES
1955 *Signs, Language and Behavior.* New York: George Braziller, Inc.
MÜLLER, F. MAX
1878 *Lectures on the Origin and Growth of Religion.* London: Longmans, Green & Co., Ltd.
MURDOCK, GEORGE P.
1949 *Social Structure.* New York: The Macmillan Co.
MURIE, ADOLPH
1944 *The Wolves of Mount Mckinley.* ("Fauna Series," No. 5.) Washington: Government Printing Office.
NADEL, S. F.
1952 "Witchcraft in Four African Societies," *Amer. Anthrop.* 54:18-29.
1954 *Nupe Religion.* Glencoe, Ill.: The Free Press.
NAROLL, RAOUL
1956 "A Preliminary Index of Social Development," *Amer. Anthrop.* 58:687-715.
NASH, MANNING
1958 *Machine Age Maya.* Glencoe, Ill.: The Free Press.
1961 "The Social Context of Economic Choice in a Small Society," *Man* 61:186-91.
NEEL, JAMES V.
1950 "The Population Genetics of Two Inherited Blood Dyscrasias in Man." In CSPSQB 1950, pp. 141-58.
NETTL, BRUNO
1956 *Music in Primitive Culture.* Cambridge: Harvard University Press.
NEWMAN, MARSHALL T.
1962 "Ecology and Nutritional Stress in Man," *Amer. Anthrop.* 64:22-34.

NORBECK, EDWARD
   1961   *Religion in Primitive Society.* New York: Harper & Row.
NORBECK, EDWARD, D. WALKER, and M. COHEN
   1962   "The Interpretation of Data: Puberty Rites," *Amer. Anthrop.* 64:463-85.
NOTTINGHAM, E. K.
   1954   *Religion and Society.* Garden City, N. Y.: Doubleday & Co., Inc.
OLMSTED, D. L.
   1950   *Ethnolinguistics So Far.* ("Studies in Linguistics," Occasional Papers No. 2.) Norman, Okla.: Battenburg Press.
OPLER, M. K. (ed.)
   1959   *Culture and Mental Health.* New York: The Macmillan Co.
OPPENHEIMER, FRANZ
   1914   *The State.* Indianapolis, Ind.: The Bobbs-Merrill Co., Inc.
PALERM, ANGEL, and ERIC R. WOLF
   1957   "Ecological Potential and Cultural Development in Meso-America." In ANTHROP. SOC. OF WASH. 1957, pp. 1-37.
PARRINDER, GEOFFREY
   1958   *Witchcraft.* Harmondsworth: Penguin Books, Ltd.
PARSONS, TALCOTT
   1953   "Revised Analytical Approach to the Theory of Social Stratification." In BENDIX and LIPSET (eds.) 1953, pp. 92-128.
   1954   *Essays in Sociological Theory.* Rev. ed. Glencoe, Ill.: The Free Press.
PARSONS, TALCOTT, and NEIL J. SMELSER
   1957   "A Comprehensive View of Exchange Systems," *Econ. Dev. and Social Change* 7:173-82.
PAUL, BENJAMIN (ed.)
   1955   *Health, Culture, and Community.* New York: Russell Sage Foundation.
PETTER, J. J.
   1962   "Recherches sur l'écologie et l'éthologie des lémuriens malgaches," *Mem. du Musée Nat. d'Hist. Naturelle* (Paris) n.s., Sér. A, Zoologie, 27:1-46.
PIGGOTT, STUART (ed.)
   1961   *The Dawn of Civilization.* New York: McGraw-Hill Book Co., Inc.

POLANYI, KARL, C. W. ARENSBERG, and H. W. PEARSON (eds.)
1957 *Trade and Market in the Early Empires.* Glencoe, Ill.: The Free Press.

POLGAR, STEVEN
1961 "Evolution and the Thermodynamic Imperative," *Human Biol.* 33:99-109.
1962 "Health and Human Behavior," *Current Anthrop.* 3: 159-205.
1963 "Health Action in Cross-Cultural Perspective. In FREE-MAN *et al.* (eds.) 1962, pp. 397-419.

POSPISIL, LEOPOLD
1958 *Kapauka Papuans and Their Law.* ("Yale University Publications in Anthropology," No. 54.) New Haven: Yale University Press.

POUND, ROSCOE
1954 *An Introduction to the Philosophy of Law.* Rev. ed. New Haven: Yale University Press.

RADCLIFFE-BROWN, A. R.
1948 *The Andaman Islanders.* Reprinted. Glencoe, Ill.: The Free Press.
1952 *Structure and Function in Primitive Society.* Glencoe, Ill.: The Free Press.

RADCLIFFE-BROWN, A. R., and DARRYL FORDE (eds.)
1950 *African Systems of Kinship and Marriage.* New York: Oxford University Press.

REDFIELD, ROBERT
1941 *The Folk Culture of Yucatan.* Chicago: University of Chicago Press.
1960 *Peasant Society and Culture and The Little Community.* Reprinted. Chicago: University of Chicago Press.

RICHARDS, A. I.
1956 *Chisungu.* New York: Grove Press.

ROBERTS, S. H.
1927 *Population Problems of the Pacific.* London: Routledge & Kegan Paul, Ltd.

ROE, ANNE, and G. G. SIMPSON (eds.)
1958 *Behavior and Evolution.* New Haven: Yale University Press.

ROMNEY, A. KIMBALL, and PHILIP J. EPLING
1959 "A Simplified Model of Kariera Kinship," *Amer. Anthrop.* 60:59-74.

278   *Bibliography*

ROMNEY, A. KIMBALL, and R. D'ANDRADE (eds.)
1964 *Transcultural Studies of Cognition.* (Special Publication
of the *American Anthropologist.* Menasha, Wisc.: American Anthropological Association.

ROSEN, GEORGE
1957 "The Biological Element in Human History," *Med. Hist.*
1:150-59.
1958 *A History of Public Health.* New York: MD Publications,
Inc.
1960 "Psychopathology in the Social Process," *J. Health &*
Hum. Behav. 1:200-210.

RUCKNAGEL, D., and J. V. NEEL
1961 "The Hemoglobinopathics." In STEINBERG (ed.) 1961,
pp. 158-260.

SACHS, CURT
1937 *World History of the Dance.* New York: W. W. Norton
& Co., Inc.
1940 *The History of Musical Instruments.* New York: W. W.
Norton & Co., Inc.

SAHLINS, MARSHALL D.
1963 "Poor Man, Rich Man, Big-Man, Chief," *Comp. Stud.*
Society & Hist. 5:285-303.

SAHLINS, MARSHALL D., and ELMAN R. SERVICE (eds.)
1960 *Evolution and Culture.* Ann Arbor, Mich.: University of
Michigan Press.

SALISBURY, R.
1962 *From Stone to Steel.* Cambridge: Cambridge University
Press.

SAPIR, EDWARD
1921 *Language.* New York: Harcourt, Brace & Co., Inc.

SAPORTA, SOL (ed.)
1961 *Psycholinguistics.* New York: Holt, Rinehart & Winston.

SAUER, CARL O.
1952 *Agricultural Origins and Dispersals.* ("Bowman Memorial
Lectures," Series 2.) New York: American Geographical
Society.

SCHACHT, JOSEPH
1950 *The Origins of Muhammedan Jurisprudence.* Oxford:
Clarendon Press.

SCHALLER, GEORGE B.
  1963 *The Mountain Gorilla.* Chicago: University of Chicago Press.
SCHAPERA, I.
  1956 *Government and Politics in Tribal Societies.* London: C. A. Watts, Ltd.
SCHER, JORDAN (ed.)
  1962 *Theories of the Mind.* New York: The Free Press of Glencoe.
SCHLOSSER, KATESA
  1949 *Propheten in Afrika.* Braunschweig: Alfred Limbach.
SCHNEIDER, DAVID, and KATHLEEN GOUGH (eds.)
  1961 *Matrilineal Kinship.* Berkeley: University of California Press.
SCHULTZ, ADOLPH H.
  1961 "Some Factors Influencing the Social Life of Primates in General and of Early Man in Particular." In WASHBURN (ed.) 1961, pp. 58-90.
SEAGLE, WILLIAM
  1941 *The Quest for Law.* New York: Alfred A. Knopf, Inc.
SEBEOK, THOMAS A.
  1962 "Coding and the Evolution of Signalling Behavior," *Behav. Sci.* 7:430-42.
SECOY, FRANK R.
  1953 *Changing Military Patterns of the Great Plains.* ("American Ethnological Society Monograph," No. 21.) Locust Valley N. J.: J. J. Augustin.
SIEGEL, BERNARD (ed.)
  1959— *Biennial Review of Anthropology.* Stanford: Stanford University Press.
SIGERIST, E. H.
  1961 *A History of Medicine.* New York: Oxford University Press.
SIMPSON, SIDNEY P., and JULIUS STONE (eds.)
  1948 *Cases and Readings on Law and Society. Book I: Law and Society in Evolution.* St. Paul, Minn.: West Publishing Co.
SINGER, MILTON
  1961 "A Survey of Culture and Personality Theory and Research" In KAPLAN (ed.) 1961, pp. 9-90.

SMELSER, NEIL J.
  1959   "A Comparative View of Exchange Systems," *Econ. Dev.
  & Cult. Change* 7:173-82.
SMITH, MICHAEL GARFIELD
  1955   *The Economy of Hausa Communities of Zaria.* "Colonial
  Research Studies," No. 16.) London: Colonial Social Science
  Research Council.
SMITH, W. ROBERTSON
  1901   *Lecture on the Religion of the Semites.* Rev. ed. London:
  A. & C. Black, Ltd.
SPICER, EDWARD (ed.)
  1952   *Human Problems in Technological Change.* New York:
  Russell Sage Foundation.
SPIRO, MELVILLE E.
  1961   "An Overview and a Suggested Reorientation." In HSU
  (ed.) 1961, pp. 459-92.
SPUHLER, J. N. (ed.)
  1959   *The Evolution of Man's Capacity for Culture.* Detroit:
  Wayne State University Press.
STAMP, L. DUDLEY (ed.)
  1961   *A History of Land Use in Arid Regions.* ("Arid Zone
  Research Papers," No. 17.) Paris: UNESCO.
STEARN, E. W., and A. E. STEARN
  1945   *The Effect of Smallpox on the Destiny of the American
  Indian.* Boston: BRUCE HUMPHRIES.
STEINBERG, A. G. (ed.)
  1961   *Progress· in Medical Genetics.* New York: Grune &
  Stratton, Inc.
STEWARD, JULIAN
  1955   *Theory of Culture Change.* Urbana, Ill.: University of
  Illinois Press.
STONE, C. P. (ed.)
  1951   *Comparative Psychology.* Englewood Cliffs, N. J.: Pren-
  tice-Hall, Inc.
STRAUS, R., and J. A. CLAUSEN (eds.)
  1963   "Medicine and Society," *Annals Amer. Acad. Polit. &
  Soc. Sci.* 346:1-148.
STURTEVANT, WILLIAM C.
  1964   "Studies in Ethnoscience." In ROMNEY and D'ANDRADE
  (eds.) 1964, pp. 99-131.
SUTTLES, WAYNE
  1960   "Affinal Ties, Subsistence and Prestige Among the Coast
  Salish," *Amer. Anthrop.* 62:296-305.

TAWNEY, R. H.
    1926 *Religion and the Rise of Capitalism.* New York; Harcourt, Brace & Co., Inc.
TAX, SOL
    1945 "Anthropology and Administration," *Amer. Indigena* 5; 21-33.
    1955 "From Lafitau to Radcliffe-Brown." In EGGAN (ed.) 1955, pp. 445-84.
    1963 *Penny Capitalism.* Reprinted. Chicago: University of Chicago Press.
TAX, SOL (ed.)
    1960 *Evolution after Darwin.* 3 vols. Chicago: University of Chicago Press.
THOMAS, W. L. (ed.)
    1956 *Man's Role in Changing the Face of the Earth.* Chicago: University of Chicago Press.
THOMPSON, LAURA
    1961 *Toward a Science of Mankind.* New York: McGraw-Hill Book Co., Inc.
THOMPSON, STITH
    1946 *The Folktale.* New York: Dryden Press.
TOCQUEVILLE, ALEXIS DE
    1946 *Democracy in America.* New York: Alfred A. Knopf, Inc.
    1955 *The Old Regime and the French Revolution.* Garden City, N. Y.: Anchor Books.
TUMIN, MELVIN, and others
    1958 "Values in Action," *Human Org.* 17:2-33.
TYLOR, E. B.
    1889a "On a Method of Investigating the Development of Institutions," *J. Royal Anthrop. Inst.* 18:245-72.
    1889b *Primitive Culture.* 3rd ed. New York: Henry Holt & Co., Inc.
VAN GENNEP, ARNOLD
    1960 *The Rites of Passage.* Chicago: University of Chicago Press.
VINOGRADOFF, PAUL
    1959 *Common Sense in Law.* New York: Oxford University Press.
VOGT, EVON Z.
    1960 "On the Concepts of Structure and Process in Cultural Anthropology," *Amer. Anthrop.* 62:18-32.

282   *Bibliography*

WALLACE, A. F. C.
1956   "Revitalization Movements," *Amer. Anthrop.* 58:264-81.
1959   "The Institutionalization of Cathartic and Control Strategies in Iroquois Religious Therapy." In OPLER (ed.) 1959, pp. 63-96.
1961   *Culture and Personality.* New York: Random House, Inc.
1962   "The New Culture-and-Personality." In ANTHROP. SOC. OF WASH. 1962.

WALLACE, A. F. C., and JOHN ATKINS
1960   "The Meaning of Kinship Terms," *Amer. Anthrop.* 62: 58-80.

WARNER, W. LLOYD, and J. O. LOW
1947   *The Social System of the Modern Factory.* New Haven: Yale University Press.

WASHBURN, SHERWOOD L. (ed.)
1962   *Social Life of Early Man.* ("Viking Fund Publications in Anthropology," No. 31.) Chicago: Aldine Publishing Co.

WASHBURN, SHERWOOD L., and F. CLARK HOWELL
1960   "Human Evolution and Culture." In TAX (ed.) 1960, vol. 2, pp. 33-56.

WASHBURN, SHERWOOD L., and IRVEN DeVORE
1961a   "The Social Life of Baboons," *Sci. Amer.* 204:62-71.
1961b   "Social Behavior of Baboons and Early Man." In WASHBURN (ed.) 1962, pp. 91-105.

WATSON, W.
1958   *Tribal Cohesion in a Money Economy.* Manchester: Manchester University Press.

WEAKLAND, J. H.
1960   "The 'Double-bind' Hypothesis of Schizophrenia and Three-party Interaction." In JACKSON (ed.) 1960, pp. 373-88.

WEBER, MAX
1930   *The Protestant Ethic and the Spirit of Capitalism.* London: George Allen & Unwin, Ltd.

WEINREICH, URIEL
1953   *Languages in Contact.* New York: Linguistic Circle of New York.

WHITE, A. D.
1896   *A History of the Warfare of Science with Theology in Christendom.* 2 vols. New York: D. Appleton & Co.

WHITE, LESLIE A.
1949   *The Science of Culture.* New York: Grove Press.
1959   *The Evolution of Culture.* New York: McGraw-Hill Book Co., Inc.

WHITING, BEATRICE B. (ed.)

1963 *Six Cultures: Studies of Child Rearing.* New York; John Wiley & Sons, Inc.

WHITING, J. W. M., and I. CHILD

1953 *Child Training and Personality.* New Haven: Yale University Press.

WHITING, J. W, M , R. KLUCKHOHN, and A. ANTHONY

1958 "The Functions of Male Initiation Ceremonies at Puberty." In MACCOBY *et al.* (eds.) 1958, pp. 359-70.

WHORF, BENJAMIN

1956 *Language, Thought and Reality.* New York: John Wiley & Sons, Inc.

WILLIAMS, F. E.

1040 *The Drama of Orokolo.* New York: Oxford University Press.

WISSLER, CLARK

1926 *The Relation of Nature to Man in Aboriginal North America.* New York: Oxford University Press.

WITTFOGEL, KARL

1957 *Oriental Despotism.* New Haven: Yale University Press.

WORSLEY, P. M.

1956 "The Kinship System of the Tallensi," *J. Royal Anthrop. Inst.* 86:37-75.

1957 *The Trumpet Shall Sound.* London: Macgibbon & Kee, Ltd.

ZINSSER, HANS.

1935 *Rats, Lice and History.* Boston: Little Brown & Co.

INDEX

284